DEVELOPING PARTNERSHIPS WITH FAMILIES THROUGH CHILDREN'S LITERATURE

ELIZABETH LILLY
Berry College

CONNIE GREEN
Appalachian State University

TULANE UNIVERSITY
TEACHER PREPARATION &
CERTIFICATION PROGRAM

PEARSON
Merrill
Prentice Hall

Upper Saddle River, New Jersey
Columbus, Ohio

Library of Congress Cataloging-in-Publication Data

Lilly, Elizabeth.
   Developing partnerships with families through children's literature/Elizabeth Lilly,
Connie Green.
   p. cm.
  Includes bibliographical references and index.
  ISBN 0-13-031351-3
   1. Family literacy programs—United States. 2. Reading—Parent participation—United States.
3. Home and school—United States. 4. Children's literature—Study and teaching (Early childhood)—United States. I. Green, Connie II. Title.

  LC151 .L462 2004
  372.42'5—dc21

2002043201

Vice President and Executive Publisher: Jeffery
  W. Johnston
Assistant Vice President and Publisher: Kevin
  M. Davis
Editorial Assistant: Autumn Crisp
Production Editor: Linda Hillis Bayma
Production Coordination: WordCrafters
  Editorial Services, Inc.

Design Coordinator: Diane C. Lorenzo
Photo Coordinator: Kathleen Kirtland
Cover Designer: Keith Van Norman
Cover Image: Corbis
Production Manager: Laura Messerly
Director of Marketing: Ann Castel Davis
Marketing Manager: Amy June
Marketing Coordinator: Tyra Poole

This book was set in Optima by Pine Tree Composition, Inc. It was printed and bound by R.R.
Donnelley & Sons Company. The cover was printed by Phoenix Color Corp.

Photo Credits: Bill Bachmann/PhotoEdit, p. 135; Christy Stromberg Brothers, pp. 34, 65; John Brothers,
p. 92; Elizabeth Childers, pp. 48, 71; Edwin Dennis, p. 1; Jeannie Dodd-Murphy, p. 206; Sharayzell
Erskine, p. 30; Mary Cameron Ervin, p. 197; Francisco Miguel Macareno Flores, pp. 88, 139; Mike
Good/Dorling Kindersley/Media Library, p. 155; Connie Green, pp. 9, 68, 238; Rebecca Knight, p. 180;
Elizabeth Lilly, pp. 50, 72, 84, 225; John O. Lilly, Jr., pp. 26, 38, 229; Anthony Magnacca/Merrill, p. 113;
Merrill Education, p. 170; Lawrence Migdale/Stock Boston, p. 145; Margaret L. Moore, p. 150; Michael
Newman/PhotoEdit, p. 125; Kathy Parham, p. 101; Laura Poole, p. 212; Renée Robinson, p. 218; Anne
Vega/Merrill, pp. 94, 162; Patrick Wlazlinski, p. 120; Shirley Zeiberg/PH College, p. 193

Pearson Education Ltd.
Pearson Edcuation Singapore Pte. Ltd.
Pearson Education Canada, Ltd.
Pearson Education—Japan

Pearson Education Australia Pty. Limited
Pearson Education North Asia Ltd.
Pearson Educación de Mexico, S.A. de C.V.
Pearson Education Malaysia Pte. Ltd.

10 9 8 7 6 5 4 3 2 1
ISBN: 0-13-031351-3

In memory of my parents, Emily and John Lilly, where the stories began.

For my sons, Matthew and Andrew, where the stories continue.

—E. L.

To my daughters, Christy, Gael, and Emily, and to my grandchildren, Grace, Dylan, Patrick, and Rowan, whose love of language and story delight and inspire me.

—C. G.

THE EASIEST WAY TO ENHANCE YOUR COURSE
Proven Journals • Proven Strategies • Proven Media

www.EducatorLearningCenter.com

Merrill Education is pleased to announce a new partnership with ASCD. The result of this partnership is a joint website, www.EducatorLearningCenter.com, with recent articles and cutting-edge teaching strategies. The Educator Learning Center combines the resources of the Association for Supervision and Curriculum Development (ASCD) and Merrill Education. At www.EducatorLearningCenter.com you will find resources that will enhance your students' understanding of course topics and of current educational issues, in addition to being invaluable for further research.

How will Educator Learning Center help your students become better teachers?

- 600+ articles from the ASCD journal *Educational Leadership* discuss everyday issues faced by practicing teachers.

- Hundreds of lesson plans and teaching strategies are categorized by content area and age range.

- Excerpts from Merrill Education texts give your students insight on important topics of instructional methods, diverse populations, assessment, classroom management, technology, and refining practice.

- Case studies, classroom video, electronic tools, and computer simulations keep your students abreast of today's classrooms and current technologies.

- A direct link on the site to Research Navigator™, where your students will have access to many of the leading education journals as well as extensive content detailing the research process.

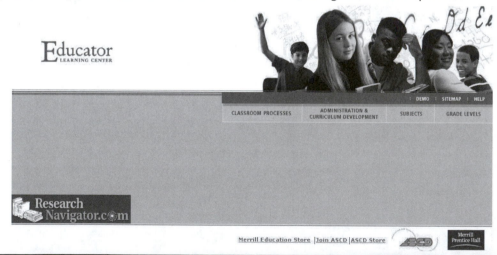

What's the cost?

A four-month subscription to Educator Learning Center is $25 but is **FREE** when used in conjunction with this text. To obtain free passcodes for your students, simply contact your local Merrill/Prentice Hall sales representative, and your representative will give you a special ISBN to give your bookstore when ordering your textbooks. To preview the value of this website to you and your students, please go to www.EducatorLearningCenter.com and click on "Demo."

ABOUT THE AUTHORS

Elizabeth Lilly, Ph.D., is an associate professor of Early Childhood and Literacy Education at Berry College. Her professional experience includes more than 20 years as a preschool, primary, and elementary teacher and teacher educator. Dr. Lilly was closely involved in the development, implementation, and evaluation of Georgia's Pre-K program. She has conducted workshops for teachers and authored publications on early literacy, family involvement, and children's literature. Her research has focused recently on story reading in linguistically and culturally diverse families.

Connie Green, Ph.D., is a professor in the Reading and Birth through Kindergarten programs at Appalachian State University. For 20 years she has worked with both undergraduate and graduate teacher education programs and has conducted research on early reading and writing in both home and early childhood settings. A former kindergarten, elementary, and preschool teacher, she continues her work in early childhood settings. Her favorite times are spent sharing books and playing with her grandchildren and hiking in the beautiful Blue Ridge Mountains.

PREFACE

Developing Partnerships with Families Through Children's Literature is a unique book that combines our interests in family involvement, emergent literacy, and children's literature. It is designed for early childhood educators, students, librarians, family specialists, and early interventionists who work with children from birth through age 5. The text blends information on contemporary families, research on early literacy, and practical strategies and resources for sharing high-quality children's literature in homes as well as in child-care and preschool settings.

Our nation has become rich with cultural and linguistic diversity as we have received newcomers from all over the world. In addition, contemporary life-styles are reflected in the changing composition of our families. Given these factors, how can teachers and child-care professionals adapt the family involvement curriculum to meet the needs and interests of all the families with whom they work?

We recommend many approaches, including the use of children's books that represent a broad range of cultures and family structures, practical and interesting ways to collaborate with families, and stories of families and teachers that reflect the joys of sharing books with young children. Each chapter highlights families reading together, children's responses to books, and suggestions for family involvement in literacy experiences. Photographs of families and their children extend the content in personal ways. A variety of professional development activities and Internet resources are recommended. Information is woven throughout the text on culturally and linguistically diverse families, multicultural literature, and resources for supporting varied family structures. We have emphasized the pleasures of reading aloud, included numerous children's books available today, and suggested appealing strategies for exploring books to support early literacy development.

Our experiences with young children and families, our own research, and the research of others have shaped our approach to early literacy and family involvement. We know that as children learn new concepts and language from books, they relate to characters and stories in affective ways. The highly personal and social context of families enhances the ways young children demonstrate their feelings about stories and their understanding of text. Building on this, we emphasize the affective nature of sharing stories with young children. Dramatizing stories, encouraging active play, engaging in related music and art experiences, and talking about books are valuable ways to support children's responses to literature.

Chapter 1 describes the language and literacy development of young children, beginning at birth and continuing until the transition to early reading and writing. Major points in the chapter are illuminated by authentic examples of language development and responses to literature recorded by parents at home.

Chapter 2 introduces readers to the exciting world of literature for infants, toddlers, preschoolers, and kindergartners. We define each genre and describe representative books. A wide variety of literature is included.

Chapter 3 contains numerous ideas for establishing and maintaining collaborative literacy partnerships with families. We present a distinctive, useful model for family involvement. Suggestions for implementing the model are described throughout the chapter.

Chapter 4 honors families from various cultural backgrounds. We discuss five major cultural groups within the United States and offer specific recommendations for involving families from each culture. Children's books from each culture are highlighted, and ways to share the books are suggested.

Chapter 5 focuses on the many types of family configurations that make up society today. We discuss special considerations to help teachers and child-care professionals work with each type of family. Books that feature varied family structures are reviewed.

Chapter 6 addresses some of the major transitions families may face. Readers will learn ways to assist families experiencing events such as the birth of a child, divorce, or moving, as well as those who are raising a child with special challenges. Books are presented to help individual children, families, or groups of children adjust to changes in their lives.

Chapter 7 describes everyday routines and experiences in the lives of families with young children. We discuss morning and evening times, going to child care or preschool, enjoying the outdoors, and learning about neighborhoods and communities. Books are recommended that depict daily events in unique ways. We address differing affective experiences of families with young children and suggest ideas for enriching family routines and daily activities with language and literature.

Developing Partnerships with Families Through Children's Literature is a celebration of children and families. We provide a treasure trove of literature and related strategies and offer personal stories about the irreplaceable comfort, knowledge, and enjoyment that come with sharing books. We hope teachers and child-care professionals will use this book as a starting point to develop their own creative approaches to involving families in literacy experiences with young children.

ACKNOWLEDGMENTS

Our sincere thanks go to the following for their contributions, support, and assistance with this book:

- The families who participated in our research study and provided us with numerous stories of sharing books with their children.
- Ann Marie Cook, Rebecca Flynn, Tiffani Bender, and Misty Capley, who worked endless hours searching the library for books, typing references, correcting various drafts, and providing feedback.
- Our students, who gave us comments on chapters in progress and shared their stories of early literacy development at home.
- Pat Farthing and Susan Golden, for suggesting books and keeping an eye out for new titles for young children.
- Stephanie Baker, for her excellent documentation and contributions on family involvement and the use of portfolios for infants and toddlers.
- Elizabeth Childers, for her wonderful stories about working with children and families learning English as a second language and the many practical strategies she shared with us.
- Paula Roten, for her insights into opening the world of reading to children who are blind or have visual impairments.
- Terri Barrett, for her contributions on emergent literacy with children who are deaf or hearing impaired and for her assistance on data analysis for our research.
- Kyley Ferris, for sharing her family activity on language development.
- Dana Lilly, for her friendship and professional collaboration.
- The reviewers of our text, who thoughtfully read drafts and offered suggestions: Sabrina Brinson, University of Memphis; Marcia Broughton, University of Northern Colorado; Janet Foster, Georgia Southwestern State University; Lynnette Harris, Eastern New Mexico University; Diane E. Karther, University of Akron; Linda Medearis, Texas A&M International; Deborah A. Moberly, Southeast Missouri State University; and Paula Packer, Lock Haven University of Pennsylvania.
- Our editor, Christina Tawney, who mentored us throughout the process of our first book.
- And, most important, our children and their families, with whom we have shared countless pleasurable hours reading.

DISCOVER THE COMPANION WEBSITE ACCOMPANYING THIS BOOK

THE PRENTICE HALL COMPANION WEBSITE: A VIRTUAL LEARNING ENVIRONMENT

Technology is a constantly growing and changing aspect of our field that is creating a need for content and resources. To address this emerging need, Prentice Hall has developed an online learning environment for students and professors alike—Companion Websites—to support our textbooks.

In creating a Companion Website, our goal is to build on and enhance what the textbook already offers. For this reason, the content for each user-friendly website is organized by topic and provides the professor and student with a variety of meaningful resources. Common features of a Companion Website include:

FOR THE PROFESSOR—

Every Companion Website integrates **Syllabus Manager™**, an online syllabus creation and management utility.

- **Syllabus Manager™** provides you, the instructor, with an easy, step-by-step process to create and revise syllabi, with direct links into Companion Website and other online content without having to learn HTML.
- Students may log on to your syllabus during any study session. All they need to know is the web address for the Companion Website and the password you've assigned to your syllabus.
- After you have created a syllabus using **Syllabus Manager™**, students may enter the syllabus for their course section from any point in the Companion Website.

- Clicking on a date, the student is shown the list of activities for the assignment. The activities for each assignment are linked directly to actual content, saving time for students.

- Adding assignments consists of clicking on the desired due date, then filling in the details of the assignment—name of the assignment, instructions, and whether it is a one-time or repeating assignment.

- In addition, links to other activities can be created easily. If the activity is online, a URL can be entered in the space provided, and it will be linked automatically in the final syllabus.

- Your completed syllabus is hosted on our servers, allowing convenient updates from any computer on the Internet. Changes you make to your syllabus are immediately available to your students at their next logon.

FOR THE STUDENT—

- **Introduction**–General information about the topic and how it will be covered in the website.

- **Web Links**–A variety of websites related to topic areas.

- **Timely Articles**–Links to online articles that enable you to become more aware of important issues in early childhood.

- **Learn by Doing**–Put concepts into action, participate in activities, examine strategies, and more.

- **Visit a School**–Visit a school's website to see concepts, theories, and strategies in action.

- **For Teachers/Practitioners**–Access information you will need to know as an educator, including information on materials, activities, and lessons.

- **Current Policies and Standards**–Find out the latest early childhood policies from the government and various organizations, and view state, federal, and curriculum standards.

- **Resources and Organizations**–Discover tools to help you plan your classroom or center and organizations to provide current information and standards for each topic.

- **Electronic Bluebook**–Paperless method of completing homework or essays assigned by a professor. Finished work can be sent to the professor via email.

- **Message Board**–Virtual bulletin board to post and respond to questions and comments from a national audience.

To take advantage of these and other resources, please visit the *Developing Partnerships with Families Through Children's Literature* Companion Website at

www.prenhall.com/lilly

BRIEF CONTENTS

CONTENTS

NOTE: Every effort has been made to provide accurate and current Internet information in this book. However, the Internet and information posted on it are constantly changing, and it is inevitable that some of the Internet addresses listed in this textbook will change.

EARLY LITERACY DEVELOPMENT

Everything's going to be hunky dory.
Give me a kiss and I'll read you a story.*

Early one morning Gail's mother entered her daughter's room and found her 6-year-old dressed in pajamas, sitting up in bed reading Mother Goose rhymes to her stuffed toys. As she watched and listened, Gail's mother realized that the poems she was hearing were not memorized. Gail was actually reading! Her mother was thrilled, not only because of Gail's facility with reading, but also by the observation that Gail was reading for pure pleasure; it was the first thing she had decided to do upon awakening.

Most parents and caregivers hope that their children will become lifelong readers who gain enjoyment and knowledge from the written word. When children have positive early experiences with reading and writing, they are more likely to be motivated to engage in literacy experiences independently. How do children enter this marvelous world of reading? How do they develop the concepts and background knowledge necessary for success in literacy? What can families do to build children's literacy knowledge during the years before formal schooling?

EARLY LITERACY

Our ideas about early literacy have come a long way since the days when young children sat on hard benches in dame schools reading from wooden paddles, called horn books, which hung around their necks. How have our ideas about early literacy developed? What researchers and educators have influenced the way reading and writing are approached today? It is important for teachers who work with young children and their families to be familiar with the history of early literacy as a foundation for current practices.

Maturationist Theory

Arnold Gesell (1925), the leader of the *maturationist movement,* compared cognitive maturation to physical maturation. Children would be "ready" to read, according to Gesell, when they had developed certain prerequisite skills that could be evaluated by readiness testing. According to this theory there is little teachers and parents can do to hurry the process of development. Reading readiness and readiness testing were central themes of early reading instruction until well into the 1950s.

Behaviorist Theory

Reading programs based on *behaviorist theory,* which are still used by some school systems today, are fast-paced, teacher-directed approaches based on the

---

*From *Don't Spill It Again, James* by Rosemary Wells, copyright © 1977 by Rosemary Wells. Used by permission of Dial Books for Young Readers, a division of Penguin Putnam Inc. All rights reserved. Reprinted by permission.

behaviorist science of the 1970s. Children learn language by repeating words and sentences modeled by their teachers, and working through sequences of reading skills in workbooks and programmed texts. The act of reading is seen as a series of isolated skills addressed by teachers hierarchically and scientifically.

Connectionist Theory

Another current theory of literacy acquisition is the *connectionist theory* (Adams, 1990). Proponents of this part-to-whole theory declare that literacy knowledge is built on a sequence of skills and experiences. Children are taught reading and writing through direct, explicit skill instruction following a predetermined scope and sequence. There is an emphasis on mastering the alphabetic code, reading words, automaticity of reading, over-learning, and reading for fluency and comprehension (Adams, 1990; Morris, 1999). Young children who do not reach the reading and writing benchmarks for their grade level within a reasonable time receive individualized remediation.

Social Constructivist Theory

The *social constructivist theory*, based on Vygotskian principles, adds a cultural dimension to the conversation about children's acquisition of literacy (Vygotsky, 1978). The basic tenets of this theory are that (a) children construct knowledge within a socially mediated cultural context, (b) language is a key component in children's appropriation of knowledge, (c) knowledge is constructed most effectively when adults *scaffold*, or support, children's development at appropriate levels, and (d) children acquire knowledge with the assistance of an adult or more experienced peer within a continuum of behavior called the *zone of proximal development* (Bodrova & Leong, 1996).

Children who come from homes and communities in which adults model and discuss reading and writing have quite different literacy schemas and practices than do children whose caregivers interact less with the tools and processes of literacy (Heath, 1982). Thus, children's development of language and literacy processes reflects the total cultural milieu in which they are raised (Bodrova & Leong, 1996). Emma, age 3 1/2 years, for example, has noticed her mother writing letters and bills, which she leaves clothes-pinned to the mailbox on their front porch for the postal carrier. Emma decided one day to write a letter to Elizabeth, her neighbor. Her "letter" was a crayon drawing, which she folded and clipped to the mailbox, just as her mom had done.

The relationship between social context and literacy development is based firmly on language, as supportive adults help young children reach higher levels of learning through scaffolding—assisting young learners with initial attempts at a task (Bodrova & Leong, 1996). When Maggie and her mother read *Yoko* (Wells, 1998) Maggie asked, "Why did Mrs. Jenkins *fret* about Yoko?" Natalie explained that "fretted" was just like "worried," and Maggie asked why Mrs. Jenkins was worried. During this exchange, and many more like it, Maggie's language and concepts were being *socially constructed* (Vygotsky, 1978), or learned with the assistance of someone more knowledgeable. Children are not passive learners; they reconstruct language as they learn and apply it, making it their own.

Critical Theory

Critical theory addresses the social and cultural backgrounds children bring with them when they come to school, and involves an understanding of the inequalities of certain groups in acquiring literacy (Freire, 1985; Gee, 1996). Young children from nonmainstream environments may have very different ways of "taking meaning" from the environment and from language than the mainstream population (Heath, 1983). Home literacy can take many forms that do not match the discourse of school communities (Taylor, 1997). Teachers who adhere to critical theory are sensitive to the ways some groups of children with diverse backgrounds "read the world" differently than mainstream children, putting them on an unequal footing in early literacy development (Freire, 1985). These teachers support a multicultural approach, address issues of social justice and nonviolence, and help children become critical thinkers and readers. Proponents of critical theory advocate social change and gender equality within the literacy curriculum (Shannon, 1998).

Emergent Literacy

The work of Marie Clay, a New Zealand educator, heralded changes in the way researchers and teachers viewed early reading. Her studies indicated that children know a great deal about reading and writing before they come to school, and they are able to experiment with and apply their knowledge in various ways (Clay, 1975). *Reading readiness* seemed to be an inaccurate term, since Clay's research showed that there was *not* a specific sequence of skills children needed to master prior to reading and writing. The children she studied seemed instead to "emerge" into literacy—with writing, reading, and oral language abilities developing together.

Emergent literacy was recently defined as "the view that literacy learning begins at birth and is encouraged through participation with adults in meaningful activities; these literacy behaviors change and eventually become conventional over time" (Neuman, Copple, & Bredekamp, 2000, p. 123). From a very young age, children who are exposed to oral and written language gradually gain control over the forms of literacy. Print-related knowledge develops similarly to the way children learn oral language (Morrow, 1997). When children are actively engaged with interesting and meaningful reading and writing experiences, they develop literacy knowledge early in their lives.

CAMBOURNE'S CONDITIONS FOR LITERACY DEVELOPMENT

Brian Cambourne (1988) proposed that children acquire early facility with oral and written language most easily when certain conditions are present in their environments, both at home and school. How can families and teachers use Cambournes's eight conditions of literacy development to help children develop language and literacy in pleasurable and meaningful ways?

1. *Immersion*—Children need to be surrounded by interesting, high-quality children's books and different kinds of text (e.g., charts, labels, newspapers, magazines). Read aloud every day to children, sing to them, play word games, and use movement and dance to generate lively engagement in language, literacy, and stories.

2. *Demonstration*—Model reading and writing for children. Let them see you writing notes, letters, stories, recipes, and lists. Make sure they notice you reading to yourself, for pleasure, for information, for directions, and for other purposes. Show them how to hold a book, turn the pages, and read aloud.

3. *Engagement*—Help children become active learners who see themselves as potential readers and writers. Set up a risk-free environment so they can experiment with language and literacy. Provide easy access to paper, pencils, crayons, markers, books, and other literacy materials.

4. *Expectation*—Set realistic expectations for language and literacy development. Become familiar with the developmental stages of emergent literacy, and support children in appropriate tasks. Expect that they will become accomplished readers and writers in their own time.

5. *Responsibility*—Give children choices about books to read. Set up the environment to promote self-direction. Provide easy access to books and literacy materials on low shelves and in baskets and show children how to take care of them.

6. *Approximation*—Accept children's mistakes when they are learning to talk, read, and write. Congratulate them on their accomplishments. Guide them gently into accuracy and soon they will begin to self-correct.

7. *Use*—Create a climate for functional and meaningful uses of oral and written language. Encourage children to read along with you; help you write notes, letters, and lists; and engage in lots of conversations.

8. *Response*—Listen to children, welcome their comments and questions, and extend their use of oral and written language. Celebrate the enormous language and literacy learning that is occurring daily!

Source: Adapted from Cambourne, B. (1988). *The whole story: Natural learning and the acquisition of literacy in the classroom.* Auckland, NZ: Ashton Scholastic.

A Balanced Approach

In sum, current research reveals that "learning to read and write is a complex, multifaceted process that requires a wide variety of instructional approaches" (Neuman et al., 2000, p. 39). The debates over which method of teaching reading may be put to rest by the studies show that no single method is best for all children all the time. Many teachers now incorporate a "balance" of research-based strategies, believing this to be the most effective way to approach literacy development (Tompkins, 2003). There are three basic principles in a balanced approach to literacy: (a) developing skills and strategies while nurturing a love of literature, (b) varying instructional approaches to fit the needs of the children, and (c) immersing children in a variety of reading materials (Fitzgerald, 1999). The balanced approach to literacy instruction incorporates the best in research, stresses the role of the teacher as an informed decision maker, allows the teacher flexibility in building a literacy program, and is based on a comprehensive view of literacy that includes reading and writing (Spiegel, 1998).

LEARNING TO READ

We now know that children do not learn to read and write spontaneously. Children come to preschool and kindergarten having been exposed to various language and literacy environments at home (Heath, 1983; Taylor, 1997; Teale & Sulzby, 1986). Adult support is needed to maximize children's learning as they actively construct knowledge about the way reading and writing work. The values, attitudes, and expectations toward literacy that are acquired in the home can have a long-term effect on learning to read (Snow, Burns, & Griffin, 1998).

Family members and teachers offer a critical role in supporting children's learning, scaffolding new skills, and understanding of reading and writing processes (Neuman et al., 2000). The guidance adults give to young children to help them succeed at reading and writing does not have to take the form of direct, formal instruction, but may be informal, playful, and casual. It may mean pointing out words that start with the same sound as the child's name or making up rhymes to go with a silly word in a poem. All instruction should be sensitive to the child's developmental level and culture and build on prior experiences. The best reading and writing education builds on what children already know and can do (Neuman et al., 2000). Literacy results from the ongoing interplay of learning and development in a supportive environment.

What experiences in the preschool years lay a favorable groundwork for reading and writing when children reach school age? A recent report by the National Research Council (Snow et al., 1998), along with a joint position statement by the International Reading Association (IRA) and the National Association for the Education of Young Children (NAEYC), provides insight into developmentally appropriate practices for early literacy education. These reports synthesized many research studies on reading and writing and made recommendations for teachers, administrators, policymakers, and families for

Laura, age 4. "I know how to read."

helping young children acquire a strong foundation for literacy. A summary of the recommendations of these studies and other research follows.

The Role of Oral Language

A strong foundation in *oral language* is a prerequisite for learning to read and write (Snow et al., 1998; Glazer, 1989; Morrow, 1997). The close emotional relationship between parent and child makes them ideal partners in the "early language game" (Butler, 1998). The back-and-forth responses of parent and child have also been described as a "dance" (Stern, 1977), where turn-taking, phonetics, syntax, and semantics are learned in a loving, natural way. When babies are deprived of this rich language stimulation, they are at risk for later difficulties in learning, particularly in reading and writing (Butler, 1998).

In all families, caregivers who add simple books to the language environment of infants and toddlers furnish a new dimension to the child's language. The contributions of books to language learning are multifaceted (Schickendanz, 1999). The musical rhythms, rhymes, alliteration, and sounds of book language have a different quality than spoken language, thus introducing the young child to phonemic understandings that go beyond ordinary language sounds. Through hearing stories children also learn the meaning of new vocabulary, how to interpret complex sentences, and how to use decontextualized language (language that refers to objects and events not in the here and now). Maggie, age 2½, used decontextualized language when she commented, "We have lots of plates, so we can have lots of friends over." She was recalling both the book *One of Each* (Hoberman, 1997) and the dishes in the kitchen, but she was not directly looking at either when she made this observation.

Children whose first language is not English face unique challenges upon entering child-care and preschool settings. Tabors (1997) refers to the "double bind" these young children find themselves in while trying to acquire English as a second language. On one hand, they cannot learn English without social interaction with English-speaking peers and adults; on the other hand, they have limited ways of socially engaging with speakers of English, due to the communication challenges.

A new preschool teacher, whose class was composed of mainly non-English-speaking 3- to 5-year olds, told us her biggest fears were that the children would feel like no one understood them and that they would be scared in a new place. When one of the children, a "talkative" little girl, began to sit away from her playmates, slouching, and frowning, the teacher tried to find out her problem. "I sat beside her, touched her shoulders, and asked what was the matter. Tears came to her eyes and she talked for two solid minutes about something. She pointed, used her voice inflection, and made facial expressions. I understood, but didn't recognize a word." Through the child's nonverbal communication, the teacher realized that she had "lost" her new friend to another playmate. The teacher helped dry her eyes, and together they found other new friends for the child.

Recognizing the challenges of second-language learners, teachers can develop oral language skills in English by:

1. Using running commentaries while engaged in activities or tasks to directly connect objects and actions to language.

2. Taking time during snack and lunchtime to initiate conversations and promote interactions among English speaking and non-English-speaking children.

3. Helping establish play relationships between children during outside or inside playtimes.

4. Organizing circle time to include songs and movements with highly predictable structures, allowing children to catch on to words, phrases, and movements that are repetitive.

5. Paying particular attention to book-reading times to help keep children focused on stories (Tabors, 1997). See chapter 4 for a detailed description of supporting non-English speaking children during read-aloud times.

The Importance of Reading Aloud

The single most important activity caregivers and teachers can do to help children become successful readers is to *read aloud* to them every day (Morrow, 1997; Neuman et al., 2000; Sulzby, 1985). In addition to the language of books, young children can learn how books work, the way to physically handle books, and what to expect in stories. By 3 to 4 months, babies start to focus on the pictures in books and will soon reach out to turn the pages themselves. Although older infants and toddlers rarely sit still very long to hear stories, it is important to encourage parents to keep reading, even for just a minute or two at a time.

By the time a child is 2 or 3, family reading routines will be established, such as at naptime or bedtime reading, and children who have been read to since infancy will begin to finish familiar lines in stories, memorize books, and pretend read to themselves. Pretending to read books and hearing stories read aloud helps children develop a global knowledge of books and a "sense of story," an idea of what typically happens in narrative (Neuman et al., 2000). Children who enjoy books and stories are familiar with the language of books and story schema and have some control over book-handling concepts such as holding the book correctly and turning the pages from right to left, have established a "literacy set," according to Don Holdaway (1979). In other words, the reading-like behaviors they are displaying indicate that they are all set to emerge into real reading.

A reciprocal relationship between caregiver and child is built during read-aloud times. Parents influence the child, but the child's behaviors and interests also have an impact on the types of books and literacy materials the parents share (Whitehurst et al., 1994). When 5-year-old Benjamin became interested in owls, his parents located books about owls in the library and

Pretending to read favorite books helps children develop a sense of story.

RECIPE FOR READING WITH YOUR CHILD

Ingredients Needed:

1 adult

1 book

1 child (add more if you prefer)

1 comfortable place to sit

Mike, age 4.
"Mom is reading
to Mike."

Directions: Select a good book. Find a cozy spot. Let your child sit in your lap or close beside you. Open the book. Begin reading. Enjoy!

found a Web site that had pictures of owls and accompanying sound bytes. Benjamin was able to learn how books and electronic resources can be used to answer questions and gain insight on subjects of interest.

What types of books appeal to young children? Recent brain research suggests that we make meaning of new ideas and experiences when they are relevant, emotionally engaging, and organized in patterns (Jensen, 1998). Good children's literature often includes all three criteria for making meaning. Select books for reading aloud that:

- Are relevant to the child and have interesting language.
- Have quality illustrations.
- Portray intriguing characters.
- Sometimes include humor.

The language and repetition of books create patterns that appeal to children and help them learn. Chapter 2 will provide more extensive information about selecting and using children's books.

Providing a Print-Rich Environment

Researchers in the area of early literacy have also found that young children benefit by being exposed to a *print-rich environment* (Harste, Woodward, & Burke, 1984; Holdaway, 1979). When there are books, magazines, newspapers, advertisements, and/or electronic print resources around the home and preschool, children develop the idea that letters and words are important and that they convey meaning. *Environmental print* is a similar term that refers to written language found in many places in the home and community. It might include print on billboards, stores, food containers, and clothing. When adults point out the labels on soup cans or cereal boxes they are helping children become aware of the way

Teachers can make simple books of environmental print to use at home and school to help children learn letters, words, and alphabetical order and encourage oral language development.

print is used to gain meaning. In Figure 1.1 we provide a letter to families about using environmental print to support children's emergent literacy. Teachers can make books of environmental print to use for a variety of purposes.

Adult Modeling

Adults *model* the uses of written language when they read and write in the presence of children, making the processes of literacy clear. A parent might sit down to write the grocery list, ask the child what they need from the store, then write "tofu" and "black beans" for the child to see. Through this example important *concepts about print* are brought to the child: Oral language can be written down, letters follow letters in a linear sequence, and written language

---

Dear Families,

Every day children see print around them in their homes and neighborhoods. We call this *environmental print*. Children may notice it on signs, labels, advertisements, and packages. Shapes, colors, and pictures that accompany environmental print are visual cues to help children remember the letters and words. Here are a few hints to help your child read the print in her world:

1. Point out signs on stores, businesses, or restaurants as you drive. McDonald's, Kmart, or Home Depot are some examples. Talk about the letters that are familiar to your child, such as those in her name. As you shop, help your child read labels on the products.

2. When you eat breakfast in the morning, ask your child to help you identify the food container(s). For example, Honey Nut Cheerios, Raisin Bran, Quaker's Oatmeal, or Cream of Wheat might be easily recognized if they are favorite breakfast choices.

3. When you finish using a food container, such as a cereal box, can, or egg carton, cut out the labels. Make a small booklet with your child by pasting one label on each page. Use the booklet to help her learn letters, words, or alphabetical order.

4. Take a walk around your neighborhood and see what signs she recognizes. You might find stop signs, billboard advertisements, and storefronts. Call attention to these environmental words, talk about letters, shapes, and colors, and see if she can begin to "read" any of them.

Happy reading!

[Teacher's name]

FIGURE 1.1
Teacher to Family: Using Environmental Print

can be reconstructed when you read it back (Clay, 1991). As adults take dictation of children's letters to relatives, they can model the sequencing of words in sentences, directionality of lines of print, and checking one's writing for errors.

When adults begin reading to children in infancy, by the time they are about age 2, the toddlers often begin to distinguish between pictures and print. Words, letters, capitalization, and punctuation can be pointed out in environmental print or books when the child is developmentally ready. Adults who are unable to read may be very motivated to help their children learn to read; however, they will need extra support from teachers (see Figure 1.2).

At 2½, Grace and Dylan were fascinated by the book ***Chicka Chicka Boom Boom*** (Martin & Archambault, 1989) both because of the playful language ("Skit

---

What can teachers do if parents and caregivers of children in their programs have limited literacy skills? Can they still be involved in their children's literacy development? Looking back on my career I am reminded of two different situations with families that point out the importance of working respectfully with caregivers who have low literacy skills.

Many years ago I worked as a kindergarten teacher in a very poor community in Florida. One of our goals was to teach the children to write their names. I worked with Elroy for weeks, having him trace and copy just the first letter in his name. He dutifully tried, but as the months passed it seemed that he was making very little progress toward mastering this important skill. Finally, I requested that the school social worker bring his grandmother (with whom he lived) to school.

I was prepared to tell her ways that she could help her grandchild by reading to him, writing grocery lists in front of him, and labeling things in the environment with written signs. I also needed her permission for Elroy to see a resource teacher for special help. When the grandmother arrived for the conference I showed her Elroy's work and asked if she would sign a paper to allow another teacher to help him. She nodded and asked if she could make the mark. Not knowing what she meant, I nodded too, and watched as she drew an "X" at the bottom of the form.

Several years later, as part of a research project, I interviewed Head Start parents about their reading-aloud practices with their children. One father of 11 children told me that he was not able to read much himself, but that he wanted to participate in our project because he desired something better for his children. He hoped they would learn to read and write, because he knew the importance of literacy.

Parents with limited literacy skills can look at books with their children, making up stories to go with the pictures. Wordless picture books are a particularly good resource to use as a basis for creating stories. Caregivers can also be encouraged to tell stories and talk with their children about daily activities. Teachers can provide information about adult literacy and English as a second language classes, or programs such as Parent Read.

FIGURE 1.2

Teacher to Teacher: What If Parents Can't Read?
Source: Connie Green.

skat skoodle doot. Flip flop flee") and the colorful alphabet letters climbing up the coconut tree. It wasn't long before they recognized many of the letters their mothers pointed out to them. Playful, active interactions with print on a regular basis are an important component of literacy development (Neuman et al., 2000).

The Alphabetic Principle

The National Research Council recommendations state that letter knowledge is one of the basic prerequisites for success in literacy learning (Snow et al., 1998). Many experiences with environmental print, books, and other literacy materials give children the opportunity to become familiar with letters and sounds. Through their own active learning and adult scaffolding, young children become aware of the *alphabetic principle*, the awareness of the systematic relationship between letters and sounds (Neuman et al., 2000). Children will become familiar with the shapes and names of letters when they play with magnetic letters, alphabet puzzles, and matching games, or form letters out of clay. The Montessori system uses sandpaper letters and the movable alphabet to provide kinesthetic stimulation for learning letter forms (Humphryes, 1998). Children who enjoy technology might learn to recognize letters from computer games or by printing out the same letter in different fonts (Schickendanz, 1999). Children can learn letter features by sorting letters that extend below or above the line or matching capital to lowercase letters.

Experiences with print should include opportunities for children to learn the sounds associated with letters in the English orthographic system. In a preschool classroom taught by one of the authors, 3- and 4-year-olds were invited to sign in as they arrived at school each day (Green, 1998). This gave them an opportunity to associate the written letters with the sounds they heard in their names. Taking dictation from children and providing information about letters and sounds is another way to help children develop the alphabetic principle. One mom wrote a story for her 3-year-old, pointing out each time she wrote a word that started with the same letter as his name or the names of other family members. This helped him make a connection between the sounds he heard and the written forms he watched his mother make.

Caregivers can incorporate activities that promote the alphabetic principle into daily routines. Pointing to words as you read from a restaurant menu or reading labels at the supermarket help children become attuned to the individual letters in words and associate them with the sounds they hear (Snow et al., 1998). Showing a child the difference between "chocolate" and "cherry" on ice cream containers helps them distinguish sound and visual discrepancies.

Access to Literacy Materials

To achieve literacy, children also need *access to reading and writing materials* (Green & Halsall, 1991; Neuman et al., 2000). Well-stocked home and classroom libraries give children the opportunity to look at books frequently and develop habits of lifelong reading. In some homes where books are not readily available, literacy materials may include advertisements, instruction manuals, calendars, or recipes (Taylor, 1997). These can be valuable resources for learning about the forms and functions of literacy within the child's community. Wise teachers will gain information about their students' home literacy environments and build continuity between home and school.

Durkin (1966) described the early readers in her research study as "paper and pencil kids." These children, who became accomplished members of the literacy community at an early age, had ready access to literacy materials they could use for creating pictures, signs, labels, letters, and lists. Figure 1.3 is a sample letter to families that suggests inexpensive supplies to use at home to support emergent literacy development. Markers, crayons, pencils, various colors and sizes of paper, envelopes, paint, and clay are excellent materials for art and writing. Books, magazines, and other forms of print are usually found in abundance in homes of children who succeed in reading and writing. Chil-

---

Dear Families,

As children begin to recognize letters and play with print, they may enjoy exploring new materials that support emergent literacy. The following list includes inexpensive tools that can be used for creating letters and words. Remember that young children need time to experiment with literacy materials. It is not necessary for adults to provide formal instruction in the alphabet.

* Magnetic letters—fun for making words on the refrigerator or other metal surface.
* Sandpaper letters—children can feel the form of the letter.
* Chalkboards or whiteboards—good for experimenting with letter forms or for leaving family messages.
* Water painting—children like to paint the house or sidewalk with this harmless "paint."
* Alphabet puzzles—help children recognize and match letter forms.
* Alphabet cookie cutters with play dough or damp sand—tactile surface provides a medium for children to feel letter shapes.
* Alphabet blocks—good for letter recognition and writing names.
* Markers, crayons, paints, paper, envelopes—encourage drawing and writing stories or letters. Children can make their own note paper with rubber stamps or stickers.

Sincerely,

[Teacher's Name]

FIGURE 1.3

Teacher to Family: Emergent Literacy Materials

dren who are allowed to play with print by filling in order forms the parent doesn't need, writing on canceled checks, or making signs to inform others are given an early entry to the world of literacy. Parents may demonstrate how they fill in calendars, compose thank-you notes, or send e-mail messages on the computer. When children see print used in purposeful ways, they are more likely to make meaningful approximations of literacy themselves.

LANGUAGE DEVELOPMENT

One morning Maggie's mother asked her young daughter what she would like for breakfast. Maggie hesitated for a moment, then said, "I thought, but not for very long," (about her breakfast) quoting a phrase from **Piggy in the Puddle** by Charlotte Pomerantz (1989). One of the most important and obvious benefits of sharing literature with young children is the impact books have on language development. Young children delight in the sounds of poetry, try out new vocabulary, and acquire understanding of concepts as they experience the language of books. Some children add their own words or verses to favorite rhymes or songs, as Dylan did when he sang about "Ringo, Singo, and Tingo", after his mom sang from the songbook **Bingo** (Wells, 1999). Sharing poetry in books and rhymes by Dr. Seuss, A. A. Milne, Jack Prelutsky, and "Mother Goose" encourages children to play with language and invent their own variations and verses (Neuman et al., 2000).

Even before they begin talking, children are developing *receptive language*, an understanding of words and their meanings. Gabrielle (15 months) demonstrated her receptive vocabulary when she pointed to her own nose, ears, and so on, as her mother read a book about body parts. When asked, "Where is the cow (horse, pig)?" in a farm animal book, Gabrielle pointed to the animals and made their sounds. In Figure 1.4 a preschool teacher describes family activities to support young children's language development. *Expressive language* is another term for spoken language. When Gabrielle could name the body parts and animals, she demonstrated her ability to use expressive language. Children's receptive language learning is usually several months ahead of their expressive language. It is obvious that literature fosters the development of both types of language. Figure 1.5 provides a letter to families that describes playful and enjoyable *daily* language experiences.

Language acquisition is not only important for oral communication; it is also a first step in becoming literate. Research has shown a clear link between the size of a child's vocabulary and early reading ability (Snow et al., 1998). According to Rosenblatt (1978), reading is an interaction between the reader and written text. When we read, we are not just decoding print; we are reconstructing the author's meaning based on our knowledge of language patterns and meanings (Goodman, 1967; Rosenblatt, 1978). Children's knowledge of lan-

One family activity I use frequently involves asking the parent/caregiver to generate a list of all the words the child has said. At the same time I generate a list of the words the child has used at school. Then we compile our lists and count the words in the child's expressive vocabulary. Several months later we make new lists to see the progress quantitatively. With Hispanic/Latino families we make lists of the child's expressive English vocabulary and expressive Spanish vocabulary.

Another activity involves the parent and child creating a book together. The child chooses pictures of interest from magazines, usually an object or character he or she names, and the parent cuts the picture out. Together they glue the picture on construction paper and write a word or phrase underneath. I put a photo of the child on the front cover, laminate and bind the pages, then allow the child to show his/her book to the class before taking it home. Parents and children really enjoy this early literacy activity.

FIGURE 1.4

Teacher to Teacher: Language Development at Home
Source: Kyley B. Ferris, Early Head Start Teacher, Asheville, NC.

guage patterns and familiarity with syntax (language structure) and semantics (meaning) helps them anticipate and interpret written language as they begin to read (Morrow, 1997).

The literary language found in books is often quite different from spoken language. In books, children hear phrases like "once upon a time," "many years ago," "in the arms of their happy parents," and words such as "fretted," "homeward," and "plunking" rarely used in oral language conversation. Children who have acquired background knowledge of literary language are better prepared for the organization and vocabulary found in text. In the following paragraphs we will look at the four areas of language learning children acquire during the preschool years—phonological knowledge, syntax, semantics, and pragmatics—and ways these facets of language can be enhanced through literature experiences.

Phonological Knowledge

Phonological knowledge refers to the ability to differentiate between speech and nonspeech sounds, distinguish between phonemes (speech sounds), and attend to slight differences in the way words are pronounced, depending on context (McGee & Richgels, 2000). This knowledge is generally acquired through speaking and listening. There are two important types of phonological knowledge: phonological awareness and phonemic awareness. *Phonological awareness* is "awareness of anything to do with the sounds of language, from intonation patterns and the sounds of words and syllables, to the sound of a phoneme [the smallest unit of sounds in a language]" (Richgels, 2001, p. 275).

Dear Families,

Children who speak clearly and confidently are better able to express their needs and desires, develop friendships, and are more competent at acquiring new skills. Oral language is the foundation for reading and writing. Children who have acquired strong vocabularies, speak in complex sentences, and differentiate among the sounds of language usually become successful readers. It is also likely that children who are successful speakers have heard stories read aloud from an early age and have participated in conversations from the time they were small.

How can families help their babies, toddlers, and preschoolers become capable language users?

• Begin talking to your child from the time of birth. Respond with soothing words to your baby's cries, coos, and laughter. Respond with enthusiasm to new sounds and treat them as meaningful. Treat early babbles and coos as real language by responding in a conversational way during feeding, diaper changes, and other routines.

• Provide your baby with many experiences that you can talk about. On walks around the neighborhood talk about flowers, trees, pets, houses, and signs. Identify and describe foods at the grocery store. Children learn vocabulary within the context of meaningful experiences.

• Play with your child, using language to describe what both of you are doing. Any type of healthy play provides fertile ground for language experiences.

• Encourage your child's natural instinct toward dramatic play as an important source for developing creativity and language. Children are thrilled when family members take on roles in their play. But remember—let your child take the lead.

• Read to your child often and in many different situations. Many families read regularly at naptime or bedtime; others find opportunities to share books while waiting for appointments, in the car while another adult is driving, or early in the morning before the day's activities begin.

• Limit television viewing and computer games. Young children learn best through active, physical involvement and engaging in language with people who can model turn-taking and introduce new ways to use words and sentences.

Sincerely,

[Teacher's Name]

FIGURE 1.5
Teacher to Family: Supporting Oral Language

Most children gradually develop an awareness of the phonological structure of speech during the preschool years (Snow et al., 1998). *Phonemic awareness* can be considered a subset of phonological awareness and refers to the ability to hear and distinguish phonemes; for example, whether two words begin or end with the same sound or have the same vowel sound. "The entry to phonemic awareness typically begins with an appreciation of alliteration, for instance that 'boy' and 'butterfly' begin with a /b/" (Snow et al., 1998). In addition to hearing alliterative sounds, children who are phonemically aware recognize rhymes, can substitute sounds in spoken words (*cat* to *bat*), hear syllables (ba-by), and orally segment words (b-a-t).

Phonemic awareness that young children acquire before and while they learn to read is correlated with successful reading (Snow et al., 1998). While there is much emphasis placed on developing phonemic awareness in kindergarten today, *it is not necessary that it be taught as an isolated skill.* Embedding phonemic awareness activities in natural language and literacy practices provides daily learning opportunities for young children.

The following examples demonstrate the way young children develop phonemic awareness by being exposed to literature before coming to school. In the bathtub, after reading *Pete and P.J.: Sing, Dance and Read With Me* (Bousman, 2000), Nate quoted the phrase, "wishy-washy wish washy wee!" demonstrating an enjoyment of language sounds. Looking at the rain, Maggie observed, "The rain is turning from 'drip drip to splash splash'," an adapted quote from Shirley Hughes's book *An Evening at Alfie's* (1985). An excellent book for developing phonemic awareness is *What in the World?* by Eve Merriam (1990). Lines like "What in the world goes gnawing and pawing scratching and latching sniffing and squiffing nibbling for tidbits of leftover cheese? Please?" (Merriam, 1990, unnumbered) stimulate sensitivity to sound and the ability to discern the differences between sounds. See Figure 1.6 for a list of books that promote phonemic awareness.

Baby-O (Carlstrom, 1992)
Barnyard Banter (Fleming, 1994)
Carrot/Parrot (Martin, 1991)
Chicka Chicka Boom Boom (Martin & Archambault, 1989)
Each Peach Pear Plum (Ahlberg & Ahlberg, 1978)
Higgle Wiggle Happy Rhymes (Merriam, 1994)
In the Tall, Tall Grass (Fleming, 1991)
Jake Baked the Cake (Hennessey, 1990)
Pigs in the Mud in the Middle of the Rud (Plourde, 1997)
Poems for the Very Young (Rosen, 1993)
Read-Aloud Rhymes for the Very Young (Prelutsky, 1986)
Sheep in a Jeep (Shaw, 1986)
Silly Sally (Wood, 1992)
Sleepytime Rhyme (Charlip, 2000)
To Market, to Market (Miranda, 1997)

FIGURE 1.6
Books for Developing Phonemic Awareness

The association between sounds and written letters are sometimes referred to as *grapho-phonic relationships* (McGee & Richgels, 2000). In English two or more speech sounds usually are associated with each letter. Beginning readers must learn the different occasions when each sound is used. Having a strong foundation in oral language from conversations with adults and hearing books read aloud provides a framework for learning grapho-phonic relationships.

Syntax

Syntax refers to the grammatical rules of language and the way words are arranged in sentences. Exposure to a wide variety of literature introduces children to interesting and unique syntax that is different from the structure of spoken language. "Children who have been read to a great deal will already know, in some way, that the language of books is different from the language that they speak. They will be developing 'an ear' for bookish or literary forms of language" (Clay, 1991, p. 28). A young mother shared the following example of her son's "bookish language." For several days after he heard **Yertle the Turtle and Other Stories** by Dr. Seuss (1966), Nate would repeat phrases from the book, following the sentence structure. According to his mother, "Nate put great emphasis on the line 'the turtles were happy, quite happy indeed.'"

Semantics

Semantics refers to the meaning connected with language. Understanding vocabulary and making sense of phrases and sentences are part of semantics. Many young children seem to constantly be asking questions in an effort to better understand language and the world around them. The day after hearing **Tasty Baby Belly Buttons** (Sierra, 1999) Maggie asked her mother what "in the arms of their happy parents" meant. At 2½ she often asked questions about words and sentences in books she read, clarifying definitions and making the new words part of her vocabulary. Many children learn vocabulary through the context of books. Emily loved **The Wild Baby** (Lindgren, 1981) and memorized most of it before she was 3. One day when she had lost a toy she instructed her mother, "Mama, hunt vainly" using an advanced vocabulary word she learned from her favorite book.

Pragmatics

Pragmatics is the social context of language. As they learn to speak, children gradually learn that language is used differently in different cultural or social situations. For example, we generally have different ways of communication in school, at a doctor's office, at a grocery store, or at home. Unique vocabulary is associated with each location, as well as differences in tone of voice and ways of approaching those who have more power in each situation. Most children seem to internalize these differences fairly well, given enough experiences and modeling by adults. Reading books about diverse cultures and places may also introduce children to the ways people use language in different situations. In addition, children may also acquire knowledge of the pragmatics of books, or book language, through hearing stories read aloud.

CONCEPT DEVELOPMENT

According to Piaget (1926), cognitive development occurs as children interact with their physical environment. Babies construct knowledge as they explore their surroundings—crawling, touching, smelling, tasting, looking, and listening. Piaget's theory describes how children grow and develop cognitively according to their age and developmental stage. Through his observations and conversations with children, Piaget documented the stages of cognitive development through which children progress as they acquire more sophisticated abilities to conceptualize the physical and logical world. He stressed children's capability to make meaning of their environment when given opportunities to manipulate objects and interact with others. As new information is learned, it is integrated into prior knowledge and more complex understanding evolves.

Vygotsky emphasized the social aspect of learning and the role adults and older children play in mediating the learning of the very young (Berk & Windsler, 1995). You will recall from your earlier reading in this chapter that Vygotsky's social constructivist theory considers language as a primary tool in helping children acquire higher mental functions. He used the term *zone of proximal development* to describe the continuum of behaviors between which children can accomplish a task independently and with assistance. When children confront new problems competently, they are functioning at their independent level. However, with assistance of someone more adept at the task, they become able to work at their potential level. As adults assist children in their problem solving and language learning they are scaffolding the child's learning, much as the scaffold of a building provides support while the building is under construction.

During story reading, parents can provide scaffolding to help children acquire new concepts from books by labeling objects and characters, modifying the language to make it more understandable, and adjusting their reading style to make the text more meaningful to the child (McGee & Richgels, 2000). For younger children, adults may label objects and characters, ask children to point to objects, or make a game of their interactions with beginning books. Daniel's mom, for example, structured situations during storybook reading to help him acquire skills such as counting, naming, and pointing. At her requests while reading aloud, Daniel counted animals, named foods and objects, or pointed to things he liked (Green, Lilly, & Barrett, 2002). Gabrielle's mother made a game of the text while reading a book about nature to her 14-month-old daughter. The mother wrote in her reading journal:

> I covered the dog with my hand. "Donde está el perro?" I asked. "Woof!" responds Gabrielle. She points and uncovers my hand. She looks up at me and smiles. She covers the dog with my hand as if to say, "Again!"

When adults read to infants, they may be introducing language and concepts for the first time through the pictures and words in books. As children gain new experiences, caregivers can bridge prior knowledge to new book concepts by helping children make connections between the two. Cochran-Smith (1984) described how children engage in "text-to-life" and "life-to-text" associations with books, allowing them to relate text to their own experiences. One mother explained:

> It seems to me that when Sean experiences something in life he recognizes it in his books and becomes more interested in the book. There are several books he has become more interested in *after* learning about the content in his real life experiences. For example, "Jack and Jill" became a favorite once he began falling and also climbing up and down hills. He points to his own head when he sees Jack on the ground holding his head. (Green et al., 2002, p. 256)

As children mature, caregivers bring attention to narrative elements, introduce and explain challenging vocabulary, and help children analyze the motivation of characters and logical relationships in stories (McGee & Richgels, 2000). Developing predictions and making inferences during reading helps children focus on the story and anticipate events to come. These skills have powerful benefits for later reading and many areas of learning.

When children hear books read, they may confirm concepts that are familiar to them or expand their notions of certain ideas. Stories extend the borders of our immediate world and supply language to frame our new knowledge. Alison, age 3, had never been to the beach. In preparation for a family trip, her grandmother gave her **Spot Goes to the Beach** (Hill, 1985). After reading it with her mom and dad, they talked about what she needed to pack. Alison suggested a beach ball, her bathing suit, and a small pail and shovel from the toy box. She also began using vocabulary and phrases acquired from the book, such as "sailor hat," "sand castles," and "fishing with a net." Clearly, the time spent together reading about the beach contributed to Alison's budding concept of a place she had not yet experienced.

Caregivers who describe objects and scenes in picture books, talk about new vocabulary, and relate book concepts to children's experiences are demonstrating the learning process. Through hearing stories, young children internalize ways of thinking and solving problems within their culture (Van Kleek, Alexander, Vigil, & Templeton, 1996). "The intimacy and social nature of story reading amplify children's opportunities to acquire concepts and skills, and to learn about the world and how they will navigate it" (Green et al., 2002, p. 248).

CONCEPTS ABOUT PRINT

At 2½, Grace demonstrated a beginning awareness of print when she sat down with her mother to read stories. Opening a book on her lap, she told her mother "I'll read it." After looking at it for a minute or two she turned to her mother and said, "You read the words." Grace maintained control by holding the book and turning the pages herself. Her request demonstrated her new knowledge that print (rather than pictures) produces the meaning of the story (Neuman et al., 2000).

Differentiating between text and pictures is a first step in developing concepts about print. Reading includes an understanding of many print features that are necessary to learn if children are to become independent readers and gain meaning from the books they read (Clay, 1975). In Figure 1.7, Fisher (1991) outlines the conventions of print that children become aware of during shared reading experiences, when adults and children read books together.

Teachers and caregivers can help young children develop an understanding of print conventions during regular story reading times. The purpose of these occasions is to develop awareness of print within the context of authentic reading, not to teach isolated skills. Here are some ways adults can help young children as they grow in their learning about print:

Book Knowledge
- Front and back of book
- Progression of reading left-hand page before right-hand page
- Page turning and book care
- Difference between pictures and print
- Title, author, and illustrator

Directionality
- Where to begin reading on a page
- Reading left to right
- Return sweep
- Following pages sequentially

Visual Conventions
- Concepts of letter, word, and sentence
- Spacing between words
- Punctuation
- Letter recognition

FIGURE 1.7

Concepts About Print

Source: Adapted from *Joyful Learning: A Whole Language Kindergarten* by B. Fisher, 1991, Portsmouth, NH: Heinemann, pp. 50–51.

- Point to the words in book titles, or note words that begin with the same letter as the child's name.
- After reading a book, go back and look for the main character's name.
- Four-year-olds may be able to locate a repetitive phrase, such as "Run, run" or others that appear in familiar nursery rhymes or stories.
- Challenge the child to find letters or point to separate words.
- Show toddlers how to hold books right side up and turn pages carefully from front to back.
- Move your fingers under words to show left-to-right progression.

Alphabet books are a good resource for learning letter recognition and sometimes beginning sounds. Today's alphabet books include stunning illustrations and a wide range of themes that would appeal to a variety of young readers. In chapter 2 we discuss alphabet books and related activities in more detail.

LISTENING COMPREHENSION

Teachers often report that children simply don't listen. Although up to 80% of the information we receive comes to us via listening, it is the area of language arts that is taught the least (Hunsaker, 1990; Jalongo, 2000). Adults are reported to listen with only 25% efficiency due to distractions and preoccupation with other matters. As children move up through the grades in school, they are expected to do more and more listening. In some school settings children are expected to listen as much as 50% of the time (Hunsaker, 1990). It is important, therefore, for teachers of young children to understand the listening process and know ways to develop listening.

Listening involves three components: (a) *hearing*, a physiological response; (b) *listening*, a perceptual act that involves focusing and cueing in on environmental stimuli; and (c) *comprehension*, cognitively processing the sounds and assigning meaning to the sounds (Jalongo, 2000). If we want children to become "good listeners," we must realize that there is more involved in listening than being still and quiet. Listening is an active process that includes physical and cognitive engagement.

Listening is the first area of language arts to develop. Children who have normal hearing listen to sounds while they are still in the womb, and they can differentiate among individual sounds shortly after birth. By 9 to 10 months, babies are able to follow simple directions (e.g., "Where's your nose?" "Bring Mommy the ball."). Through active listening, children process and comprehend new information, come to understand feelings, and acquire cultural beliefs (Jalongo, 2000). Maggie, age 2½ years, frequently asked questions during and after story reading. The day she listened to **The Tale of Two Bad Mice** (Potter, 1974), she asked what "odds and ends" were. We can suppose that she not only listened to the story while it was read, but she thought about it later and needed more information to help her understand the meaning.

Children also demonstrate their listening comprehension by retelling stories they have heard. As teachers, we can explain to parents the value of allowing young children to retell books from the pictures. Preschool and kindergarten children sometimes enjoy telling stories with puppets, flannel board figures, or other props. Wordless picture books provide excellent opportunities for children to retell stories or add their own interpretations of pictures in a group discussion. We will discuss wordless picture books in more detail in chapter 2. See Figure 1.8 for tips on developing listening skills.

Engaging children in participatory activities during story reading may enhance listening comprehension. For example, children may be asked to move like characters in a book, clap their hands when they hear a certain word or sound, or

---

Dear Families,

Young children are able to listen from the time they are born. You might ask, "Why doesn't my 4-year-old listen to me?" There can be many reasons that a child does not always pay attention or follow directions. The following ideas may help your child to become a more focused listener.

- Show your child that you are a good listener. When your child is talking, bend down to the child's eye level and focus on what she is saying. If you practice good listening skills, your child will, too.

- Read stories aloud and talk about the pictures and events in the story. Encourage your child to tell the story back to you. Your comments and questions can help your child stay focused on the story.

- Take a listening walk. Silently stroll with your child through a park or your own back yard. Together try to recall all the sounds you heard.

- Gain your child's attention. Minimize other sounds in the home, such as television and radio before giving directions.

- Give clear directions. Simplify directions to one or two requests. While on the child's eye level ask the child to follow the directions. Use a calm, quiet voice. Ask your child to repeat the most important parts of your directions. (You will find this isn't necessary after a while.)

- Encourage your child to listen to and identify sounds around the home, such as a dog barking, lawn mower, or water running.

- Ask your child to listen when he or she is physically able to do so effectively. Children who are tired, hungry, or overstimulated usually have difficulty focusing their attention.

- Make listening fun rather than a chore.

Sincerely,

[Teacher's Name]

FIGURE 1.8
Teacher to Families: Listening Ideas

respond in some other way. When Connie read Eric Carle's **Head to Toe** (1999) to a class of preschool children with language delays, they responded by acting out the motions of the animals in the pictures.

Children will be expected to learn by listening throughout their lives. The background they receive from hearing good literature and participating in listening activities at home and school can prepare them for more challenging experiences later in life.

LEARNING ABOUT BOOKS AND STORIES

In homes where books are readily available and reading is a familiar routine, children typically go through a sequence of stages in learning about books and stories (Holdaway, 1979; Jalongo, 2000; Sulzby, 1985). Children who have had fewer home experiences with literature might go through a similar developmental sequence, but at varying ages (Jalongo, 2000). Let's take a look at the development of emergent reading.

When literature is introduced to babies during the first weeks of life, children may perceive the difference between books and toys before they are 1 year old. When books are kept in a separate place and handled with special care, children will begin to treat them in a different way from other materials. Babies soon learn to climb into someone's lap and snuggle in when they know they are going to look at a book. Jalongo (2000) describes this *first stage* of emergent literacy as "understanding what a book is."

Children typically go through a sequence of stages in learning about books and stories.

After developing the concepts of books, young children enter the *second stage* of emergent literacy, where they learn how books work, including the top and bottom of books, and appropriate ways to manipulate books. During the first 2 years, as motor control is rapidly developing, children take pride in learning to turn pages and manipulate book parts, like lifting flaps and smelling scented pages in pop-up or toy books. As a toddler, Amy pulled tabs in **Where, Oh Where, Is Kipper's Bear?** (Inkpen, 1994), to see where the toy bear was hiding and what all the imaginary animals were saying. When Amy came to the last page, she delighted in seeing the flashlight shine as Kipper read a book under the covers. Her interest in flashlights increased with this experience.

Toddlers may also learn to follow book-related dialogue such as labeling pictures and answering questions the caregiver might ask. Reading a Sesame Street book about body parts to Dylan, his father pointed to each body part on the book characters, then asked Dylan to point to his own arm, head, neck, and so on. This toddler had learned to participate in book dialogue through words and actions.

At the *third stage*, children become listeners and participants in book sharing. If they are reading a new book, adults use highly interactive language (Sulzby, 1985), extending the child's understanding of the pictures and concepts. When they hear the same story again and again, children learn the sequence of events and the repeated language. Caregivers may hesitate at the ends of lines, and allow children to fill in familiar words or sounds. The children in the Head Start center where Connie volunteered loved the book **No, David!** (Shannon, 1999) so much that they quickly memorized the short lines on each page. Each time Connie read the book they would respond with "No, David," "David, come back here," or "Settle down," in the appropriate places.

In the *fourth stage*, children invent stories to go along with illustrations. During this stage children choose books to look at independently or may want to "read" to adults or other children. Their retellings are based on pictures, with the child producing some quotations from the book or some storylike language. Sulzby (1985) describes four categories of early story retelling that are oriented to pictures rather than print. First, children make comments about the pictures or label what they see in the illustrations. This would include comments like, "Woof-woof," "There's a kitty," or "It's a monster!" Younger children may excitedly slap the page or gesture along with their comments. Second, children retell stories by following the action in the pictures. "Monkey's jumpin' rope," and "Duck sleeping" would be examples of this stage. When Alison "read" **Spot Goes to the Beach** (Hill, 1985) to her parents by describing what she saw under each flap, and making comments like "not Spot's towel," she was following the action in the pictures. In the third category, dialogic storytelling, the child may provide dialogue for story characters and tell a somewhat disjointed story based on pictures, memorized words or phrases, and memories of the story. The fourth category, monologic storytelling, is characterized by the use of story intonation. An adult who can see the pictures can probably follow a complete story by the child.

As children begin to pay attention to print, rather than pictures and memory alone, they enter the *fifth stage* of emergent literacy. At this point children focus on a combination of print, meaning, and story knowledge. Children who are fully at the fifth stage not only recognize that the print in a book carries the story, but they also recognize some words. They combine their word knowledge strategies with meaning gained from pictures and prior knowledge of the book as they retell stories.

At the *sixth stage*, children attempt to read accurately by using their knowledge of letters, sounds, and words. They may no longer make up parts of the story because they are so focused on the phonetic relationships and word knowledge. Some meaning may be lost at this stage because of the emphasis the child is placing on the parts of written language.

Children coordinate their knowledge of print and story conventions in the *seventh stage* of emergent literacy. They use various reading strategies when they seem most appropriate, allowing them to focus on words, sound–symbol relationships, and meaning simultaneously. They incorporate prior knowledge and prediction and seek out new information into their reading. Table 1.1 summarizes the stages of emergent reading.

Through many experiences with literature, children grow in their understanding of the story *schema*, or the framework of the story. They become aware that stories have a beginning, middle, and end; a setting; a sequence of action; characters who solve problems; and often repetition, dialogue, and interesting language. Having a sense of story prepares children for understanding new literature they encounter (Cochran-Smith, 1984). As they become familiar with the way stories are organized, children will be able to anticipate or predict the actions of characters and consequences of those actions. This is a lifetime strategy that good readers use to help them comprehend new material.

Future teacher Christina Champion wrote about the importance of reading in her childhood:

> Reading was a major part of my life growing up. Every night before bed, my dad would lie with me and read my favorite book. I usually enjoyed books that dealt with animals or little girls. He would have me identify the front, back, and inside of the book. My father also taught me that you read from left to right. As he read to me he would be very animated and excited about the story. I was so mesmerized by his story reading that it completely captivated me. I always looked forward to the nightly readings that took place in my home. My parents also read a great deal themselves, so I witnessed their love of books and desire to read. Magazines and books decorated my father's study, and it amazed me that he actually read every book that lined his bookcases.

BOND BETWEEN CAREGIVERS AND CHILDREN

Recent research on brain development has underscored the importance of attachment and positive affect during the early years (Jensen, 1998; Shore, 1997). "Children learn in the context of important relationships" (Shore, 1997, p. 29).

TABLE 1.1

Stages of Emergent Reading

Stage	Approximate Age	What Happens?	How Can Caregivers Help?
1. What is a book?	Birth–2	Children perceive differences between books and toys, learn to enjoy books, appreciate story time with caregivers.	Frequent lap reading. Keep books within range of children's interests. Never force reading. Store books separately from toys and model caring for books.
2. Learning how books work and responding to books	1–3	Children manipulate books, learn where to begin reading, turn pages, and move parts of books. They label pictures and actions and respond by pointing, vocalizing, and moving their bodies.	Point out characters, objects, and actions in pictures. Encourage children to demonstrate receptive language by pointing and expressive language by naming objects. Promote movement with stories and dramatization.
3. Listening and participating	2–5	Children enjoy and learn from repetition of stories. They begin to use dialogue, follow the sequence of a story, and repeat playful language.	Use interactive language and expand on what children say about pictures. Leave off words at the end of lines to see whether the child fills in the phrase. Model use of book vocabulary in new situations.
4. "Reading" by inventing stories for pictures	3–5	Children first make up stories related to pictures in books; second, focus on individual pictures, then follow actions in pictures; third, use dialogue; and fourth, give a monologue retelling of the whole story.	Encourage children to spend time alone with books, perhaps at naptime, in the car, or at bedtime. Listen to their retellings and make comments to help them move toward the next stage of retelling. Point out letters and words that support their retellings.
5. Story retelling combines focus on print, pictures, and memory	4–6	Children are developing concepts about print and words. They combine strategies of using picture clues, knowledge of story structure, and print when retelling stories.	Continue to read aloud and help children gain meaning from stories. Go back through books after reading once and point out letters, words, punctuation, and so on. Help children find letters and words they know in context.
6. Focus on letters, sounds, and words during reading	5–7	Children focus on reading words, using what they know about phonics and word recognition. Comprehension may suffer for a while when children attend to the elements of language.	While children are focused on the parts of language, adults can help them maintain interest in the meaningful parts of reading by talking about stories and participating in dramatization or related music or craft activities.
7. Coordinate knowledge of print and story conventions	5–8	Children use a variety of reading strategies to gain meaning from print. Prediction and use of background knowledge support reading.	Even though children are becoming independent readers, it is important to read books aloud that are at a slightly higher level than they can read independently. Model strategies that they may be ready to try and demonstrate your own reading processes.

Source: Adapted from *Early Childhood Language Arts* (2nd ed.) by M. Jalongo, 2000, Boston: Allyn & Bacon; and "Children's Emergent Reading of Favorite Storybooks: A Developmental Study" by E. Sulzby, 1985, *Reading Research Quarterly, 20,* pp. 458–481.

When children are securely attached to their caregivers and live in an emotionally warm environment, they are less likely to experience developmental delays than children who feel physically or psychologically threatened. Nurturing early childhood environments also seem to "protect" children from adverse effects of later stressful situations.

It is never too early to begin reading to children. Possibly before birth, but certainly in the first days after birth, infants respond to the sounds of their parents' voices and often attend to songs or poetry. Some parents may unexpectedly find themselves reading aloud from novels as they hold their newborns and find that the sounds of reading sooth the little ones (Campbell, 1999). These first encounters with language and with trusting relationships build a strong emotional foundation for the young child (Butler, 1998).

Reading aloud to very young children has sometimes been called "lap reading" because adults and older children seem to innately know that sharing books is also a good time for being close. When a baby or young child is nearby, the caregiver can show affection while sharing the sounds and rhythms of language found in good literature. Children who have experienced lap reading again and again come to associate hearing stories with nurturing, cuddling, and being loved. As her mother reads the classic baby book, **Pat the Bunny** (Kunhardt, 1968), 15-month-old Gabrielle makes a game out of the page where

It is never too early to begin reading to children. This special time together builds a strong emotional foundation for infants.

she puts her finger through the mother's wedding ring. "I pretend to gobble up her finger with my fingers behind the page," her mother reports. "Jomp, jomp!" she laughs, repeating the game over and over. Later, Gabrielle sits contentedly on her 5-year-old brother's lap while he identifies objects in a picture book for her.

> It seems that language learning has a great deal to do with emotion and the development of relationships. This is seen to perfection in the interaction between parent and baby; eyes locked together, the adult almost physically drawing "verbal" response from the baby, both engulfed by that unique experience of intimate and joyful "connecting" which sets the pattern of relationship between two people. (Butler, 1998, p. 4)

Families can grow together and learn about one another as they read together (Taylor & Strickland, 1986). Parents learn their children's story preferences and how to adapt reading aloud to meet each child's personality and developmental needs. Children come to know their families' values and interests from the books they share, and the conversations they have around those books (Calkins, 1997). Over time the language and characters of books may become an important part of family history, as children and adults recall favorite storybook figures and sayings.

Maggie, age 3, expressed the concept of attachment beautifully when she kissed her mother's hand and nose and said, "Now you have a kissing hand, and it won't even come off when you eat. I promise!" Maggie and her mother had recently read **The Kissing Hand** by Audrey Penn (1993).

Each family that shares books together establishes rituals and routines around reading. Five-year-old Benjamin eats more slowly than his parents, so Dad reads a book or two to him while he finishes his breakfast. Grace has a pile of books on the nightstand by her bed, so that she can look at them in the morning if she wakes up before her mother. Many families sit together on the sofa or lie together in bed and read stories in the evening. These reading routines may last a lifetime. College students have told us that their parents engrained the habit of reading every night so firmly that even as adults they can't sleep unless they have read something.

Of course, not all books evoke feelings of contentment. As every early childhood teacher knows, the preschool years are a time when children's fears are at a peak. Listening to stories about monsters helps some children learn to cope with anxieties. Sitting on a familiar lap while reading about scary creatures can assist children in confronting their anxieties and learn ways to cope. "The adult's presence produces a sense of safety, and this feeling of security is of paramount importance because in the years when picture books are used, representations are not yet fully distinguished from the objects they represent" (Spitz, 1999, p. 16).

The positive affect children experience during lap reading, and activities that accompany or follow stories, may be one part of developing the secure attachments that are so important for emotional and cognitive well-being. The

Illustration by Emily Katherine Green. Reproduced by permission.

physical, emotional, and intellectual presence of an adult is critical to the healthy development of children. An adult's supportive presence is needed for learning and for experiencing the pleasure of literature, which are inseparable. When adults share the love of literature with children, they build a foundation for reading while transmitting their own pleasure in language, story, and imagination (Spitz, 1999).

ENJOYMENT

Three-year-old Alison was intrigued by the story *You Can't Catch Me* (Doyle, 1998) and "read" it to her parents by selecting and naming certain pictures that she recognized. They ended each scenario with "I caught you," giving Alison a big hug. Later, Alison acted out the story as she ran away and was chased and caught by Mom. The pleasure of a good story was expressed through Alison's exuberant enactment.

The comfort of touch and the soothing sound of a familiar adult voice make reading a gratifying experience for young children. Some books bring out giggles, while others incite tears. Regardless of the emotions, sharing stories together as a family can be so pleasurable that one mother called it "our golden time," a time of deep enjoyment of each other's company and the literature that was being shared (Taylor & Strickland, 1986).

Many children and families encounter what Taylor and Strickland (1986) call "breakthrough books," stories that truly enchant a child and parent, and may be read three or four times a day for several weeks. Sometimes these books provide security, like ***Goodnight Moon*** (Brown, 1947) or ***Hush! A Thai Lullaby*** (Ho, 1996), where the calming words, repetition, and relationships of characters assure the young child that she will be cared for and loved. Other books may appeal to children because of the language, rhyme, or humor. Nate laughed every time his parents read from ***Chicka Chicka Boom Boom*** (Martin & Archambault, 1989). Sometimes illustrations, like the energetic and lively art of Janet Stevens in ***Tops and Bottoms*** (1995) and ***Cook-a-doodle-doo*** (Stevens & Crummel, 1999) or the vivid colors of Denise Fleming's captivating pictures in ***Mama Cat Has Three Kittens*** (1998) and ***Barnyard Banter*** (1994), attract children to new stories. Visual images have the power to captivate the imaginations of the young and amplify the message of text.

When reading to young children it is important for caregivers and teachers to begin by sharing the joy of literature, rather than approaching the experience with a lesson to teach (Jalongo, 1988). If adults are passionate about the books they read, their enthusiasm will influence the children with whom they share stories.

A group of Head Start children heard Connie's voice chanting, "Caps, caps for sale, fifty cents a cap." Several of them left the block and model train centers to squeeze close to listen and participate in actions or conversation around the classic ***Caps for Sale*** (Slobodkina, 1947). As Connie and the children shared this experience they were joined in a caring relationship. Mem Fox (1993), children's author and literacy expert, describes the importance of the relationship between children and adult readers.

> When I read to children, what I want most from them at the end is a sigh of contentment because we have shared a little of life together. . . . The sigh is important. It's a signal that the reading or listening to literature has been a deeply felt pleasure. (p. 122)

Pleasure was demonstrated frequently during Benjamin's family story reading times. The day Benjamin and his mom read five ***Peanuts*** cartoon books together, his mother wrote this journal entry: "In the evening the whole family ate popcorn and watched a *Peanuts* video. When it was over we talked about roasting marshmallows in the fall. We laughed and laughed because Benjamin can say 'Blaagh!' just like Snoopy." Family book reading can be a relaxing and entertaining experience at the same time that it fosters language learning, develops a lifelong love of literature and inspires playful thinking.

Parents who enjoy reading will transmit a love of literature to their children.

IMAGINATION AND CREATIVITY

Well, he was humming this hum to himself, and walking along gaily, wondering what everybody else was doing, and *what it felt like, being somebody else*, when suddenly he came to a sandy bank, and in the bank was a large hole. (Italics added.)*

Just as Pooh wonders what it would feel like to be somebody else, young children are curious about how the world seems from another point of view. Through play, children take on the role of another person or animal, learn to use symbols, and assimilate new information about the world in which they live. Play fosters optimum development when it stretches the child cognitively and socially, spurring the imagination and engaging the mind. Johnson, Christie, and Yawkey (1999) define dramatic play as nonliteral, intrinsically motivated, having a process (over product) orientation, freely chosen, and having a positive affect for the child. The focus of play is on "exploring rather than on accomplishing predetermined ends or goals" (McLane & McNamee, 1991, p. 2). The ability to represent with symbols and create imaginary worlds is first used in play and later applied to reading and writing tasks.

Book-related dramatic play refers to children acting out the meaning they discern from the text or illustrations of storybooks (Rowe, 1998). Young chil-

*From *Winnie-the-Pooh* by A. A. Milne, illustrated by E. H. Shepard, copyright 1926 by E. P. Dutton, renewed 1954 by A. A. Milne. Used by permission of Dutton Children's Books, an imprint of Penguin Putnam Books for Young Readers, a division of Penguin Putnam, Inc. All rights reserved. Reprinted with permission.

dren may take on the persona or actions of a character, follow the theme of a story, and/or act out parts of a story plot when they participate in book-related dramatic play. Children 2 and 3 years of age typically engage in individual pre-tense, enacting stories by themselves or seeking out an audience in a nearby adult (Rowe, 1998). Sometimes the child announces his or her role and assigns another role to the adult who becomes a co-player in the drama. Nate's mother provided an excellent example. "Nate has really gotten into pretending and casting lately. When he acts out **Puppy Love** (King-Smith, 1997) he is always Dodo, I am Little Elsie, and Dad is Fly, the German shepherd. He gets on the bed in the study and says it is a dog bed, then he tells me to lay on the bed." See Figure 1.9 for more on literature and movement.

Book-related dramatic play appears to be, at least in part, an aesthetic expe-rience where the child actually "lives through" the plot of the book (Rosenblatt,

---

Recent brain research confirms what many parents and early childhood educators have long known: Learning begins with movement. As we observe young children on the playground or in an open indoor space we see them running, climbing, dancing, twirling, and simply taking pleasure in physical expression. The area of the brain that controls movement is the same section that is responsible for cognition. Physical and mental activities go hand in hand.

Traditionally, in early childhood classrooms, teachers wait until children are seated quietly in a circle with hands on their laps before beginning story time. Re-search indicates that this may not be the most effective way for toddlers, preschoolers, and kindergarten children to interact with literature. Many recently published books for young children engender creativity and movement. "Physical responses are not only enjoyable; they also help children associate words with feelings and movements" (Green, 2002, p. 14). Children might move like animals described in a poem, act out a dance illustrated in a picture book, and enact the sequence of a folktale. Dramatiz-ing stories and poems increases comprehension as children come to understand meaning though their interpretation of events and feelings conveyed in the words and pictures in books. Bouncing, twirling, clapping, and swaying also form the basis of motions children will need later as they catch a football, swing a bat, or dance (Green, 2002).

Here are a few good books to help you begin joining literature and movement:

The Baby's Game Book (Wilmer, 2000)	*From Head to Toe* (Carle, 1999)
Bouncing Time (Hubbel, 2000)	*Higgle, Wiggle, Happy Rhymes* (Merriam, 1994)
Clap Your Hands (Cauley, 1992)	
Dancin' in the Kitchen (Gelsanliter & Christian, 1998)	*Let's Dance* (Ancona, 1998)
	Pete's a Pizza (Steig, 1998)
Frog Legs: A Picture Book of Action Verse (Shannon, 2000)	*Twist with a Burger, Jitter with a Bug* (Lowery, 1995)

FIGURE 1.9

Teacher to Teacher: Literature and Movement

Source: Adapted from "Moving to Literature" by C. Green, 2002, *Texas Child Care Quarterly,* 26(1), pp. 12–21.

1978). Enjoyment and understanding of the meaning of stories is facilitated by the multisensory experience of enactment. Children also explore their personal questions by acting out segments of information books (Rowe, 1998). Shortly after Alison's first check-up at the dentist, her mom read **My First Dentist Visit** (Allen, 1988) to her. As soon as they finished the story, Alison acted out her experience, making the "brrrr" sound of the polisher and talking about the dentist's chair and the surprise she chose. They often read the book just before it is time for Alison to brush her teeth. In this case, a 3-year-old made connections between her own prior experience and the text, coming to a better understanding of visiting the dentist by integrating the two.

During play, children develop their use of symbols, starting with toys that look like the objects they represent (e.g., tea cups) and moving to more abstract symbols (a block for a telephone) at about the age of 2. According to Vygotsky (1978) toys provide a pivot that separates objects from their meaning. By 2½, Nate used his index finger as a pivot, to represent favorite book characters. Benjamin, at 5½, had a more advanced command of symbolic representation and enjoyed creating his own props for book fantasy play. After reading **The Best Halloween of All** (Wojciechowski, 2000) Benjamin draped sheets, towels, and pillowcases on his body and invented several mask possibilities. Then he told his mother, "I want this to be serious. Will you help me?" She agreed, and he finally decided to be a robot with a paper bag costume. They cut holes in the bag and also made a paper hat. Benjamin drew buttons and levers all over it with his crayons.

Book-related dramatic play supports understanding of character, provides a vehicle for applying the language of books, and is a motivating way for children to become involved in literature. Children can act out poetry, information books, folk tales, fantasy, or realistic fiction. The reenactment of characters and plots using the language of books can provide a bridge to reading (McLane & McNamee, 1991). Within the context of play, children experience literature and deepen their comprehension of books and recall of stories.

SUMMARY

Learning to read is one goal most families have in common for their children. Educators who work with very young children recognize the value of language and literacy experiences that occur in the home before children are introduced to formal instruction. Families lay the groundwork for successful readers and writers when they snuggle close to their children and share stories, encourage language and play related to stories, emphasize rhymes and interesting sounds, point out environmental print, and informally introduce their children to writing. Teachers can support families by suggesting and providing developmentally appropriate books and recommending materials and activities parents can do at home to encourage oral language, listening, and emergent reading and writing.

When reading is a joyful experience it affirms the bond between children and their families and motivates children to read independently. As one mother said when discussing reading aloud to her five children: "They think it's the best thing in the world we could do for them. They like it better than eating ice cream."

FOR PROFESSIONAL DEVELOPMENT

1. Select a book for each of the following age groups: infants, toddlers, preschoolers, and kindergartners. What characteristics of the book make it appealing and appropriate for this age group? Share at least two of the books with children. How did they respond to the books? What did you do to encourage the children's involvement? Do you think these books were good choices to read aloud? Why or why not?

2. Observe a parent or caregiver reading aloud to a young child. What do you notice about the way this pair interacts while reading and listening to stories? What was the emotional tone of the experience?

3. In a family setting, tape record the spoken language between a parent or caregiver and a young child (with their permission, of course). What did you notice about the adult's language that supported or limited the child's language? What did you learn that will influence the way you talk with children?

4. Observe three children interacting with books. Document their emergent reading behaviors. Refer to Table 1.1 and describe which of the stages of story retelling best represents the children's engagement with books.

INTERNET RESOURCES

http://www.ala.org

> The American Library Association has superb literacy resources for families, teachers, librarians, and parent educators. Their program, "Born to Read: How to Raise a Reader," targets new and expectant parents who are considered "at risk." There are numerous links to other notable sites.

http://www.rif.org/

> Reading Is Fundamental is an organization that promotes family literacy through programs and information about reading with young children. Especially helpful is their "Reading Planet" link that offers books, activities, Web resources and literacy information for families.

http://cbcbooks.org/

> The Children's Book Council is dedicated to encouraging literacy and the enjoyment of children's books. In addition to a wealth of information on books, the Website features authors and illustrators, an online catalog of books, and information on National Children's Book Week.

SHARING THE MAGIC OF CHILDREN'S LITERATURE

Grandmother stands at the sink washing dishes from lunch. Andrew, age 5, pulls up a stool behind her, stands on it, and reaches around her to pat the folds of skin beneath her chin. In a wondrous voice, as Andrew pats and pulls gently, he declares, "Grandmother, you feel just like the saggy, baggy elephant!"

Grandmother loved telling this family story about Andrew's comparison of her to the saggy, baggy elephant in Rudyard Kipling's tale, one of his favorite stories for naptime reading at her house. Children like Andrew, who have daily experiences with quality literature, often naturally incorporate literary language into their conversations and make text-to-life and life-to-text connections (Cochran-Smith, 1984; Green, Lilly, & Barrett, 2002). At a very early age, Andrew had discovered the power of literature to give us language that helps describe our inner thoughts and feelings, even as it delights and entertains us.

Mem Fox, popular author of children's books, has written a book for parents and teachers titled *Reading Magic* (2001). She describes reading aloud as a magical, exuberant, joyful time that has an enormous impact on early reading development. We agree! Books give us endless hours of enjoyment, develop our imagination and creative spirit, help us learn about ourselves and our world, and become our "friends" for a lifetime. Let's take a look into the enchanting world of children's literature.

THE INFLUENCE OF STORIES

Where did stories begin? Gail Haley, award-winning author of *A Story, a Story* (1970) retells the African tale of Nyame, the Sky God to whom all the stories of the world belonged. They were kept in a golden box by his throne. Tricked by Ananse, the Spider man, Nyame's stories were brought to Earth and released all over the world.

In early societies, storytellers were important transmitters of the beliefs, attitudes, and values of a culture. In our quest for answers about our origin, the laws of nature, and human behavior, stories were the vehicles that gave us explanations. In public forums and within the family unit, stories were shared and passed from one generation to the next, shaping the lives of the listeners in countless ways. Today stories continue to play an important role in many cultures, weaving words into lessons for daily life.

Gary Nabhan, who writes about the value of the natural world for young children, helped guide his own children to discover the wonders of nature as he coupled his knowledge of natural history with ideas, images, and stories from his own childhood. Explaining the importance of stories in his life, he says:

My own childhood mental maps of the West were fuzzy except when I could connect them to the stories I knew: the unfolding of our journeys from Denver to Pocatello, the paths of Lewis and Clark or the Oregon Trail traced on the maps, geological "creation legends" absorbed from my father. We learn our homeland from stories, just as we learn nearly everything from stories. (Nabhan & Trimble, 1994, p. 20)

Reeny, that unforgettable 5-year-old in Vivian Paley's book, **The Girl with the Brown Crayon** (1997), shows definitively how stories capture our imagination and become a part of our lives. Through her encounters with Leo Lionni's books, Reeny entices her kindergarten friends and teacher into a yearlong relationship with his stories. Daily experiences in Reeny's preschool classroom began to be interpreted by the children in the context of Lionni's stories, allowing them a common framework within which to share their budding thoughts about life and relationships.

With so many technological influences in children's lives, a story is a gift that some children are rarely given. Stories have the power to transport us, inform us, and make our lives magical. There are no knobs to turn, no keys to punch, no screen to watch—just printed words and illustrations on a page. What is it, then, that explains the unique power of literature to influence and shape our lives in so many ways? Kay Vandergrift, noted authority in children's literature, believes that the literature we love is never forgotten as the stories become woven into our lives. "[p]art of the beauty and the magic of story is that it becomes lived experience that one can go back to and dwell in again and again" (Vandergrift, 1980, p. xv).

What are your earliest memories of stories? How often were stories— written or oral—a part of your daily life? Did any become treasured memories? As you read this chapter, think of the part stories have played in your life and consider the ways you can bring stories into the lives of the children you teach.

THE GENRES OF CHILDREN'S LITERATURE

We know that early exposure to books is a primary building block in supporting emergent literacy. Additionally, the availability of high-quality books in many genres is important. Unfortunately, recent research has highlighted the inequities of children's access to books in child-care centers in the United States (Neuman, Celano, Greco, & Shue, 2001). In one study, television sets were more predominant than books in low-income child-care centers (Neuman & Celano, 2001). Differences have been found between low- and middle-income communities in literacy resources, public libraries, and the amount and quality of literacy materials in public schools (Neuman et al., 2001). One group of researchers (Stanovich, 2000; West & Stanovich, 1991) posited an "environmental opportunity hypothesis" based on their findings that differing access to books exacerbates the gap between children who develop a positive attitude toward reading and those who do not. How can we close the gap?

One way to begin is to build your knowledge base about children's literature. When you learn the qualities that represent the best in children's books and become familiar with the wide range of books available for children, you will be able to share the information with families, as well as make good choices about what books to include in your child-care center or preschool. Look through the children's books you already have available. Are they worn and ragged, pulled apart by too many little eager hands? Are they almost brand-new because they have not been used very much? What types of books

TABLE 2.1

Overview of Genres of Children's Literature

Genre	Characteristics	Types	Notable Authors for Young Children
Traditional Literature	• Handed down orally • No known authors • Basis of our literary heritage	• Folktales • Fables • Myths • Legends and epics	Tales retold or interpreted by: Jan Brett Tomie dePaola Gail Haley Trina Schart Hyman Steven Kellogg Janet Stevens Ed Young Paul Zelinsky
Fantasy	• Contains elements of traditional literature • Identifiable authors • Make-believe is combined with believable • Illuminates life in magical ways	• Animal fantasy • Talking toys and dolls • Miniature beings • Magical powers • Peculiar characters and imaginary worlds	Sandra Boynton Eric Carle Lucy Cousins Denise Fleming Mem Fox Kevin Henkes William Joyce Keiko Kasza Leo Lionni Nancy Tafuri Rosemary Wells Audrey and Don Wood
Poetry	• Concise language • Sensory images • Rhythmical quality • Evokes emotions • Personification • Figurative language	• Ballads • Limericks and riddles • Concrete poems • Free verse • Haiku • Cinquain • Narrative	Kay Charo Jane Dyer Eloise Greenfield Mary Ann Hoberman Lee Bennett Hopkins Eve Merriam Jack Prelutsky
Realistic Fiction	• Honestly portrays life • Helps children see others like them • Gives children insight into lives not like their own • Reflects current issues	• Family stories • Developmental milestones • Friends • Special challenges • Transitions • Daily lives	Eve Bunting Shirley Hughes Pat Hutchins Ezra Jack Keats Pat Mora Cynthia Rylant David Shannon Bernard Waber Vera B. Williams Harriet Ziefert Charlotte Zolotow

Genre	Characteristics	Types	Notable Authors for Young Children
Historical Fiction	• Helps children imagine life in much different times from today • May provide a link to grandparents, older relatives or friends • Makes the past come alive	• For young children use books about the recent past	Eve Bunting Barbara Cooney Donald Hall Gloria Houston
Informational/ Concept Books	• Contain concepts and facts • Subjects are ourselves, our families, nature, animals, the world • Promote a disposition for inquiry	• Concept books • Photographic essays • Identification books • Life-cycle books • Activity and how-to books	Byron Barton Joanna Cole Donald Crews Lois Ehlert Lindsey George Gail Gibbons Ruth Heller Tana Hoban Bruce McMillan Margaret Miller Ann Morris Helen Oxenbury

do the children choose? Do you have enough variety to meet the needs of all the children and families? What do you need to know about children's literature to help you make educated choices?

Children's literature is categorized into genres, or types of literature, each having definitive characteristics or features. Typically, children's literature is classified in the following ways: picture books, poetry, traditional literature, modern fantasy, contemporary realistic fiction, historical fiction, and informational books. Table 2.1 provides an overview of the genres and includes many notable authors for young children. Picture books and culturally diverse literature span the genres (see Figure 2.1).

FIGURE 2.1
Genres of Children's Literature

As you read on, consider the criteria for evaluating picture books in all genres, as listed in Figure 2.2. Take note of the books and related experiences that appeal to you and begin a list of your favorites to share with children and families.

---

1. *Format*
   - Size, shape
   - Dust jacket
   - Page design
   - Illustrations
   - Paper quality
   - Binding

2. *Plot or Story Line*
   - Draws reader/listener right in; interesting
   - Well-constructed; original
   - Contains action; builds suspense
   - Comes to a satisfying conclusion

3. *Setting*
   - Central to story
   - Time and place related to plot, characters, theme

4. *Characters*
   - Memorable main character(s)
   - Clearly delineated through actions, dialogue, and/or other characters' reactions to the main characters
   - Support the development of the story

5. *Theme*
   - May or may not have a theme
   - Worthwhile for children
   - Is not overtly moralistic or didactic

6. *Style of Writing*
   - Engages the child's attention
   - Well-written
   - Dialogue illuminates characters and story
   - Matches illustrations

7. *Additional Considerations*
   - Is the book visually enticing?
   - How would you rate the "read-aloud" appeal?
   - Is the story told with integrity?
   - How does the story compare with others on the same topic or in the same genre?
   - How do you think children will respond to the book?

FIGURE 2.2
Evaluating Picture Books

PICTURE BOOKS

Picture books are defined by format rather than content. Text and illustrations are integrated uniquely to represent a story, theme, or concept in approximately 32 pages. In the overall design of the book, illustrations are dominant, extending the text in a meaningful way. The most appealing picture books represent a successful interdependence of text and illustrations. When a toddler is entranced by the pictures as you read the text, and puts the book back in your hand after you've finished reading and put it aside, she is relating on a very basic level to the magic of a well-written picture book. There are various subcategories of picture books that provide a wide range of visual, auditory, and tactile stimulation for very young children.

Books for Babies

Lily's mother and older sisters read aloud to her from the day she arrived home from the hospital. At first, her mother sang lullabies and read aloud the novel or magazine she was reading to herself. The sound of her voice seemed to comfort Lily during restless times. Soon Lily's sisters introduced her to some of their favorite childhood books and the new cardboard books that had been purchased in anticipation of her arrival. By the time she could sit up independently, Lily was so familiar with the way books worked that she could turn the pages and even seemed to comment on pictures with her babbles. When Lily was 2, her vocabulary included many words that came directly from books she had read and adapted to new situations.

One of the fastest growing segments of the publishing industry is the production of books for babies and toddlers. Educators, librarians, and even politicians are encouraging parents, grandparents, and caregivers to read to children beginning at birth. When children are introduced to books in a playful manner during infancy, they become accustomed to reading as part of the daily routine. In *Babies Need Books* (1998), Dorothy Butler recommends sharing books with infants from the first days after birth. Babies can learn a lot about books during the first few months, as their families start them on a life-long habit of reading. Take a look at the benefits of early book experiences:

- Learning to listen
- Language development
- Developing sensory awareness
- Visual focus
- Recognition of objects pictured in books
- Reinforcement of basic concepts
- Extending concrete experiences
- Supporting emotional development through lap reading

For suggestions on reading with babies and toddlers who have hearing impairments see Figure 2.3.

Increasing numbers of children with hearing loss can listen to stories by means of hearing aids or cochlear implants. Sitting on an adult's lap provides a good environment, as the reader's voice is near the little one's ear. A naturally expressive reading style is appropriate, with no need for increasing volume. Pictures can give a context for the child who is just starting to process information through hearing. The adult's proximity to the child and reducing background noise will increase the learning opportunities and enjoyment of books. There are visual ways to enrich the experience of sharing books for the child who cannot learn to understand language through listening alone.

Sharon and Craig started to sign with Emily during her first year of life. When Sharon first started reading to Emily, she had to plan how to hold her so that Emily could see the signs and the pictures in the book at the same time. Sharon held her daughter on her lap with her left arm, propped up the book, and signed with her right hand. By signing throughout the day, Sharon was able to communicate with Emily in a way that supported her natural learning. Emily became a very competent signer, and could converse at length about her life experiences.

Sharon deliberately used books to facilitate language development. Sometimes she would rephrase books because of her limited sign vocabulary. When Sharon later learned the signs for the terms in the book, and used them, Emily would protest, wanting the familiar sentences or phrases. Many hearing children also protest when their parents divert from familiar text.

Just before Emily turned 3, Sharon and Craig decided to change their mode of communication to cued speech to help Emily lip-read and speak more easily. Cued speech is a phonetically based visual communication of hand shapes, hand placement, and movement. As Craig and Sharon became more fluent, cueing became incorporated into book reading time. Now Emily had to see Sharon's face when she read to her, so mother and daughter sat opposite each other on the bed. But Emily was used to sitting on a lap for book reading and was not happy with this arrangement; so Dad was routinely brought into the activity to hold Emily on his lap while Mom held the book in her left hand and read, cueing with her right hand. Although Craig wanted to practice cueing and reading with Emily, when he started Emily took the book away and gave it to her mother, choosing to stay with the familiar routine.

Two of Emily's favorite books are *Brown Bear, Brown Bear, What do You See?* (Martin, 1967) and *Go Away, Big Green Monster* (Emberly, 1992). She initially learned to read these books in sign, and at first did not want them to be cued to her. She now accepts new books being read with cues and has learned to accept the familiar ones being read with cues. Emily still remembers the early signs she learned and will recite the books to herself with sign.

FIGURE 2.3

Teacher to Teacher: Reading with Children with Hearing Impairments

Source: Theresa M. Barrett, Office of Education, North Carolina Department of Health and Human Resources. Reprinted by permission.

Toy and Board Books

Frequently, a baby's first encounter with books involves literature that encourages interaction between the adult and the infant. These picture books for the youngest children, sometimes called participation books, range from sturdy cardboard to squishy bathtub books. Cloth books, scratch-and-sniff, lift-the-flap, pop-up, and shape books also are included in this picture book category.

Babies take pleasure in participating as books are being read aloud. A toy book that combines textures to feel with flaps to lift is **Fuzzy Yellow Ducklings** (Van Fleet, 1995), which introduces shapes, colors, animals, and textures in an intriguing way. Die-cut pages let the reader take a peek at a part of the animal, which is fully revealed as the flap is lifted. Descriptive adjectives introduce each shape and animal in a menagerie sure to keep toddlers engaged. A fold-out final section presents all the animals together, with questions about colors, shapes, animal names, and numbers.

Eric Hill, author of the "Spot" books, has written a series of engaging cardboard lift-the-flap books, such as **Spot Goes to School** (2001a), **Spot Goes to the Farm** (2001b), **Goodnight Spot** (1999), and **Spot's First Words** (1986). The large, bold letters, simple text, and brightly colored pictures make the books easy to read to babies. In **Where's Spot?** (1980), a mother dog looks for her puppy all

MORE FAVORITES

Toy and Board Books

Catch the Ball! (Carle, 1998)

Dear Zoo (Campbell, 1982)

Go Away, Big Green Monster! (Emberly, 1993)

Hey Diddle Diddle (Winter, 1999)

I Smell Honey (Pinkney & Pinkney, 1997)

Little Monsters (Pienkowski, 1986)

Pajama Time! (Boynton, 2000)

Peek-a-Moo! (Cimarusti, 1998)

This Little Baby Goes Out (Breeze, 1990)

This Little Piggy (Manning, 1997)

The Very Hungry Caterpillar (Carle, 1969)

The Very Lonely Firefly (Carle, 1995)

Where Is My Baby? (Ziefert & Taback, 2002)

Who Said Moo? (Ziefert & Taback, 2002)

Very young children are often fascinated by books that show babies engaged in familiar activities.

through the house. At 14 months old, Gabrielle loved for her mother to read **Donde Está Spot?** (1996), the Spanish version of *Where's Spot?* Her mother wrote about Gabrielle's interaction with the book: "She likes opening and closing the flaps in the book. At the end of the book she likes to praise Spot. "Mu be!" ("Muy bien!")."

Erin, a 16-month-old, has recently been entranced with **Where Is Baby's Belly Button?** (Katz, 2000), another simple lift-the-flap book written in a question–answer format. Her nana brought it to Erin when she visited. Nana commented to the authors that she must have read it "a hundred times" to her granddaughter during the short visit! She often read it with variations, substituting Erin's name in the text and asking her to point to her belly button, eyes, mouth, feet, and other body parts mentioned. The repetition of the text ("Where are baby's [Erin's] eyes? Where are baby's feet?") made it easy for Erin to respond. She loved to lift the flap, and joined in on some of the easier words, since she had recently begun to use one-word utterances.

A favorite board book of ours is **Wrapping Paper Romp** (1998b) by Patricia Hubbell. Lively illustrations combine with a rhythmical text to describe a toddler's joy of a new present. The wrapping paper, however, brings more excitement than the present! **Pots and Pans** (1998a) is another board book by Hubbell that celebrates an everyday occurrence in some households. Again, the lyrical text filled with descriptive words makes it an enjoyable read-aloud, while the pictures capture all the exuberance of a toddler "making music" with noisy, clanging pots and pans.

Babies are often fascinated by other infants. Sean's mother observed that her 17-month-old son was interested in cardboard "chunky" books because he could see other babies in action. Helen Oxenbury has written a collection of board books for the very youngest that shows babies engaged in familiar activities such as taking a walk, riding in a car, or getting dressed. *Tickle, Tickle* (Oxenbury, 1987) features babies from other cultures laughing, sleeping, and splashing in the tub. Babies and toddlers will be delighted to see others like themselves in *Dressing* (1981a), *Family* (1981b), *Friends* (1981c), *Playing* (1981d), and *Working* (1981e).

Many popular authors have had their books reprinted in board book formats, some more appropriately than others. When selecting board books, make sure there is a small amount of print on each page, the subject is clearly meant for toddlers, and the illustrations convey the topic simply and effectively.

Concept Books

Concept books are those that introduce information about colors, shapes, animals, the natural world, and other topics of interest. As single concepts are explained in lively and interesting ways, young children become active learners. Concept books have been referred to as stepping stones on the path to informational books children will use as they mature (Darigan, Tunnell, & Jacobs, 2002).

Tana Hoban is a master of concept books presented through photography. In *Red, Blue, Yellow Shoe* (1986) Hoban displays single pictures of familiar items on each page, accompanied by a dot of color and the name of the color. Each object (e.g., shoe, mitten, flower, teddy bear) is the color of the dot on the bottom of the page. *Over, Under, and Through* (1987), Hoban's book about positional words, was used by a preservice teacher when she engaged 4-year-olds in an author/illustrator study on Tana Hoban. Abbye first read the book and talked about positional words, allowing the children to move around and show examples in the room. After this short introduction, she led the children outside to the playground and, using an instant camera, took pictures of them *under* the sliding board, climbing *over* the balance beam, going *through* the tires, and other playful positions. Back in the room Abbye spread out all the pictures; asked each child individually to identify him/herself; and requested that they dictate a sentence, phrase, or word that described the position they were demonstrating. She then displayed photos and captions on a documentation board for the children and families to enjoy. It was a wonderful example of using literature in a developmentally appropriate way to achieve required objectives, including positional words, movement, language development, and emergent literacy. Other popular concept books by Hoban are *Exactly the Opposite* (1990), *Look Book* (1997), and *Just Look* (1996).

Children acted out positional words on the playground after reading Tana Hoban's concept book Over, Under, and Through.

Nina Crews has produced a photographic essay concept book, **A High, Low, Near, Far, Loud, Quiet Story** (1999) that pictures a mother and her two children engaged in daily activities. Beginning with morning, photographs capture opposites throughout the day, ending with nighttime. Using this book as a model, caregivers or teachers could point out opposites during a day at home, child care, or preschool. If a camera is available, it would be easy to make a book of photographic opposites, featuring the children with whom you work.

Vehicles, big machinery, and various means of transportation are often interesting to toddlers. Dylan, 21 months old, began to recognize the big yellow school bus that passed his house every day after reading Donald Crews's book **School Bus** (1984). He later began using the word *bus* as it came down the street, applied it to other buses that provided transportation in his suburban community, and used phrases from the book such as "going this way" when he saw the buses coming and going. Two other books by Crews, **Freight Train** (1978) and **Truck** (1980), capitalize on this interest, while familiarizing children with related concepts.

MORE FAVORITES

Concept Books

Building a House (Barton, 1992)

Color Dance (Jonas, 1989)

Color Farm (Ehlert, 1990)

Color Zoo (Ehlert, 1989)

Machines at Work (Barton, 1997)

Mouse Paint (Walsh, 1989)

My Car (Barton, 2001)

My Five Senses (Miller, 1998)

My Very First Book of Colors (Carle, 1985)

Planes (Barton, 1998)

Puffins Climb, Penguins Rhyme (McMillan, 2001)

A Rainbow All Around Me (Pinkney, 2002)

Red Is Best (Stinson, 1988)

Spots, Feathers, and Curly Tails (Tafuri, 1988)

Trucks (Barton, 1998)

What Is Round? (Dotlich, 1999)

What Is Square? (Dotlich, 1999)

What's On My Head? (Miller, 1998)

Alphabet Books

The first alphabet book for children, written by Kate Greenaway in the late 1800s, was titled **A Apple Pie** (Greenaway, 1993). It was a story alphabet book about children who baked and shared an apple pie. ABC books have come a long way since then! Many of today's alphabet books are visually enticing and immediately draw children into the world of letters and sounds through their formats, illustrations, and language. The subjects for modern ABC books range from humorous stories, riddles, and rhymes to concept acquisition and information about the natural world. Young children are invited to become involved in the text while developing letter recognition and phonemic and phonological awareness, predictors of children's ability to learn to read (Adams, 1990; Snow, Burns, & Griffin, 1998). Alphabet books can be used creatively to draw attention to letters and the sounds they represent, giving children numerous opportunities to play with language. See Figure 2.4 for a list of alphabet book activities.

Be selective when choosing ABC books. For the youngest children, look for letters that stand apart on the page, objects that are common, and subjects that are familiar (Huck, Hepler, Hickman, & Kiefer, 2001). Older preschoolers may enjoy more complex illustrations, depending on their prior experiences with the alphabet.

Try some of the following ways to extend children's enjoyment of alphabet books:

- Make a photographic alphabet book of the children's pictures and their names.
- Use environmental print to make an alphabet book. Labels from food containers are familiar to children and easily accessible.
- Develop a series of thematic alphabet books, such as ones on babies, animals, or household objects. Use photographs or drawings.
- Experiment with different media and artistic techniques to make a textured alphabet book that encourages tactile experiences with the objects and letters.
- For children who are learning English as a second language, label objects in class- and teacher-made alphabet books in their home language as well as in English.
- Make a sign language alphabet by using photographs of the children's hands as they sign.
- Provide copies of the alphabet books for family check out. Include a tip sheet for adult caregivers on enjoying the books at home.

FIGURE 2.4
Teacher to Teacher : Alphabet Book Activities

Alphabet letters are coupled with clever, humorous illustrations in **Helen Oxenbury's ABC of Things** (Oxenbury, 1983). For each letter, both uppercase and lowercase letters are given, accompanied by one or more objects that represent the letter. **Maisy's ABC** (Cousins, 1995) is one in a series of Maisy-the-mouse books that have become favorites with preschoolers. Bold primary colors, cartoonlike figures, flaps to lift, and tabs to pull combine to make this ABC book appealing.

A wildly popular ABC book is **Chicka Chicka Boom Boom** (Martin & Archambault, 1989). As the letters go up and fall off the coconut tree, the musical cadence of the verse cajoles readers of all ages to join in. **Alphabetics** (MacDonald, 1986) is a playful and creatively designed alphabet book in which the letters tumble around and emerge as part of the picture they represent. For example, "n" turns upside down through a series of pictures and becomes a "nest." The letters are clearly recognizable, and the objects stand out on a white background, making it easy to identify them.

Two early childhood students used Lois Ehlert's book, **Eating the Alphabet** (1989) as the basis for a kindergarten lesson on the alphabet. As they read the book, many children chimed in with comments on their favorite foods that were featured in the book. Some of the foods, however, were new to the kindergarteners and required short explanations from the early childhood students. After reading the book and talking about the foods, the children illustrated their own alphabet book of foods. At the end of the week, a tasting party was held to try out a few of the foods mentioned in the book. The children tasted the foods, dictated describing words, illustrated their choices, and then graphed them on a class chart.

MORE FAVORITES

Alphabet Books

A My Name Is Alice (Bayer & Kellogg, 1992)

"A" You're Adorable (Kaye, Wise, & Lippman, 1998)

Action Alphabet (Rotner, 1996)

Allison's Zinnia (Lobel, 1990)

Alphabet City (Johnson, 1995)

Alfie's ABC (Hughes, 1998)

Appalachian ABC's (Hall, 1998)

The Butterfly Alphabet (Sandved, 1996)

A Farmer's Alphabet (Azarian, 1981)

Handsigns: A Sign Language Alphabet (Fain, 1993)

K Is for Kiss Good Night: A Bedtime Alphabet (Sardegna, 1994)

K Is for Kwanzaa (Ford, 1997)

Mary Had a Little Lamb (Hale, 1990)

Navajo ABC: A Dine Alphabet (Tapahonso, 1995)

Old Black Fly (Aylesworth, 1992)

On Market Street (Lobel, 1981)

Zoe and Her Zebra (Beaton, 1999)

*A **Is for Africa*** (Onyefulu, 1993) is a culturally specific alphabet book for older preschoolers. The author, who is from Africa, writes a short explanation about the book at the beginning, accompanied by an outline map of Africa. The photographs for each illustration capture the landscape, people, customs, foods, and housing in Nigeria, and represent the diversity throughout the continent.

Counting Books

When her children Matthew and Andrew were small, Elizabeth (one of the co-authors) would often recite "One, two, buckle my shoe…" as she helped them learn to tie their shoes. Soon it became a favorite jingle to chant around the house. She also mentioned that "Five Little Monkeys" was her mantra at bedtime, as the boys went into overdrive activity on the bed while putting on their pajamas.

Numbers are everywhere in a child's environment: on the clock, on the front of their homes or apartments, on billboards, on the dashboard of the car, even on the buttons on the television remote control! The concept of counting is best learned through manipulating concrete objects, of course, but counting books offer opportunities to introduce and reinforce one-to-one correspondence, recognition of numbers, counting sequentially, sets, sorting, and other essential mathematical concepts. Look for counting books that clearly present the objects to be counted, make sure that sets or groupings are obvious, and try to select books that feature common objects for the youngest children to count (Huck et al., 2001).

Very young children will enjoy Tana Hoban's **Count and See** (1972), which photographically presents common objects, street scenes, everyday situations, and diverse children. A companion book is *1,2,3* (1985) by Hoban. Familiar objects are presented in photographs (toes, fingers, shoes, etc.), as well as the number names and numerals, making the book easy to use.

Denise Fleming's book, **Count!** (1992) combines colorful, action-packed illustrations with descriptive text to help youngsters learn about counting from 1 to 10 and then by 10s to 50. Animals and insects are featured on double-page spreads, accompanied by the corresponding numeral, number words, and set. Fleming's use of handmade pulp paper in bright primary colors makes the objects easy to count.

Bedtime is the subject of two counting books featuring families. **The Midnight Farm** (Lindbergh, 1987) is a soothing lullaby that describes nighttime among the animals on a farm. The beautifully muted two-page spreads by Susan Jeffers take the reader on a midnight trip around the farm with a mother and son, while the text weaves in a counting rhyme as the pair encounters animals on their nocturnal exploration. **Ten, Nine, Eight** (Bang, 1983) conveys tenderness, security, and the loving relationship of father and

MORE FAVORITES

Counting Books

Big Fat Hen (Baker, 1994)

Counting to Christmas (Tafuri, 1998)

Let's Count it Out, Jesse Bear (Carlstrom, 1996)

Mouse Count (Walsh, 1995)

One Red Sun (Keats, 1999)

Over in the Meadow (Keats, 1971)

Roll Over: A Counting Song (Peek, 1999)

Ten Black Dots (Crews, 1986)

Ten Cats have Ten Hats: A Counting Book (Marzollo, 1994)

Ten Little Bears: A Counting Rhyme (Hague, 1999)

Ten Rosy Roses (Merriam, 1999)

The Very Hungry Caterpillar (Carle, 1969)

daughter as they get ready for bed. The numerals clearly stand out on a white background, accompanied by a short, descriptive phrase about the objects to be counted. The illustrations are presented in warm colors and simple vignettes. Both of the books would be soothing to read to children at the end of a long day.

A family shops together and prepares a meal in **Feast for Ten** (Falwell, 1993). It's tempting to try to feel the textures in the collage illustrations, made from different types of fabric. The numerals stand out clearly and the objects are easy to count. The story line offers a warm affirmation of African American family life as each of the family members participates and cooperates.

Wordless Books

One day as Connie was observing her kindergarten students, she overheard Carter and Jim as they intently studied the pictures in **Frog Goes to Dinner** (Mayer, 1974). Carter suggested, "You read to me, and I'll read to you." Jim, a charming redheaded boy with a language delay, eagerly agreed. For 10 minutes the two boys took turns describing the pictures and inventing a story for this wordless picture book.

Based on Carter and Jim's idea, Connie brought many more wordless picture books into the classroom in the weeks to come and set aside short periods of time for pairs of children to "read" the books together. Sometimes she purposely grouped a student with a rich lexicon with one whose vocabulary was not as extensive, in an attempt to expand language development of the second child. Even when the pairing was random, or the children looked at the books independently, they seemed to benefit in many ways. They used expressive language as they created stories, listened carefully to each other, and followed the elements of story grammar as they described beginning, middle, and ending of a story, character traits, and details of a setting.

Wordless picture books can prepare children for reading in the following ways:

- Learning about story sequence. *Moonlight* (Ormerod, 1982) develops understanding of temporal sequence by showing a child's evening rituals and preparation for bed.

- Noting details in a story. In *Peter Spier's Rain* (Spier, 1982), each illustration depicts subtle aspects of color and movement to indicate impending weather changes.

- Determining main idea. *First Snow* (McCully, 1985) portrays a little mouse building up courage to ride a sled down a hill for the first time. Children might conclude that it is good to try new activities.

- Making inferences. By observing the pictorial sequence of events in *Four Hungry Kittens* (McCully, 2001), children can infer that the kittens are lonely and wandering around the barn because their mother has been accidentally locked in a closet.

MORE FAVORITES

Wordless Books

Father Christmas (Briggs, 1973)

Good Dog Carl (Day, 1985)

In the Pond (Cristini & Puricelli, 1984)

Oops! (Mayer, 1977)

Pancakes for Breakfast (dePaola, 1990)

Rosie's Walk (Hutchins, 1998)

The Snowman (Briggs, 1978)

Sunshine (Omerod, 1981)

Will's Mammoth (Martin, 1989)

Window (Baker, 1991)

- Drawing conclusions. By examining the picture in **Deep in the Forest** (Turkle, 1976), children will conclude that the roles of the people and bears are reversed from the story of the three bears.

- Observing cause and effect. By following the antics of the mischievous bird in **April Wilson's Magpie's Magic** (Wilson, 1999), children can see how his shenanigans bring on the conclusion of the book.

Wordless picture books allow children to be creative—there is no right or wrong way to tell the story. They are as equally accessible to children with little English or those with developmental delays, as they are to gifted children. Additionally, parents and caregivers with limited English can easily "read" the stories to their children, interpreting the illustrations in their own ways. Although currently there are few wordless picture books depicting diverse cultures, most have universal themes such as preparing for bed, the natural world, or experiencing new situations.

Imagination and independent thinking are supported as children describe actions and relationships in the illustrations or dramatize the stories. Adults can also foster literacy by audiotaping children's storytelling based on wordless books or writing their stories on sticky notes and temporarily attaching them to the pages of the book.

Mother Goose Rhymes

About the time he turned 2 years old, Dylan's favorite book was a collection of Mother Goose rhymes. When he brought the large volume to his parents, he often requested his favorite nursery rhymes by name—"Baa-Baa" (Baa-Baa Black Sheep), "Dumpy-Wumpy" (Humpty-Dumpty), "Hot Buns" (Hot Cross Buns), and "Fly" (Sing a Song of Sixpence).

FIGURE 2.5
Mother Goose Collections

The Glorious Mother Goose (Edens, 1998)
Here Comes Mother Goose (Opie, 1999)
The Movable Mother Goose (Sabuda, 1999)
The Original Volland Edition Mother Goose (Grover, 1984)
The Real Mother Goose (Wright, 1916)
Sylvia Long's Mother Goose (Long, 1999)
Tomie dePaola's Mother Goose (dePaola, 1985)
Wendy Watson's Mother Goose (Watson, 1989)
Willy Pogány's Mother Goose (Pogány, 2000)

Why are nursery rhymes so appealing to young children? The ear-catching music and lilt of the rhymes makes them enjoyable to children from infancy through the primary grades. Many of the rhymes have tunes that are easy for children to learn. (If families are unfamiliar with the music, there are many tapes and compact discs available.) Children enjoy acting out the poems, since many of them involve movement (e.g., *Jack Be Nimble, Wee Willie Winkie, Ring around the Rosie*). The characters and situations are silly, the content highly varied, and their humor and nonsense lift the spirits. Finally, the illustrations in many collections, created by award-winning artists, introduce children to times and places that can only be reached in the imagination. Depending on the illustrator, children may be exposed to art as diverse as depictions of the 18th-century English countryside in Blanche Fisher Wright's illustrations of **The Real Mother Goose** (Wright, 1916), art-deco designs from the 1920s in **Willy Pogány's Mother Goose** (Poga'ny, 2000), or the whimsical animals portrayed in **Sylvia Long's Mother Goose** (Long, 1999). Figure 2.5 lists several Mother Goose collections.

What are the best ways to share Mother Goose rhymes with children birth to 5 years old? The presentation of the rhymes should vary, depending on the age of the child. For infants and toddlers, who are rapidly learning new vocabulary and concepts, it helps to point to the pictures of the words you are saying. If a body part is mentioned, touch it on yourself or the child. Dramatize whatever you can with movement and sing those poems that have tunes. A good example is "Patty-Cake," where adults clap and roll the baby's hands at the appropriate times.

Mother Goose poems are a great way to introduce the concepts of rhyming words and alliteration. Families with preschool children may find that the alphabet, counting, and days of the week rhymes provide a pleasant format for teaching these skills. Children will continue to increase their vocabularies and add new concepts as they ask questions and adults point out interesting aspects of the illustrations and language. Adults can also ask children what they think is happening in the pictures or why they believe characters acted in a certain way.

With so many versions of Mother Goose available, how do families know which one to choose? The following criteria may be useful:

- How old is the child? Shorter, movement-oriented rhymes with animal characters are more appealing to younger children. Kindergarten children may enjoy more diversity of rhymes.
- Will the pictures appeal to the child and adults who read the book? Families can choose from different historical time periods and whether or not they want animal pictures.
- What rhymes are included in the collection? Are they all traditional, or are some lesser-known poems included?

Whatever books families choose, one can be sure that reading Mother Goose will be magical time for children and adults alike.

Predictable Books

Predictable books are those in which the text is highly structured, patterned, cumulative, repetitive, or rhyming. They provide wonderful opportunities for language play and development and phonological and phonemic awareness. Because of the text structure, the books support predicting and confirming, two skills necessary for successful reading.

MORE FAVORITES

Predictable Books

The Bag I'm Taking to Grandma's (Neitzel, 1995)

Buzz, Buzz, Buzz (Barton, 1995)

Farmer Duck (Waddell, 1992)

Feathers for Lunch (Ehlert, 1990)

I Went Walking (Williams, 1990)

If You Give a Mouse a Cookie (Numeroff, 1985)

The Jacket I Wear in the Snow (Neitzel, 1989)

King Bidgood's in the Bathtub (Wood, 1985)

Let's Go Visiting (Williams, 1998)

Millions of Cats (Gag, 1928)

New Shoes, Red Shoes (Rollings, 2000)

Off We Go! (Yolen, 2000)

Pigs in the Mud in the Middle of the Rud (Plourde, 1997)

Rachel Fister's Blister (MacDonald, 1993)

We're Going on a Bear Hunt (Rosen, 1989)

A kindergarten class made an innovation of *Brown Bear, Brown Bear, What Do You See?* (Martin, 1992) during an ocean unit.

One of the most well-loved predictable books is Bill Martin Jr.'s **Brown Bear, Brown Bear, What Do You See?** (1992). Kim, a kindergarten teacher, used the patterned text to create a child-made book beginning with "Ocean, ocean what do you see?" Each child drew a particular sea creature they had been studying, Kim wrote the repetitive phrase on each page, and the pictures were assembled into a small book to place in the reading center. Books that are child-created based on patterned text are called "innovations."

Jamberry (Degan, 1983) is a rollicking, rhythmical celebration of berries and berry-picking. Bruce Degan wrote it based on his experiences as a child who went searching for berries in the fields with his grandparents. One mother recorded comments in her reading journal about her 17-month-old son's experiences with *Jamberry*:

This was my third time reading the book to him. He showed interest until the end. We take him in our yard and let him pick berries and eat them as he does the picking. We started that before the book was given to us, which may help make this book interesting to him.

Farm animals are the subject of a cumulative book written by Nancy Tafuri. **This Is the Farmer** (Tafuri, 1994) illustrates the animals in a chain of events that is set off by the farmer. The format of the book is larger than usual, with big, bold, black type and colorful two-page spreads. A mouse appears after a few pages and is seen on every subsequent page, sometimes in hiding.

Animal mothers and babies are featured in Deborah Guarino's predictable book, **Is Your Mama a Llama**? (1989), delightfully illustrated by Steven Kellogg. When 4-year-old Lacy heard the book for the first time, she commented to her mother that the words rhymed. The question–answer format encourages children to chime in, while the clues given in the text support prediction.

An afternoon nap on granny's bed becomes really crowded in **The Napping House** (Wood & Wood, 1984) when each page adds another sleepy character—a boy, dog, cat, mouse, and, finally, a flea! The reader's perspective moves with every additional character until we are at last looking down on the piled up bed. As all jump off, the perspective moves back downward and the colors start shifting to bring the end of the nap and a sunny day. This book is a great one to use for role-play with young children.

Song Picture Books

Mackenzie and Maddisen's mom played classical music for the twin infants at naptime each day. Before she was a year old, Mackenzie learned how to activate a musical toy with the punch of a large button. When she could barely stand, she would turn it on and move her little body to the rhythmic beat of the music. Whether soothing a fussy baby at naptime with music, distracting a toddler from a tantrum by singing a song, or chanting a short ditty to make diaper changes less frustrating, caregivers often incorporate music and rhythm into the day.

Children as young as 2 can sometimes be heard singing or reciting simple lyrics to their favorite songs (Jalongo & Ribblett, 1997). Music is a natural and easily available source of language learning in homes, child-care centers, and preschools. The link between music and literacy development has recently gained attention (Barclay & Walwer, 1992; Jalongo & Ribblett, 1997; Hansen & Bernstorf, 2002). Song picture books are often illustrated versions of well-known songs, chants, or fingerplays. Building on children's prior knowledge of the words and tunes, the books immediately engage children's interest and invite participation by singing and movement. Song picture books can be used to reinforce emergent literacy by promoting phonological and phonemic awareness, building vocabulary, encouraging fluency, and presenting opportunities for creative movement and language play (Hansen & Bernstorf, 2002; Jalongo & Ribblett, 1997).

The Lady with the Alligator Purse (Westcott, 1998) easily lends itself to dramatic reenactment. When the children in Elizabeth's kindergarten class in South Georgia were studying the swamp, she put the song on chart paper and used it frequently with the children for role play and literacy development. It was a favorite song with the children throughout the unit. Putting the words on the chart helped focus children's attention on phrases, words, and letters, while supplying a visual script to support learning the song.

A favorite song, ***There Was an Old Lady Who Swallowed a Fly*** (Taback, 1997), can now be found in variations. It follows the traditional song version and is cleverly illustrated using die-cut pages, mixed media, and collage. Another adaptation describes the old lady's diet a little differently. ***There Was an Old Lady Who Swallowed a Trout!*** (Sloat, 1998) adds a Pacific Northwest menu to the old lady's meal. She swallows a trout, salmon, otter, seal, and other fishy creatures, but when she finally swallows the whole ocean, she laughs and spits out all the creatures. Engaging children in music and literacy through song picture books is inexpensive, entertaining, educational, and gives some "oomph" to an otherwise ordinary day at home or school.

See Figure 2.6 for tips on successful read-aloud techniques.

MORE FAVORITES

Song Picture Books

Abiyoyo (Seeger, 1994)

Arroz Con Leche: Popular Songs and Rhymes from Latin America (Delacre, 1989)

Baby Beluga (Raffi, 1992)

The Bear Went over the Mountain (Wells, 1998)

De Colores and Other Latin-American Folk Songs for Children (Orozco, 1999)

Do Your Ears Hang Low? A Love Story (Church, 2002)

Down by the River: Afro-Carribean Rhymes, Games, and Songs for Children (Hallworth, 1996)

Fiddle-I-Fee: A Farmyard Song for the Very Young (Sweet, 2002)

Five Little Ducks (Raffi, 1998)

Go Tell Aunt Rhody (Aliki, 1986)

Hush Little Baby (Long, 1997)

The Jolly Mon (Buffet & Buffet, 1988)

Joseph had a Little Overcoat (Taback, 1999)

Mama Don't Allow (Hurd, 1984)

Mary Wore Her Red Dress and Henry Wore His Green Sneakers (Peek, 1998)

Miss Mary Mack (Hoberman, 1998)

Rock-a-Bye Baby (Winter, 1999)

The Teddy Bears' Picnic (Kennedy, 2002)

The Wheels on the Bus: The Traditional Song (Zelinsky, 1990)

It is probably safe to say that most parents and caregivers today recognize the value of reading to young children. They may even know that it is the most important thing they can do to help their children become independent, lifelong readers. But do all parents and caregivers know how to read aloud well and inspire excitement about books? If not, early childhood teachers and librarians can help family members develop the art of reading aloud.

Well-loved children's author Mem Fox describes effective techniques for reading aloud in her book *Reading Magic* (2001), and on her Web site, www.memfox.com. According to Fox, there are six things readers can do with their voices to make the reading aloud experience enjoyable for young listeners.

- Make your voice loud or soft, fast or slow, high or low, and use dramatic pauses.
- During the dark passages in a story, slow down and pause to create anticipation.
- Speed up your voice during exciting, quickly paced episodes, and use a low voice for frightening parts.
- A higher voice might be used for portraying a child or little animal's part, while a lower voice might be used for adult characters and villains.
- Try to think about the words you are reading and what meaning they convey; then change your voice to express that meaning.
- When reading aloud, the two most important sentences in the book are the first and last. The beginning sentence sets the tone and "grabs" the child into the story. Be sure that you read the first sentence slowly and dramatically to captivate your listener(s). The last line, a "farewell," also should be read slowly, to give the child a chance to enjoy the final moments of a well-read tale. Expressive reading makes the child enthralled with the book and eager to hear more (Fox, 2001).

As parents and caregivers read aloud, they can help children understand three "magical secrets" of literacy: (a) the magic of print, (b) the magic of language, and (c) the magic of knowledge about the world (Fox, 2001). Adults can point out these secrets of reading in playful ways when discussing the books and going back through them after reading aloud. Knowledge of each of these secrets is essential to children as they begin to read independently.

Parents and caregivers of preschoolers sometimes complain that their children want to hear the same story read over and over again. Although the adults may think that they can't bear to read a certain book one more time, it is important to take a deep breath and dive right into the old favorite again. The book may be meeting a psychological need or the child may simply find security and pleasure in hearing a familiar story over and over. Rereading (and rereading and rereading) is a vital step in helping children learn to read.

Reading together is a way families can show their love and grow together. "For when parents and children read stories together, they create their own stories, original stories that are filled with the special kind of magic that all families can share" (Taylor & Strickland, 1986, p. 111).

FIGURE 2.6
Teacher to Teacher: Reading Aloud

POETRY

Poetry is distinguished from the other genres by its form. Whether sparse, strong images dominate or longer, more developed refrains emerge, poetry wastes no words. Through poems, children can recognize familiar feelings or see the world with new eyes. The musical cadence, rhyme, and rhythm of poetry read aloud can soothe a fussy baby or enchant a curious toddler. As we watch newborns move their bodies in response to the rhythm of our voices, it seems that humans are innately attracted to poetry.

Poetry is an excellent way to spark children's awareness of language and sounds (Burns, Griffin, & Snow, 1999). Young children who hear poetry read aloud learn to experiment with language, make up words, and have well-developed vocabularies. Playing with language is a natural activity for young children; poetry reflects this playfulness. Marie, 3½, an avid poetry fan, requested "sneaky snacks" when she was hungry and "nippy-naps" when she was tired. Stretching the imagination, evoking familiar sensations, and illuminating our emotions, poetry is a magical combination of language to share with children.

Books of poetry are available for children today and can be found in the following categories: anthologies, collections of poems by a single author, poetry collections about a single theme, and versions of single poems. Cynthia Rylant has written a lovely book of poems for children, ***Good Morning, Sweetie Pie***

MORE FAVORITES

Poetry

Close Your Eyes (Marzollo, 1998)

Each Peach Pear Plum (Ahlberg & Ahlberg, 1978)

The Fish Is Me: Bathtime Rhymes (Philip, 2002)

Honey, I Love and Other Love Poems (Greenfield, 1978)

I Love You: A Rebus Poem (Marzollo, 1999)

I See the Moon: Good Night Poems and Lullabies (Pfister, 1991)

Poems to Read to the Very Young (Wilkin, 2001)

Talking Like the Rain: A First Book of Poems (Kennedy & Kennedy, 1992)

The Three Bears Rhyme Book (Yolen, 1987)

Welcome Baby: Baby Rhymes for Baby Times (Calmenson, 2002)

Whiskers and Rhymes (Adoff, 1988)

(2001). The eight poems celebrate a toddler's daily life, beginning with the morning and ending at bedtime. In *A Child's Calendar*, (Updike, 1999), each poem captures the essence of the months all year long in five short verses. The illustrations by Trina Schart Hyman are a visual treat. Lee Bennett Hopkins, a popular writer of poetry for children, collected poems to share in his book, ***Side by Side Poems to Read Together*** (1988). Hopkins says the poems, "are meant to be read aloud—spoken, shouted, sung, enjoyed" (1988, unpaged).

TRADITIONAL LITERATURE

Folktales, fables, myths, legends and epics—the body of folklore we call *traditional literature*—are stories that originated orally and have no identifiable author. Told around cottage fires and in the great halls of castles, stories became the vehicle for transmitting the beliefs, attitudes, and values of a culture. Entertaining adults and children alike, traditional literature became the basis of our literary heritage.

Ask a child to tell you a story and chances are she will begin, "Once upon a time…" Familiar archetypal characters (e.g., the hero, fairy godmother, wicked witch, beautiful princess) that populate traditional literature help children easily relate to the stories. The brevity and fast-paced plots of folktales assist children as they learn character traits and story structure in memorable and enjoyable ways. Good is usually rewarded, evil is ultimately punished, and everyone lives "happily ever after."

In addition to forming the foundation of our literary heritage, traditional literature also serves as a rich body of multicultural information. The Grimm brothers, who were among the first to collect and record folktales, believed that as people migrated from place to place they changed the stories to better fit the audience. This theory accounts for folktale variants that, presumably, were crafted by storytellers to reflect the native people, culture, and geography of a certain place. Consider the many versions of "Cinderella" that have been published: ***Mufaro's Beautiful Daughter*** (Steptoe, 1987); ***The Egyptian Cinderella*** (Climo, 1989); ***The Rough-Face Girl*** (Martin, 1992); and, ***Yeh-Shen: A Cinderella Story from China*** (Louie, 1982). One of the values of folktale variants lies in the cultural identification these universal stories bring to specific groups of children. Looking at the illustrations, a child who has recently moved to the United States may see geography, clothing, artifacts, food, or climates that are familiar. The text presents relationships, language, customs, and attitudes that may trigger recognition and bring comfort and security to children who have recently immigrated. Folktale variations give children of all cultures a foundation for understanding the lives of others.

Bruno Bettleheim (1976) states that fairy tales are "magic mirrors" that help children cope with the dreams and struggles of childhood. Preschoolers often become enraptured by the magical nature of folk and fairy tales, vividly recasting everyday events and traumas into stories made more exciting and satisfying by imaginative creatures and heroic deeds. Considering the stark reality of many children's daily lives, traditional literature offers an acceptable escape into a world of make-believe.

Toddlers will love being introduced to nursery tales by Helen Oxenbury. She has published two small versions that contain watercolor illustrations and simple retellings. Little ones will meet Goldilocks, the Three Little Pigs, Red Riding Hood, and others in **First Nursery Stories** (1994) and **Favorite Nursery Stories** (1995).

As a young girl, author/illustrator Trina Schart Hyman wanted to be Little Red Riding Hood so much that her mother made her a red hooded cape to wear in her fantasy play. Her rendering of the Grimm Brothers' tale is enchanting and true to the original version. Hyman's **Little Red Riding Hood** (1983) was a Caldecott Honor book. In contrast, James Marshall's retelling, **Red Riding Hood** (1987), is a comical version with cartoon-like illustrations. When the wolf arrives at Granny's house, ahead of Red Riding Hood, Granny is really upset because he has disturbed her reading! He eats her anyway, along with Red Riding Hood when she arrives. At last, they are rescued by the faithful woodcutter. Another of Marshall's retold tales, **Goldilocks and the Three Bears** (1988), won a Caldecott Honor medal.

The many published versions of "The Gingerbread Boy" keep youngsters on their toes looking for similarities and differences. Set in New York City, Richard Egielski's **The Gingerbread Boy** (2000) takes readers on a romp past alley

The Gingerbread Man is easily adapted for story retelling on a flannel board.

rats, construction workers, and street musicians until he meets his fate in Central Park. A recipe for gingerbread cookies is included. In Jan Brett's adaptation, **The Gingerbread Baby** (1999) the main character is a gingerbread baby in the Swiss Alps, who escapes from the oven before he is fully baked and eludes his animal and human pursuers before being outwitted by Matti, the young boy who had mistakenly let him out. Matti makes an elaborate gingerbread house into which the gingerbread baby runs, thinking it is a refuge. Brett's use of the side panels on each page to extend the story line, and the gingerbread house which has a flap to lift, make this story irresistible.

Eric Kimmel has put a new twist on the tale by changing the gingerbread boy to a tortilla and situating the story in South Texas. In **The Runaway Tortilla** (2000), the tortilla decides she is much too beautiful to eat, so she rolls out the door past trotting donkeys, slithering rattlesnakes, and leaping jackrabbits, among others. She finally meets her demise after being tricked by a coyote. The stylized illustrations combine with counting skills, action words, Southwest vocabulary, and several Spanish words to make this a rollicking retelling of a familiar tale.

MORE FAVORITES

Traditional Literature

Baby Rattlesnake/Viborita de Cascabel (Ata, 1996)

Borrequita and the Coyote: A Tale from Ayutla, Mexico (Aardema, 1998)

Chicken Little (Hobson, 2000)

Cuckoo/Cucu (Ehlert, 1997)

Foolish Rabbit's Big Mistake (Martin, 1985)

The Gingerbread Man (Aylesworth, 1998)

Jack and the Beanstalk (Kellogg, 1991)

Lon Po Po: A Red Riding Hood Story from China (Young, 1989)

The Mitten: A Ukranian Folktale (Brett, 1990)

Moon Rope: A Peruvian Folktale (Ehlert, 1992)

Strega Nona (dePaola, 1975)

The Tale of Rabbit and Coyote (Johnson, 1994)

Tops and Bottoms (Stevens, 1995)

Town Mouse, Country Mouse (Brett, 1994)

Two of Everything: A Chinese Folktale (Hong, 1993)

Paul Zelinsky has retold familiar fairy tales and illustrated them with beautiful oil paintings. ***Rapunzel*** (Zelinsky & Grimm, 1997) won the Caldecott Medal. The illustrations in ***Rumplestiltskin*** (Zelinsky, 1986) and ***Hansel and Gretel*** (Zelinsky, 1999) are equally stunning. Figure 2.7 offers suggestions for using folktales in storytelling.

Storytellers and children develop a magical relationship as they share the drama of a fine tale. In storytelling there is nothing to separate the teller from the audience; eye contact is maintained and the audience can participate with gestures and repeated phrases. Beginning tellers can choose from family or personal stories, folktales, stories they enjoyed as children, or the wide variety of contemporary stories available.

Preparing for storytelling:
1. Read or listen to the story many times. You may want to rewrite the tale to make it your own.
2. Do not try to memorize the whole story. Learn only important parts word for word, such as beginnings or endings.
3. Map the sequence of the story or write down key points in order. Avoid having too many notes, as you might be tempted to read them, rather than tell your story.
4. Learn repetitive parts. There are often repeated rhymes in folktales that should be memorized.
5. Plan gestures and expressions to emphasize points and add drama.
6. Project your voice, but keep it natural. Use appropriate inflections and body language.
7. Practice in front of a mirror or a friend who will honestly critique your work.

Telling your story:
1. Arrange the area to be as free of clutter as possible, so that listeners concentrate on the story.
2. Make eye contact with your audience and tell the story *with them.*
3. Take your time, pause, and provide descriptions that allow your listener to visualize the story.
4. Encourage your audience to participate and respond. If you are using props with young children, you might give them opportunities to hold the props or move them in some way.
5. Pay special attention to the conclusion. Leave time for responses at the end.
6. Be yourself and enjoy the experience!

Storytelling tips were adapted from
www.aaronshep.com/storytelling
A good resource for storytellers, which includes hints on telling stories with and without props, is:
Bauer, C. F. (1993). *Caroline Feller Bauer's Handbook for Storytellers.* Chicago: American Library Association.

FIGURE 2.7
Teacher to Teacher: Storytelling

MODERN FANTASY

Talking toys and animals, preposterous situations, imaginary worlds, and magical powers are all found in the world of fantasy. Readers are encouraged to suspend disbelief and enter into realms where characters, settings, and events defy the laws of the real world. Closely akin to traditional literature in the motifs they contain, stories of fantasy differ in that their authors are known. For example, **Charlotte's Web** (White, 1952), **Alice's Adventures in Wonderland** (Carroll, 1865), and **Winnie the Pooh** (Milne, 1926) are classic stories of fantasy that have known authors, yet retain many characteristics of traditional literature.

Where the Wild Things Are (Sendak, 1963) is a modern fantasy that satisfies a young child's feelings of aggressiveness toward being punished. After Max is sent to his room, his imaginative adventures with the "wild things" allow him to act out his feelings in an acceptable way through his fantasy, bringing him back to reality with a loving gesture from his mother.

Goodnight Moon (Brown, 1947) is a fantasy that dozens of caregivers could probably recite by heart! The repetitive refrain encourages little ones to join in, while the color illustrations darken to indicate the nightfall as the rabbit

Children's views of themselves and their families are often played out in the world of animal fantasy.

says goodnight to objects in his room. The mouse moves in each double-page color spread, intriguing young readers and honing their observational skills. Vocabulary development is naturally supported as adult readers ask, "Where's the mouse?" or ask children to point to and name objects.

Children's views of themselves, their immediate environment, and the relationships with siblings and caregivers are often played out in the world of animal fantasy. Several endearing animal characters that illustrate elements of fantasy grounded in child-like reality are Olivia, Max and Ruby, and Chrysanthemum. In **Olivia** (Falconer, 2000), a Caldecott Honor book, clothes scattered across the endpapers give the immediate impression that someone is on the move! This bundle of energy is Olivia, a preschool pig who romps through her days with such zeal that she earns a time out after trying to imitate artist Jackson Pollock on the bedroom wall. The black-and-white drawings, brightened by strategic spots of red, dance off the page with Olivia's exuberance. Three-year-old Emma's mom commented that they both identified with Olivia as they read the book. Mom said that Emma is just like Olivia—she wears out her mom and dad and tries to change outfits "about twenty times a day!" For those who enjoyed **Olivia**, there is a sequel, **Olivia Saves the Circus** (Falconer, 2001).

MORE FAVORITES

Fantasy

Blueberries for Sal (McClosky, 1948)

Cloudy with a Chance of Meatballs (Barrett, 1978)

Curious George (Rey, 1973)

Frannie B. Kranny, There's a Bird in Your Hair! (Lerner & Goldhor, 2001)

Frederick (Lionni, 1973)

George Shrinks (Joyce, 1985)

I Love You Little One (Tafuri, 2000)

Imogene's Antlers (Small, 1986)

The Jolly Postman or Other People's Letters (Ahlberg & Ahlberg, 1986)

Koala Lou (Fox, 1994)

Madeline (Bemelmans, 1976)

Make Way for Ducklings (McCloskey, 1941)

Piggies (Wood & Wood, 1991)

The Runaway Bunny (Brown, 1972)

10 Minutes Till Bedtime (Rathmann, 2000)

The Wolf's Chicken Stew (Kasza, 1996)

Yoko's Paper Cranes (Wells, 2001)

Rosemary Wells brings us Max and Ruby, those spirited siblings who make everyday activities truly adventurous. Toddlers won't be able to resist *Goodnight Max* (Wells, 2000), a participation book that features 14 items to touch as Ruby tries to put Max to bed. Wells has also written Max and Ruby books that present more complicated story lines, while retaining Ruby's bossiness and Max's ability to outwit his big sister. *Bunny Money* (Wells, 1997b) is a hilarious tale that explores the ups and downs of shopping with a limited amount of money. The author includes the directions for "making money" at the end of the story. *Bunny Cakes* (Wells, 1997a) presents an often-encountered dilemma of emergent writers: No one can read what early writers write!

Chester and Wilson, Lilly, Chrysanthemum, Julius, Owen, and Sheila Rae—the famous cast of mice characters who populate Kevin Henkes's modern fantasy stories—bring refreshing and realistic insights to the world of children. From sibling rivalry to misbehavior in preschool, Henkes uses humorous text and lively illustrations to illuminate a wide array of childhood dilemmas. Children identify readily with the characters, especially in *Julius, the Baby of the World* (1990), *Chrysanthemum* (1991), and *Owen* (1993).

CONTEMPORARY REALISTIC FICTION

In contrast to modern fantasy, realistic fiction contains no talking animals or toys, no excursions to imaginary worlds, and no unlikely events. Firmly grounded in plausible events and populated by characters that could be real people, realistic fiction allows young children to see themselves and others in situations that are presented in credible ways. Contemporary realistic fiction offers children the disparate qualities of affirming their own feelings while giving glimpses into lives unlike their own.

Writers of realistic fiction for very young children develop stories based on family life, social and emotional development, and people and events in a child's immediate environment. Featuring families of diverse cultures, varied lifestyles, and differing socioeconomic levels, subjects of realistic fiction range from the birth of a new sibling to homelessness.

For the youngest, *Baby Says* (Steptoe, 1988) is the story of an older brother who is trying to construct a building block masterpiece while baby brother, from the playpen, tries to disrupt the process. Although exasperated at first, big brother relents when he gets a kiss and hug from the baby, and the two join in the block play together.

Helen Oxenbury has written a series of books about Tom and his monkey, Pippo. The simple board books follow the daily adventures of the pair, describing events that many preschoolers are likely to recognize. *Pippo Gets Lost* (1998a) and *Tom and Pippo Go for a Walk* (1998b) capture the playfulness and simplicity of childhood.

Ezra Jack Keats's realistic stories about Peter and his friends have entertained young children for years. Known for his use of collage, Keats was one of the first authors of children's books to feature African American children in an

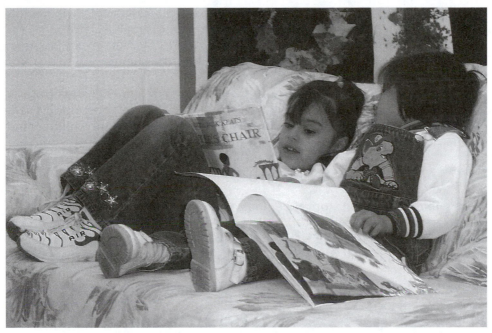

Ezra Jack Keats's stories of realistic fiction help children explore issues such as the arrival of a new baby in Peter's Chair.

MORE FAVORITES

Contemporary Realistic Fiction

All By Myself! (Aliki, 2000)

Cherries and Cherry Pits (Williams, 1986)

Dear Juno (Pak, 1999)

Ira Sleeps Over (Waber, 1972)

Matthew and Tilly (Jones, 1991)

Mommy Doesn't Know My Name (Williams, 1996)

"More, More, More," Said the Baby (Williams, 1990)

No Nap (Bunting, 1996)

Oonga Boonga (Wishinsky, 1998)

Someday a Tree (Bunting, 1993)

Starting School (Ahlberg & Ahlberg, 1988)

The Stray Dog (Simont, 2001)

These Hands (Price, 1999)

Tucking Mommy In (Loh, 1987)

What Shall We Play? (Heap, 2002)

William's Doll (Zolotow, 1972)

inner-city neighborhood. *The Snowy Day* (1962), a Caldecott Medal winner, lets us share the excitement of a new snowfall in the city through a child's eyes. *Pet Show* (1972), *Goggles* (1969), and *Peter's Chair* (1967) chronicle everyday situations and explore issues common to many children, such as sibling rivalry, peer acceptance, and bullying.

Throughout the rest of the chapters, you will encounter many books of realistic fiction to use with young children and their families concerning a variety of topics. It is important to become well-acquainted with the children and families in your program to use realistic fiction most effectively.

HISTORICAL FICTION

Stories that combine historical settings, events, and/or people with fictional characters are considered historical fiction. When choosing historical fiction, it is important that the setting is historically accurate and the characters behave in ways that are typical of the time period. As well, the characters' dialogue, clothing, and relationships should reflect an historically accurate perspective. Many of the books in this genre are more appropriate for elementary-age chil-

Jackdaws help young children learn about the past by providing concrete objects to examine and discuss.

dren, but we believe that children as young as 5 can appreciate the stories in historical fiction, noting some of the differences between "then" and "now." Historical fiction can make the past accessible to young children.

During a thematic unit for kindergartners in South Georgia, Elizabeth used **When I Was Young in the Mountains** (Rylant, 1982). The topic was the Okefenokee Swamp, a nearby large wetland area and wildlife refuge that was occupied at times by homesteaders and cypress loggers. She writes:

> Since much of the available literature on the Okefenokee pioneers and structures was geared to adult readers, we read *When I Was Young in the Mountains* (1982) by Cynthia Rylant. Although the story does not take place in the same setting, it is from a similar time period. The children made immediate connections between the book and our pioneer cabin and artifacts. Upon completing the cabin, the children used it for dramatic play and as a reading center. Our jackdaw [a collection of objects about a particular time period], cabin, and related reading allowed the children to imagine life as pioneers, and thus became a rich springboard for relevant and meaningful ways to explore times past. (Dodd, 1999, p. 138)

Elizabeth asked families to donate items for the class jackdaw. Items included mason jars, a washboard, an old lamp, a kettle, cooking utensils, and a quilt. The jackdaw allowed the children to enjoy learning about "long ago" in a concrete way, while helping them connect to the illustrations and text in the books they read.

MORE FAVORITES

Historical Fiction

Cecil's Story (Lyon, 1991)

Charlie and His Wheat Straw Hat (Hiser, 1986)

Cowboys (Round, 1991)

I Go with My Family to Grandma's (Levinson, 1990)

Island Boy (Cooney, 1991)

Miss Rumphius (Cooney, 1982)

The Ox-Cart Man (Hall, 1979)

A Picnic in October (Bunting, 1999)

Prairie Primer A to Z (Stutson & Patent, 1999)

Solomon Grundy (Hoguet, 1986)

When Addie was Scared (Bailey, 1999)

The Year of the Perfect Christmas Tree: An Appalachian Story (Houston, 1988)

INFORMATIONAL BOOKS

Children are naturally curious. How many times have you heard a young child ask, "Why?" or "Where?" or "How?" Although parents may tire of answering the endless questions, the inquisitiveness of a young child is the basis of complex cognitive thought. As children interact with their environments and talk with others about what they observe and experience, they begin to develop a schema of themselves, others, and their world.

Informational, or nonfiction, books cover countless topics (e.g., animals, nature, activities, concepts, music, art) and are readily available to help parents and teachers explain the wonders of the world to young children. Not only do informational books provide lots of facts to satisfy inquiring minds, they also present text structures and formats that are different from narrative (story) text. Familiarity with the expository text structure of informational books aids the development of reading, writing, and content acquisition in young children (Pappas, 1993; Richgels, 2002).

Today's informational books are visually attractive, have appealing formats, and skillfully blend facts and illustrations to appeal to youngsters. For toddlers, there are many concept books available, as we discussed in a previous section. When children begin to explore their surroundings and develop cognitively, there are many exceptionally well-written and illustrated informational books from which to choose.

When looking for informational books to use with young children, make sure the facts are accurate and up-to-date. For example, the brontosaurus dinosaur was renamed a few years ago, based on additional bones found in a fossilized dinosaur. Consider the author's background, the clarity of illustrations, the format, and the presentation of information.

Gail Gibbons is a well-respected author of informational books. *The Milk Makers* (1985), *Spiders* (1993), and *Fire! Fire!* (1984) are three good examples of Gibbon's ability to present information in reader-friendly ways. Joanna Cole is another popular author of nonfiction. *My New Kitten* (1995) is a photographic essay that discretely, but accurately, describes a mother cat having kittens.

Books featuring information about our bodies are interesting to young children. *Two Eyes, a Nose, and a Mouth* (Intrater, 1995) includes close-up photographs of diverse faces, including children and adults. The text uses a variety of words to describe eyes, noses, and mouths, at the same time emphasizing the unique physical features that each of us possess. *Eyes, Nose, Fingers, and Toes* (Hindley, 1999) is written for toddlers. The whimsical illustrations depict ways children use their bodies. Toddlers play "peek-a-boo," yawn, laugh, sing, smile, stretch, and wiggle their way through the book.

Lois Ehlert has written several informational books for children, illustrated with collage and mixed media in nontraditional formats. When reading *Snowballs* (1995), for example, you must turn the book vertically to look at the two-page spreads. In *Nuts to You!* (1993) and *Red Leaf, Yellow Leaf* (1991) Ehlert

MORE FAVORITES

Informational Books

Apples (Gibbons, 2000)

Chickens Aren't the Only Ones (Heller, 1999)

Everything Has a Place (Lillie, 1993)

Everywhere Babies (Myers, 2001)

Fire! Fire! (Gibbons, 1984)

Growing Vegetable Soup (Ehlert, 1987)

In the Snow: Who's Been Here? (George, 1995)

In the Woods: Who's Been Here? (George, 1995)

Mice Squeak, We Speak (dePaola, 1997)

Play (Morris, 1998)

Tools (Morris, 1992)

When This Box Is Full (Lillie, 1993)

uses die-cut pages to increase the reader's engagement in the story. In most of her informational books, Ehlert extends the text by including additional facts or photos at the end of the book.

ENGAGING CHILDREN IN LITERATURE

Reader Response Theory

A former student, who is now a preschool teacher, corresponds frequently with us via e-mail. One day she wrote:

> I only have a minute, but I wanted to tell you what this little boy said on Monday. We were reading and reading and reading during rest time. He is a unique learner and has a very hard time calming down, so we read. I suggested that we read another book and he said, "I can't, I'm full." I have laughed for three days now—I wish you knew Peter. He's the kind of kid that makes you cry twice a week and love your job the other three! (Elizabeth Childers, personal communication, March 7, 2001).

Stories evoke myriad responses from young children. When a familiar, loved book is read aloud, a child's body language, facial expressions, and linguistic responses offer immediate impressions about their attachment to the story. One of the first phrases young children use to express their satisfaction with a good book is, "Read it again!" The life experiences, knowledge, emotions, and associations a reader brings to the text help construct meaning each time it is read, thus creating a transaction between the reader and the text. Louise Rosenblatt (1976) refers to this as "reader response theory." As stories are read and discussed, literature comes alive in ways that are personal for each reader.

Young children often immerse themselves in the story, often "becoming" the characters and incorporating literary language and book-related play into their daily lives. Mom and Maggie (age 2½) read **Bunny Cakes** (Wells, 1997a) one afternoon. The next day, Maggie made "cakes" during her playtime and told Mom she needed "silver stars, birthday candles, sugar hearts, and buttercream roses" just like in the book. Then she made "caterpillar icing" and asked which cake her mom wanted.

Readers' responses to literature are individual, active, and meaningful. Responses are influenced by sociocultural context as well as developmental ages and stages. Reader response theory helps explain why children may react to the same story in different ways. For example, depending on a child's experiences and moods, a story that engenders a particular response one day may spark quite a different reaction when read later. As you interact with children daily, take time to listen to their conversations about books, encourage discussions about text and illustrations, and observe their many responses. An understanding of reader response, coupled with knowledge of the wide range of children's literature available, will help as you choose and share books with children.

Illustration by Emily Katherine Green. Reproduced with permission.

Types of Responses

The variety of children's responses to literature has been well-documented by researchers. In a yearlong study of Leo Lionni's books with kindergartners, Vivian Paley (1997) led the children as they engaged in literary discussions, art, dramatic play, and writing. Paley discovered that the children discussed Lionni's books in great detail, closely examined his illustrations, and made connections from the books to their life in the classroom.

Rowe (1998) investigated the book-related dramatic play of 2- and 3-year-olds in a home and preschool setting. She found that the children directly connected books to their play. They experienced books in kinesthetic and affective ways, used book-related play as a means of inquiry, and linked their world to the book-reading events through play and language.

Preschoolers in a study by Green and Halsall (1991) used language and concepts from books during their play and in their conversations. Their interactions with stories resulted in book-related dramatic play and conversations with adults that helped the children make sense of developmental and moral issues. Enactment of folk and fairy tales was a frequent response found in this study. Shelby Wolf described the importance of literature in the lives of her two young daughters in *The Braid of Literature* (Wolf & Heath, 1992). Enactment of favorite books was a primary vehicle through which the girls explored relationships, literary language, and life in general.

In our own research on family storybook reading (Green et al., 2002), parents kept journals to document children's responses to books during and after story-reading events in their homes. Analysis of the data indicated that children's responses fell into five categories: (a) literary language, (b) concept acquisition, (c) book-related dramatic play, (d) affective associations, and (e) book-related activities. In other words, during and after sharing books with their parents, the children in our study used language from the stories; acquired new concepts about themselves, others, and the world around them; acted out characters or situations in the stories; used literature to help them understand emotions and relationships; and, participated in activities uniquely related to the stories they had heard (e.g., art activities, cooking, family outings). Take a look at Table 2.2 for specific examples of children's responses to books.

Strategies for Engagement

How does research help us plan appropriately for young children? The studies described above highlight the importance of providing literature and experiences that will help strengthen literary, language, and life connections. The findings remind us to be astute observers of children's responses to literature and encourage parents and caretakers to be more aware of responses to books they read to their children. You may want to set up a

TABLE 2.2

Children's Responses to Literature

Category	Description	Examples
Literary Language	Book-specific vocabulary, syntax, phonetic play, dialogue, informational passages, and narration used in play, self-talk, or in conversations with others	• Dylan's mom read *Go Away Big Green Monster* and now he frequently says, "Go away, Mama." • After reading *In the Night Kitchen*, Nick and his mom made dumplings. As they worked with the batter, Nick said, "Stir it, stir it, make it, bake it," adaptations of the story text. • As mom reads *Is Your Mama a Llama?* Lacy comments about how the words rhyme.
Concept Acquisition	Using literature, social interactions, and related environmental explorations to build concepts and acquire skills; contains both interpersonal and intra-personal planes; involves text-to-life and and life-to-text experiences and and associations	• After hearing *Three Billy Goats Gruff*, Grace is asked if she knows that goats eat grass; Grace says, "Like baa-baa sheep." • Listening to *Monday's Child*, Sean points to the animals, people, and different objects as his mother asks him questions. • Aaron loves to hear *Have You Seen My Cat?* His mom reports that after several readings he says, "My cat" and goes to find Lucy (his cat); he meows for her; and they count her kittens.
Book-Related Dramatic Play	Enactments related either explicitly or implictly to the text or illustrations of books or to the read-aloud experience	• Grace manipulated a small clock while reciting "Hickory, Dickory, Dock." • Aaron pretended to sweep the kitchen floor with a broom and "fly" after listening to *Witchy Broom*. • Brad used a sheet to build a tent in the living room, wore his toy camping gear and backpack, and used stuffed toys to help "find a king" after hearing *The Rescue of Babar*.
Affective Associations	Using literature to understand relationships, feelings, self and others, and social and moral issues	• Masha's mom often reads *The Kissing Hand* to her the night before she goes to her dad's house for two days. They give each other "kissing hands"when they say good-bye.

Category	Description	Examples
		• Angela's mother chose *Happy Adoption Day* to read to help her understand in a positive light what it means to be adopted. • A few days after reading *Are You My Mother?* Nick turned to his mom in a restaurant and said, "You're my mother."
Book-Related Experiences	Activities uniquely related to the books children hear, including arts, crafts, cooking, family outings, etc.	• Missy's parents took her to eat sushi after reading *Yoko.* • After reading *Sweet Dream Pie,* Brad and his mom made a pie with special ingredients. • Maria and her mom went to the pond to feed the ducks after reading *Mira Cómo Crecen Patitos (Look How They Grow).*

Source: Green, C. R., Lilly, E., & Barrett, T. M. (2002). Families reading together: Connecting literature and life. *Journal of Research in Childhood Education, 16,* 254. Reprinted by permission.

home–school dialogue journal in which you and the parents record short anecdotes about children's responses to literature. This exchange of information will help you learn what types of books are being read at home, as well as what responses and activities occur as a result. You can use this knowledge to recommend appropriate books and related experience to families. Additionally, it will help you plan more effectively for literature experiences at preschool or childcare.

Stephanie Baker, who works with infants at a developmental day school in North Carolina, keeps a portfolio for each child in her care. The portfolios are composed of letters to families and children, photographs, summaries of observational notes, developmental or educational information for families, and samples of children's artwork. Figure 2.8 shows an example of an entry Stephanie made in the portfolio for Courtney, an infant with Down syndrome.

Children with sensory impairments may need special adaptations for book reading. See Figure 2.9 for ideas about reading with children who have visual impairments and encouraging their responses to literature.

In addition to reading aloud, there are endless possibilities for links to literature that encourage responses. Take a look at Figure 2.10 for response possibilities for home and school. Remember, though, that the primary purpose of reading with young children is for enjoyment. Plan only those response activities that occur naturally from books.

The following is a letter to parents about their baby daughter's response to literature. It was written by her child-care provider.

Courtney showed an interest in books from the day we first introduced them to her. She appeared to enjoy the one-on-one closeness of looking at a book with her caregiver. We began pointing to objects in the book and naming them. Quickly she picked up on that and began pointing at objects with us. Next, she began taking our hands and making us point at all the objects on the page. She then began initiating looking at books on her own once she became mobile and knew how to crawl to them. Every day we have observed her go and pick out a book, sit down, turn the pages, and point to objects while at the same time vocalizing. A week or two before she left the baby room, I tried something new with her. I handed her a book upside down. I wanted to see how she would respond. She immediately looked inside the book and turned it around the right way. She continued bringing us books to look at with her. She especially loved singing books. Some of Courtney's favorite books were

> The Itsy-bitsy Spider
> Peek-a-boo Books
> Feel Farm Animals Books
> Counting Books

FIGURE 2.8

Teacher to Family: Response to Literature

Source: Stephanie Baker, Infant Specialist, Ashe Developmental Day School, Jefferson, North Carolina. Reprinted by permission.

Parents and teachers know the importance of reading with children and the benefits the children gain; however, sometimes parents of children with visual impairments wonder how they can share this experience of reading a storybook with their child. As with all children, you want to choose books that interest your child and involve her in the story. The following are specific ideas and suggestions for reading with a child who is visually impaired or blind:

- Choose books with simple, bright pictures.
- Outline pictures with a bold black pen, if they need extra contrast, or use puff paint to give the pictures a texture.
- Provide something to touch that is related to the story. For example, if your child's favorite book is about a teddy bear, give him a teddy bear to hold while reading the story.

FIGURE 2.9

Teacher to Family: Reading to Children Who Have Visual Impairments

Source: Paula Roten, Certified Teacher of the Visually Impaired, Governor Morehead Preschool, North Carolina. Reprinted by permission.

- Story boxes can be created using a shoebox and items that relate to the story. Pull out the items from the box as you read the story.
- Make up your own stories around your child's toys.
- Make books for your child; there are various ways to do this.
- Allow your child time to explore books and turn the pages.
- Use simple, textured books.
- Use print and Braille books (books with print and Braille on the same page). Your child can feel the Braille while you read the print.
- If your child is going to be a Braille reader, allow him or her time to "scribble" on a Braille writer and "read" the story back to you.
- If your child is unfamiliar with an idea or concept presented in a story, allow her a chance to explore or experience the idea first-hand.
- There are courses for parents and teachers to learn Braille. You could Braille your child's favorite stories.
- Most important, make reading time enjoyable.

Resources

1. American Printing House for the Blind, Inc.
        1839 Frankfort Avenue
        P.O. Box 6085
        Louisville, KY 40206-0085
        1-800-223-1839

Offers numerous items related to Braille and visual impairments, books, videos, toys and materials. The video *Discovering the Magic of Reading* is an excellent resource for teachers and families.

2. National Braille Press
        88 St. Stephen Street
        Boston, MA 02115
        1-800-548-7323

Their resources include the book *Just Enough to Know Better: A Braille Primer*, a wonderful source for families.

3. Seedlings Braille Books for Children
        P.O. Box 2395
        Livonia, MI 48151-0395
        1-800-778-8552

Offers print/Braille books for infants through adulthood.

4. American Foundation for the Blind Press
        11 Penn Plaza, Suite 300
        New York, NY 10001
        Beginning With Braille
        By Anna Swenson

This book has a wonderful resource section.

FIGURE 2.9
Continued

Help families extend enjoyment of literature at home. For some activities, you may need to send home materials if they are not available in the home. You may wish to send home the books you are using at school, so families can have the opportunity to read them with their children and do related activities.

At Preschool or Child-Care Center	At Home
• Storytelling	• Tell family stories or make up stories
• Book-related dramatic play	• Help your child act out favorite books
• Story retelling	• Encourage your child to tell the story to you
• Shared book experience using big books	• Make "little books" with your child
• Art projects	• Help your child draw pictures about favorite stories
• Cooking	• Let your child help you make simple recipes
• Music and movement	• Sing songs to your child and make up movements
• Story dictation	• Write down stories your child dictates to you.
• Puppets	• Make puppets from small paper bags and have a play
• Flannel-board stories	• Use the small flannel board in the take-home packet to help your child retell the story

FIGURE 2.10
Teacher to Teacher: Ideas for Responses to Literature

SURROUNDING CHILDREN WITH GOOD BOOKS

Selecting Quality Literature

Award Books

Take a peek into the children's section of a bookstore today and you'll see vast quantities of books—in stacks, on racks, on tables, and sometimes scattered on the floor. It's often confusing to sort through the jumble and sheer volume of children's books. How can parents, caregivers, and teachers ferret out books that will appeal to infants, toddlers, and preschoolers?

An easy way to begin collecting quality books is to consult the award lists. One of the best-known awards for children's picture books is the Randolph Caldecott Medal, awarded to the illustrator of the most distinguished picture book published each year in the United States. It is named for Randolph

Caldecott, an English illustrator in the late 1800s who was among the first to be noted for the lively action in his pictures. Although given primarily for the illustrations, Caldecott-winning books successfully integrate text and pictures. The Caldecott medal is gold and features an illustration from Randolph Caldecott's book, **The Diverting History of John Gilpin** (1878). It is stamped on the cover of award-winning picture books. Caldecott Honor Books display a silver version of the medal on the covers.

The Coretta Scott King Award was established in 1970 to recognize an African American author or illustrator. The award symbolizes the life and work of Martin Luther King Jr. and his wife, who continued to work for peace and brotherhood after her husband's death. Due to the nature of the award, given for books that encourage appreciation of all cultures and support the pursuit of the "American Dream", the Coretta Scott King Award books are more appropriate for elementary-age children. There are, however, several fine books in this collection that preschoolers would enjoy.

Print and Technological Resources

The Reading Teacher, published by the International Reading Association, publishes children's book reviews. In every October issue, there is a special feature on the "Children's Choices" for the year, favorite books chosen by teams of children all around the country. The November issue presents the "Teachers' Choices" for each year, selected by a cross-section of U.S. teachers.

Reading Rainbow is a children's television program on PBS that highlights several books on each show. The companion Web site [http://pbskids.org/readingrainbow/] is packed with information about broadcast schedules, book lists, and teacher resources.

Other sources for children's books and ideas are found in journals such as *Young Children, Childhood Education* and magazines like *Booklinks* or *Cricket*. Additional lists of books can be found in reference books located in public or university libraries. Two especially good reference books are *A to Zoo* and *Best Books for Children*. The Internet is filled with Web sites about children's books. See the resources at the end of the chapter for appropriate Web sites.

Software products for young children have increased in the past few years. Parents and teachers may become confused when trying to sort out the array of products marketed for young children, which vary considerably in quality (Burns et al., 1999). Look for computer programs that:

- Have developmentally appropriate content.
- Are user-friendly.
- Support the daily routines of the classroom.
- Enrich curriculum content.
- Reflect cultural diversity (e.g., available in multiple languages, gender equitable, portray people of varying abilities, contain diverse families).
- Promote positive social values (NAEYC, 1996).

Compiling a Classroom Library

A first-year preschool teacher called us soon after she started preplanning period. She was shocked to find out that the preschool had very few children's books available, many of which were inappropriate or of poor quality. Additionally, the majority of her children were Hispanic, who spoke no English. How, she asked, would she ever be able to stock the classroom library with quality books?

A beginning book collection can be small but effective in helping children develop literacy; however, there are a number of resources that will help boost your book collection. The public and school libraries are often the fastest and most convenient places to start. At times, public libraries offer "backdoor book sales" where you can pick up books inexpensively. There may be bookstores in your community that offer discounts to teachers. Book clubs (Scholastic, Trumpet, Troll) offer bonus points for free books, depending on the number of books you order.

Fund-raisers and grants to buy books are other ideas. Parent organizations may help organize and implement the fund-raiser for you as part of their

This inviting library corner offers low shelves, high-quality literature, and a rocking chair for young readers.

service to the school. A reading council in South Georgia held "Literacy Day at the Mall" every February, which was supported by a grant from "Reading Is Fundamental."

Some towns have "Community Partners in Education," a program that organizes collaboration between local businesses and schools. If such a program exists in your community, ask your community partner for book donations. Service organizations in the community may be another source for books or monetary donations.

Ask your administrators if there are opportunities for local, state, or federal grant funding. One kindergarten teacher wanted to start a classroom library for check-out because the school librarian decreed that kindergartners were too young to check out books. Faced with the dilemma of limited books, Kathy found out that she could submit a grant to the curriculum coordinator. She did, and was awarded $1,500 for her efforts!

Creating a Literature-Friendly Classroom

Children who come to child care or preschool with rich literacy experiences most likely live in homes where books are plentiful and within easy reach. In their homes you might see baskets of books on the den floor, a low bookshelf in the child's bedroom filled with interesting titles for naps and bedtime reading, a plastic crate of books in the kitchen, and waterproof baby books in the tub alongside the bath toys. The daily literacy environment that teachers set up is equally as important. Surround children with a variety of good books in all genres that are accessible, provide time to browse and read, give children choices, initiate book discussions, and make time for book-related activities. Morrow (1997) recommends five to eight books per child, with a core collection of high-quality books. Additionally, there should be a revolving collection suited to the children's interests, topics or concepts being discussed, and special events in the children's lives.

The library corner or book nook needs to be inviting and easy to navigate for all children. Below are some suggested items to include:

- Carpet
- Rocking chair
- Colorful pillows and cushions
- Beanbag or overstuffed chair
- Low shelves with titles facing outward
- Good lighting
- Book-related posters and props (e.g., flannel board, puppets, finger puppets, accessories for book-related dramatic play)
- Plants
- Big books, regular books, child-authored books, and so on
- Audio equipment for books on tape

Even infants can enjoy "browsing" through books if you let them crawl among a few sturdy books on soft mats or quilts. Of course, chewing, crinkling, and shaking of books often accompanies the read-aloud time, so make sure the books are nontoxic and can withstand close examination by eager little hands. Storing additional books in clear vinyl pockets hung low on the walls will protect them while allowing the youngest readers to see the covers (Dombro, Colker, & Dodge, 1997).

You may want to set up a family lending library (Brock & Dodd, 1994) to encourage family check-out of the books from your classroom. Families may need assistance in choosing books as well as locating them. Making books readily available to families will encourage reading at home. We provide more information on a Family Lending Library in chapter 3.

SUMMARY

From earliest times, stories have wrapped themselves around the audience and woven themselves into their lives. Children's books continue the oral tradition and bring enjoyment in many different genres. Responses to stories are influenced by many factors. Teachers who are familiar with the quality and variety of children's books available today can engage children in responses to literature in developmentally appropriate ways and recommend books to families that meet their needs, interests, and lifestyles.

FOR PROFESSIONAL DEVELOPMENT

1. Evaluate several picture books according to the criteria in the chapter.
2. Plan a library center for a child-care center or preschool room. Draw a floor plan, include a list of books and materials, and plan ways to involve families in the center.
3. Choose five books from different genres and plan book-related props for them.
4. Plan a book display for a child-care center or preschool room. Gather materials and books, set up the display, and include a list of related books to give to families.
5. Select a folktale, practice telling it, and share it with young children.

INTERNET RESOURCES

http://www.aaronshepard.com/storytelling

Aaron Shepard's Storytelling Page provides ideas for selecting and telling stories, as well as a variety of stories children will enjoy.

http://www.carolhurst.com

> Carol Hurst's Children's Literature site offers a large selection of books for children, ideas for using them at school and home, and links to many other children's literature sites.

http://www.ucalgary.ca/~dkbrown/

> The Children's Literature Web Guide is maintained by an individual at the University of Calgary. It contains commentaries on new books, a discussion board on children's literature, quick references to awards and best-sellers, and many links to other Web sites about children's literature.

Linking Home and School Literacies

Families engage in widely different literacy experiences and practices in their homes and communities. Yetta Goodman (1997) refers to the various ways children become literate as the "multiple roads to literacy" (p. 56). She advocates conscious acknowledgment of the legitimate and unique ways families promote literacy. Honoring the divergent literacies within families and communities requires teachers to become knowledgeable about and respectful of the nonschool literacy lives of the children and families with whom they work. Further, it necessitates continuing, positive, and responsive communication and collaboration among home, school, and community settings.

HOME LITERACY

In the daily home lives of many families, parents read newspapers, books, magazines, recipes, and repair manuals; write checks and keep financial records; sort through the mail and answer letters; check their e-mail and work on the computer; read the Bible; tell stories; and read books to their children. As families go about their lives in the community, literacy experiences occur when taking a walk, driving, shopping, going to church, or playing in the park. Literacy styles and values are often modeled in context for children, thus demonstrating reading and writing in meaningful ways. For example, when Mom helps her young son write his name, read a label on a can, or notice environmental print, she is showing him that print is used to help us make sense of our world.

In other families, there may be a limited number of print and print-related experiences available for the children, even though their parents possess practical information and culturally acquired skills that are necessary for effective and productive daily living. Think of the adults you know who cannot read well—or at all—who have a wealth of knowledge about agriculture, repair, sewing, cooking, mechanical equipment, folk medicine and remedies, painting, or hunting. Children in families such as these are often the recipients of household and community "funds of knowledge" acquired through social interactions with adults in everyday contexts (Moll, Amanti, Neff, & Gonzalez, 1992). Active participation in work that requires specialized knowledge—such as planting crops or building a fence—contributes to a child's overall literacy development in countless ways.

LITERACY AT CENTERS AND PRESCHOOLS

Most infants, toddlers, and preschoolers begin their journey to literacy within the family circle, influenced by the social and cultural contexts in which they are raised. As they arrive in child-care centers or preschool settings, they possess varying degrees of knowledge about literacy. Teachers who capitalize on the diverse literacies held by the children and families with whom they work can provide appropriate experiences that build on this knowledge. Working closely with families, teachers can plan literacy goals and experiences that match children's linguistic and cultural diversity. The key is open, ongoing, and supportive communication with families.

Too often, families on the margins of society are viewed within a deficit framework. Unfortunately, this viewpoint leads to literacy programs and strategies for involving families that are designed to "break the cycle" of low literacy (Taylor, 1997). A more respectful view of families is needed to form effective literacy partnerships between home and school settings. Rockwell, Andre, and Hawley (1996) assert that "whatever the form or degree, all families have strengths" (p. 24). Swick (1991) identifies some of those strengths as love, respect, communication, togetherness, consideration, and commitment. Although not every family possesses all of these qualities, it is important to look positively at the knowledge, skills, and capabilities of individual families and to build on their strengths and abilities. Barbour and Barbour (2001) advise teachers to consider parents and caregivers as capable and active members of a partnership team. They remind us to maintain humility and compassion when working with families and to remember that most parents have the best interests of their children at heart.

The benefits of family involvement have been well-documented (e.g., Berger, 2000; Epstein, 1995; Rockwell et al., 1996; Swick, 1991). Parents and caregivers of young children who develop a working relationship with teachers:

- Receive relevant information about topics such as child development, health, nutrition, safety, and positive guidance skills.
- Learn developmentally appropriate practices for home learning experiences (e.g., playing games and supporting language and literacy development).
- Find out about local family agencies (e.g., Parents as Teachers, Parents and Children Together, health department, social services).
- Develop collaborative relationships with teachers and child-care workers.
- Become more comfortable visiting the classroom and participating in school-based decisions.

The benefits for children of home/school collaboration include:

- Increased feelings of safety and confidence in new child-care or preschool environments.
- Increased self-esteem.
- Higher academic achievement.
- More positive attitude toward school.
- Fewer behavior problems.
- More opportunities to see parents and teachers working as partners.

Teachers profit from family/school collaboration by:

- Developing a deeper understanding of children and families.
- Gaining insight into family situations that might influence children's behaviors and learning at school.
- Planning more relevant curricula.

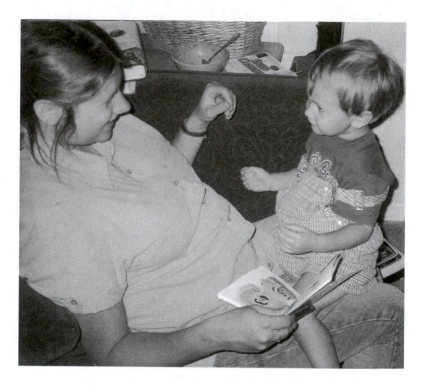

Parents who develop comfortable, collaborative relationships with teachers and child-care professionals learn many ways to support language and literacy at home.

- Including parents and caregivers as volunteers.
- Understanding and supporting the needs of diverse families.
- Gaining more positive attitudes toward families and their involvement in schools.
- Advocating for the rights of children and their families.

CHALLENGES TO BRIDGING HOME AND SCHOOL

Families may face challenges in becoming a part of their children's lives in child care or at preschool. In addition to differences in culture and family composition, adult caregivers and parents possess varying degrees of social and financial capital (Coleman, 1991) that affect their participation in their children's lives at school. For example, some adults are so intensely involved in providing basic needs for their children that there is little emotional or physical energy left to volunteer at preschool or engage in school-related activities. Additionally, limited funds or work obligations may exclude families' attendance at school events or special programs.

When planning opportunities for family involvement, take into account past school experiences, literacy levels, perceptions about how children become literate, and language barriers of primary caregivers. Factors such as the need for child care or lack of transportation may impede participation. Time, job responsibilities, or daily schedules may also interfere. Shawn, an undergraduate student in a parent-involvement class stated that she would not participate in any family meeting at her daughter's child-care center unless refreshments were offered. Shawn's college classes ended each day just in time for her to pick up her daughter, so she didn't have an opportunity to eat before attending a meeting. Providing transportation, refreshments, child care, and alternative schedules for workshops or conferences will help support busy adults. Home and school literacy partnerships can be successfully cultivated when teachers recognize the everyday challenges faced by families and plan accordingly.

Equally as important, teachers need to closely examine their own personal biases and assumptions about including families (Kieff & Wellhousen, 2000a; Rockwell et al., 1996). Prior experiences with families may lead to negative attitudes toward involvement and cause teachers to abandon their efforts. Teachers' mistaken assumptions or lack of knowledge about family lifestyles, structures, literacy levels, or culture may hinder the development of home/school relationships. Lack of training about how to work with families constrains the development of positive strategies for family involvement. Frequently, insufficient staff time for planning, time conflicts, difficulties in making home visits, or lack of funding may lead to complications in establishing effective collaboration with parents and caregivers. Despite the challenges of family involvement, teachers who reach out to families and actively facilitate positive interaction will create working relationships that benefit children at home and school.

DEVELOPING LITERACY PARTNERSHIPS

Partnerships with families are not always easy to establish. Careful planning, time, and effort to involve families in the process are needed. The cycle shown in Figure 3.1 will help you design literacy activities and experiences that actively engage families and bring home and school literacies together.

Gather Information on Families

When planning literacy experiences for the families in your program, first learn about their home literacy practices. Taylor (1983) characterizes parents' transmission of literacy styles and values to their children in terms of conservation and change. She contends that parents conserve, or keep, those traditions that were valuable to their own literacy development, such as bedtime story reading. Other events in parents' literacy histories that are not positively remembered are changed or reconstructed to prevent their children from unhappy associations with literacy. For example, a father who was not read to at home as a child may become dedicated to reading every night to his daughter.

Gather Information on Families
- Assess literacy needs.
- Prioritize needs.

Evaluate Literacy Strategies
- Gather feedback from families.
- Alter or retain strategies.
- Celebrate successes.

Plan Literacy Strategies
- Select objectives.
- Collaborate with families.
- Develop literacy
  strategies.

Implement Literacy Strategies
- Inform families.
- Try out literacy strategies.
- Monitor success.

FIGURE 3.1
Literacy Partnership Cycle

Developing literacy partnerships requires careful planning, time, and effort to involve all families.

Using a simple, open-ended questionnaire or conducting an oral interview will be helpful when compiling information on families. A family profile as shown in Figure 3.2 will help organize the information as you talk with parents and caregivers about the literacy development of their children, daily home routines, favorite books, and traditions (Brock & Dodd, 1994). An immediate outcome will be that you learn more about their lifestyles, culture, traditions, and literacy practices and can suggest books and activities to enjoy together. Long-term, the information will be crucial as you assemble literacy strategies to link home and school.

Edwards, Pleasants, and Franklin (1999) advocate the use of interviews—"parent stories"—to inform instruction and suggest community resources to families. Parent stories provide teachers with glimpses into the nonschool literacy lives of children, present a framework for positive dialogue between caregivers and teachers, and help inform decisions for literacy development. Briefly, the process of collecting parent stories involves (a) enlisting the support of your director and colleagues, (b) selecting an initial number of families with whom to collaborate, (c) conducting the interview, (d) summarizing the

---

FAMILY PROFILE
Personal Information

Child's name:
Child's date of birth:
Name(s) of adult caregiver(s):
Occupation(s) of adult caregiver(s):
Siblings (name, gender, age):
Other significant adults who live in the home (name, relationship):
Family type (e.g., single parent, grandparent-headed household):
Cultural background:
Language(s) spoken:
Education level of adult caregiver(s):

Possible Interview Questions

1. What activities do you and your child enjoy doing together at home?
2. What are your child's favorite books?
3. How often do you read with your child?
4. What time of day do you read together? Where?
5. What are your child's favorite songs? Rhymes? Games?

FIGURE 3.2

Teacher to Teacher: Family Profile
Adapted from Dodd, E., & Lilly, D. (1997). Family portfolios: Portraits of children and families. *Preventing School Failure,* *41*(2), pp. 57–62.

information into a narrative form, (e) making instructional decisions based on the data, and (f) compiling a list of local, state, and national resources to support the child and family. Important issues to consider are respecting the sometimes nontraditional literacy events described by parents, sensitivity in collecting and analyzing the families' literacy stories, and careful dissemination of the resources that may be helpful to them. A more complete explanation of parent stories can be found in Edwards' book *A Path to Follow: Learning to Listen to Parents.*

Plan Literacy Strategies

Hiebert and Raphael (1998) suggest that the literacies of children's homes and communities should be *integrated* into the classroom, to enhance emergent literacy development. They also recommend that literacies of the classroom should be *extended* into homes and communities to help establish meaningful contexts for literacy learning. With these recommendations in mind, teachers can begin to select objectives for literacy strategies that will be most beneficial to the children and their families.

Look closely at the information you received from the family profiles or parent stories to gain ideas for the most appropriate shared literacy opportunities. If the families have a strong oral tradition, your objective may be to increase opportunities for involvement with written text. Plan a family storytelling workshop, combining oral and written folktales. Parents could make oral tapes of traditional tales or write short books of family stories to place in the classroom. Investigate the community for opportunities to extend the topic. The arts council may have volunteers who will visit and share stories in the classroom. Family events within the community may be available to support storytelling.

Implement Literacy Strategies

Putting literacy strategies into practice successfully depends on families receiving accurate information and becoming meaningfully involved. If you've decided to begin home reading journals, for example, you need to plan time to talk with parents about the process and model your expectations. An informal meeting with parents will allow time for them to ask questions, find out ways to record information in the journals, and learn ways of reading and interacting with their children during story time. Teachers frequently recommend reading aloud to babies, toddlers, or preschoolers but do not always share effective ways to read aloud. As parents begin using the home reading journals, ask about their successes and challenges as you chat during drop-off or pick-up times. If some children ride the bus, make time for short telephone calls to their parents.

Evaluate Literacy Strategies

As you develop a repertoire of literacy strategies that work well for families, ongoing feedback is an integral component of success. Use both formal and informal ways of collecting comments and suggestions from parents and care-givers. One kindergarten teacher who provided home-learning activity kits for families included a short questionnaire for adults to record overall impres-sions of the activity. Another prekindergarten teacher placed journals in the home-learning kits for brief, daily remarks during the week of check-out. Con-sider the literacy abilities of the families before choosing the methods for gath-ering comments. According to the feedback received, alter or retain the strategies that work best for the families.

New ideas will emerge as you consider contributions from the families, helping you make stronger literacy connections for home and school. In the following sections, we discuss a variety of strategies to help you begin devel-oping literacy partnerships with families.

A MODEL FOR FAMILY INVOLVEMENT IN LITERACY

Epstein (1995) has proposed a model of parent involvement to promote home/school partnerships. Each level contains goals and practices that corre-spond to a continuum of parental involvement. We have adapted and defined four of Epstein's levels to apply to family literacy involvement and suggested examples of strategies for each. Some are broad enough to serve more than one level, according to the needs, interests, and lifestyles of the families with whom you work. Table 3.1 provides an overview of the four levels.

Level One: Parenting

On the most basic family level—parenting—there are myriad opportunities to help caregivers nurture their children's literacy development. Ordinary days with infants, toddlers, and preschoolers are filled with fleeting moments and sustained interactions that present windows of opportunity to notice, extend, and chronicle children's budding literate lives. Heightening caregivers' aware-ness of literacy milestones and equipping them with information and docu-mentation strategies will allow teachers to plan appropriate experiences at school that build on the literacies of home.

Literacy Portraits

Mei Ling, age 4, often plays on the home computer, according to her mom, Lina. Mei Ling is becoming a whiz at "Reader Rabbit" and "Sesame Street Math" and Lina is proud of her daughter's emerging computer skills. Lina's job requires a

TABLE 3.1

Involving Families in Literacy

Level	Description	Literacy Strategies
Level One: Parenting	Families provide the primary literacy environment for their children. Teachers can support families with basic child-rearing information and activities that are complementary with home literacy practices.	• Literacy Portraits • Family literacy workshops
Level Two: Communication	Teachers have an obligation to engage in regular written and oral communication with families. Ongoing communication creates a continuing dialogue about literacy practices that flows between home and preschool settings.	• Newsletters & calendars • Literacy Brochures • Traveling friend • Literacy Dialogue Journals
Level Three: Volunteering	Working caregivers and those who stay at home need opportunities to participate in the literacy lives of their children at daycare and preschool. A variety of experiences and times for involvement will foster family contributions.	• Literacy Helpers • Family stories • Family albums
Level Four: Learning at Home	Families vary in their perceptions about literacy, their home routines, and the ability to work with their children. Teachers need to suggest home literacy activities that are relevant to the children and families with whom they work.	• Home visits • Home-Learning Activities • Family Lending Library

lot of computer work, both at home and at work, where Mei Ling frequently visits. One day Mei Ling typed a string of letters on the computer, told Lina it was an e-mail message, and asked her to send it to her cousin in Georgia.

Children engage in a variety of literacy experiences in their lives outside of school. Teachers often have no way of learning about these experiences and are not able to take them into account when planning curriculum or activities. One way to discover and document everyday literacy experiences is through the use of Literacy Portraits. Sometimes referred to as a "literacy portfolio," a Literacy Portrait is the story of a child's journey to literacy within multiple contexts. Similar to a portfolio, a Literacy Portrait contains artifacts from home, day-care or preschool, and community settings that document early literacy development. Contributions to the Literacy Portrait come from the child, family members, the teacher, and other significant adults. The contents will vary according to the age and developmental level of the child and the caregivers' time and ability to provide the artifacts. Ultimately, the Literacy Portrait should present a representative selection of samples that celebrate the unique literacy growth of the child in multiple contexts.

How do teachers organize and use Literacy Portraits? There are three steps: (a) Compile and sort the artifacts into categories, (b) write short narrative summaries for each category, and (c) share the Literacy Portraits with families, and (d) plan for complementary literacy experiences. Making a simple chart is an easy way to brainstorm and organize literacy artifacts for inclusion. Table 3.2 lists possible contents for a child in preschool. Sharing these ideas with families will help them provide a variety of materials.

After determining which items to highlight in the Literacy Portrait, document the date of each artifact, write a brief description of the context in which it was produced, and note the contributor (parent/caregiver, child, teacher, other). You may decide to let the adult contributors write their own descriptions, or have the child dictate descriptions to you for inclusion. Select a time period during which to collect and document artifacts—a month or six weeks, for example. Analyze the data for patterns of literacy development across the three contexts of home, school, and community, and write a short narrative summary to celebrate the literacy growth of the child and share it with the child and family. Then begin the cycle again.

Two factors to consider when using Literacy Portraits are time and storage. Realistically speaking, you will not be able to concentrate on every child at the same time. Select a small number with whom to begin and add other children as time permits. Store the artifacts at school in an expanding file folder or a three-ring notebook with clear plastic sleeves for easy reference. Also think about the transitory nature of some families. If many in your program are homeless, migrant, or in jobs that require moving frequently, consider alter-

TABLE 3.2

Teacher to Teacher: Artifacts to Include in Literacy Portrait

Literacy at Home	Literacy at Preschool	Literacy in the Community
(Artifacts from child, family members, and other significant adults)	(Artifacts from child, teacher, and other adults at preschool)	(Artifacts from child, family members, and other involved adults)
• Scribbles/drawings	• Story retellings	• Awards
• Name-writing attempts	• Dictated stories	• Notices
• Baby journal entries	• Anecdotal records	• Club involvement
• Favorite books	• Photographs	• Church bulletins/ announcements
• Videotapes	• Artwork	
• Photographs	• Project activities	• Photos
• Letters/postcards	• Videotapes	• Newsletters
• E-mail messages	• Audiotapes	• Library card
• Family holiday newsletters		• Newspaper clippings
• Family recipes		

Photographs and drawings furnished by families can be used in a child's Literacy Portfolio to document literacy experiences at home.

"The bestest reader ever. I love you." Inviting parents and caregivers to become Literacy Helpers gives them multiple opportunities to participate, directly or indirectly.

I believe portfolios are a beautiful way to capture moments of infants and toddlers exploring their new world. In my classroom, I use portfolios to collect information on the children and to show families how their children are learning. I include letters to families and children, photographs, summaries of observational notes, developmental and educational information for families, and samples of children's work. The portfolios are a powerful way to illustrate the developmental processes of an infant and the changes that occur in just one year.

When a child is ready to advance to the next classroom, the family and I plan a meeting to look at the portfolio together. I ask them to take it home and return it to their child's new teacher. By the time a child enters the pre-K room, he will have a full portfolio of learning experiences and special times at Ashe Developmental Day School.

Looking at Books

(A letter to Samuel's parents that is in his portfolio)

Samuel has always been interested in books. Since he was very small he has wanted to sit in his caregivers' laps and look at books.

Exploring a book is just the beginning of pre-reading skills. When children look at books they are using skills they will later use in reading, such as learning the proper way to turn the pages, learning the names of objects, people, and animals, learning sounds, songs, and much more.

Samuel had access to age-appropriate books any time of the day. His caregivers read books to him every day, and encouraged Samuel to pick up books and explore them on his own.

FIGURE 3.3

Teacher to Teacher: Samuel's Literacy Portfolio
Source: Stephanie Baker, Infant Specialist, Ashe Developmental Day School, North Carolina. Used by permission.

nate ways to document children's literacy growth. Figure 3.3 presents one teacher's approach to a literacy portfolio.

Family Literacy Workshops

A workshop approach to family involvement should be a dynamic, relevant opportunity for families and teachers to come together informally and exchange ideas, information, materials, and resources. Workshops are successful when participants do things instead of talking about them, when teachers and caregivers are considered equals, and when all parties advocate for children (Vopat, 1994). Careful planning, organization, and knowledge of participating families are essential.

In one prekindergarten summer program that lasted six weeks, teachers planned and held four family workshops. A needs assessment was administered to determine the adult caregivers' preference for times. Results indicated that evening was the most requested time, so Thursday night was chosen. To alleviate transportation problems, a school bus was provided. Parents brought their children and their siblings to the workshop. A teacher greeted families at the sign-in table, nametags were distributed, and refreshments were served. Ice-breakers were introduced to help families become relaxed and get to know each other.

The meetings began promptly at 7 P.M. with a five-minute performance by the children, who sang songs, performed fingerplays, or showed their families some of the literacy activities they participated in during the week. Starting on such an upbeat note and featuring the children generated excitement and enthusiasm among the families. After their participation, the children went to their daytime classroom for supervised playtime while the program continued. A topic for the night was introduced, such as reading aloud, language development, or concept development. The speaker showed a 10-minute video clip of the children at preschool to provide a basis for interactive discussions of the topic, which usually lasted about 15 minutes. The adults were divided into

---

Tips for Effective Workshops

- Choose a topic based on family needs assessment.
- Arrange transportation and child care.
- Plan ice-breakers and refreshments.
- Develop content and strategies for interactive participation.
- Gather materials and technology.
- Set meeting agenda.
- Develop evaluation plans for teacher and family feedback.
- Distribute notice and advertisements.

Literacy Workshop Topics

- Reading aloud (and selecting quality books to read)
- Book-making
- Sharing poems, rhymes, and fingerplays
- Literacy through cooking
- Counting, alphabet, and concept books
- Technology and emergent literacy
- Literacy through play
- Favorite authors and related activities

FIGURE 3.4
Teacher to Teacher: Family Literacy Workshops

small groups for guided discussion to help them feel more secure in sharing comments or asking questions.

In the final portion of the evening, parents joined their children in the classroom to observe the teacher, who involved the youngsters in an informal literacy activity. Families then scattered around the room to complete a related activity. By 8:30 P.M., good-byes were said and families were given a home-learning activity related to the evening's topic.

By starting small, teachers can create interesting approaches to workshops that will be enjoyed by children and their caregivers. Make-and-take workshops are usually very popular with families. Ask parents for suggestions about topics and visit programs that effectively implement family workshops. If a university is close by, undergraduate students in classes such as emergent literacy, family involvement, or children's literature may be available to plan and deliver some workshops. Funding may be secured by writing simple grant proposals to the local school system or a community literacy agency. Teacher-tested tips and workshop topics to help you begin are given in Figure 3.4. Refer to *The Parent Project: A Workshop Approach to Parent Involvement* (Vopat, 1994) for a more comprehensive workshop model.

Level Two: Communication

Consider this scenario: Mom is reading Natasha one last bedtime story before leaving to go to her night shift at a local factory. After the story Natasha says, "Mommy, teacher says our families are making books together tomorrow. Can you and Grandma come?" What a way for Mom to find out about a special day at child care! Ongoing and timely communication with families is a fundamental tenet of positive home/school literacy partnerships. Communication is usually classified as one-way or two-way (Berger, 2000). Information that flows from school to home—notes, newsletters, calendars, and brochures—represents one-way communication. Two-way communication, which is accompanied by interaction and conversation between caregivers and teachers, helps personalize information and tailor programs to meet the unique needs of children and their families. Both types of communication are vital for building integrated, collaborative literacy partnerships with families.

Newsletters and Calendars

With the busy lives of families and teachers it is sometimes difficult for us to communicate as often as we would like. While two-way, face-to-face communication is preferable, one-way communication, such as newsletters and calendars can be a way for educators to share information and stay in touch with families. Desktop publishing options make it easy for even the novice computer user to produce attractive, family-friendly newsletters and calendars in a short time. Using colorful paper and graphics adds to the likelihood that the material will be read and the information remembered. Early childhood teachers might consider the following uses for family newsletters:

Little Sprouts Preschool

VOL. 1 No. 12	Rome, Georgia	April 30, 2003

Spring is Here!

We've been watching our flower seeds closely and drawing what we've noticed. Here's Andrew's picture:

ANDREW

Next Family Meeting

On Saturday, May 10 at 9:00am we will gather at school to weed, water and fertilize the garden. After we work, we will make garden alphabet books. Please come!

Come Join Us!

We'll be going on a field trip to McGregor's Nursery on May 14 at 11:30am. We'd love to have you join us. Please call the school secretary for details (264-5555) by May 12th if you would like to go.

Seed Packets ...

are available at school for planting at home in a garden, pot or window box. Many thanks to McGregor's Nursery for the donation!

Here are some great books about gardening to share with your child:

1. Jasper's Beanstalk- by Mick Inkpen
2. The Carrot Seed- by Ruth Krauss
3. Flower Garden- by Eve Bunting
4. Planting a Rainbow- by Lois Ehlert
5. Bumblebee, Bumblebee, Do You Know Me?- by Anne Rockwell

When writing newsletters, be sure to use straightforward language, brightly colored paper, and children's drawings.

Source: Composition and computer design by Nicole Griffith and Misty Capley. Used with permission.

TABLE 3.3

Literacy Development Through "Home Fun"

Monday	Tuesday	Wednesday	Thursday	Friday
Talk about the labels on food containers with your child. Help him find some letters that are in his name.	Look around your home or yard for objects that are circles, squares, and other shapes. Make a shape booklet.	Ask your child to tell you a story about a favorite book character. Write it down so you can read it again and again.	When you read a familiar bedtime story, leave out repeated words. See whether your child can say them.	Act out a favorite story with your child. Let her take the lead role.

- Suggest books for reading at home and accompanying activities.
- Feature an author or illustrator.
- Highlight children's artwork and writing.
- Recruit and thank volunteers.
- Share quotes from children.
- Describe a project or unit of study and recommend related books.
- Request materials.
- Make announcements.
- Share information on child development topics, such as language and literacy development, toilet training, temper tantrums, motor development.
- Suggest home-learning activities.
- Provide simple recipes children and families can make together.

Calendars can be sent home as alternatives or additions to newsletters to recommend activities that families and young children can do together at home. Kindergarten parents have told one of the authors that they enjoy calendars of home activities because they can put them on the refrigerator and choose from ideas that might be of interest to their children. While families might not do all the activities or accomplish them in the order suggested, it is a reminder to spend quality time with children each day. A format such as the one in Table 3.3 provides suggestions for "home fun" that focuses on literacy development (Berger, 2000).

When writing newsletters and calendars, remember to use jargon-free language; be sensitive to family culture and literacy levels; and limit the amount of written information you send home so families won't become overwhelmed with paper. Use brightly colored paper and let the children add illustrations. Remember to send newsletters or calendars translated into the primary home language for families who do not speak English.

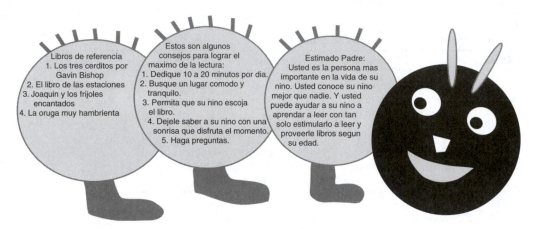

FIGURE 3.5
Literacy Brochure

Literacy Brochures

At times, teachers may wish to furnish families with literacy information that doesn't quite fit the format of a newsletter or calendar. In these cases, a Literacy Brochure is the answer. Easy to compile and reproduce, Literacy Brochures can be developed to address topics such as the stages of emergent reading, reading with children, choosing good books, appropriate books for certain ages, and obtaining a library card. Literacy brochures can be created in a variety of eye-catching shapes that attract parents' attention and are easy to read.

A group of Head Start teachers who work with migrant families in South Georgia fashioned a Literacy Brochure in the shape of a caterpillar, as seen in Figure 3.5. The teachers wrote the brochure in Spanish to help families learn about reading with their children. Information was also included on the local library. When asked why they chose the caterpillar shape, the teachers explained that migrant workers often encounter caterpillars in the fields so the shape is easily recognized and familiar.

Traveling Friend

The "traveling friend" is a creative and motivating way to encourage family participation in emergent literacy. A stuffed, washable toy is donated or purchased (yard sales are great resources) along with an inexpensive suitcase or travel bag. Put the bear, clown, or other animal in the suitcase, along with writing tools and a journal. The traveling friend takes turns visiting the children's homes throughout the year, either for a weekend or for several days. During the stay the child dictates the toy's adventures for an adult family member to write in an accompanying journal. The journal, toy, and suitcase are returned to school or child care, where the teacher reads the adventures from the journal while the child elaborates on their experiences together. It is important for the teacher to write (and laminate) a letter clearly explaining the project (Helm, 1994). Books may also be included in the suitcase for the family to read aloud to the child. Some children like to include new props, such as a toothbrush or clothes, for future creative play by other children in the class. In one kindergarten classroom the teacher posted sentence strips stating "Today P. J. Bear will visit _____." "Next P. J. Bear will visit _____." These statements not only help the teacher and class keep up with the whereabouts of their friend, they also help children learn about time sequencing and turn-taking.

The traveling friend activity has become a favorite in many early childhood programs. Teachers and children learn about the home lives of the children in the class, families spend an enjoyable time with a "visitor," and literacy development is enhanced in a meaningful, appealing way. Each class can add innovations to the theme to make it a unique project.

Literacy Dialogue Journals

When a new baby arrives home, many parents begin documenting the details of her life right away in baby books. A smile, a gurgle, grasping at Dad's finger, attempts at walking—all these are treasured "firsts" for the parents or caregivers. In a similar manner, literacy dialogue journals contain notes, anecdotes, and observations by primary caregivers of the blossoming literacy lives of their children. Broadening the concept of baby books a bit, literacy dialogue journals are written exchanges of information between caregivers and teachers that document a child's important literacy milestones.

Most caregivers relish the request to talk about their children. The use of literacy dialogue journals encourages parents to continue providing information but somewhat removes the immediacy of a response from the teacher. For example, one Saturday morning while Nana is washing the breakfast dishes, she notices that 17-month-old Shelley has crawled to the basket of books near the sofa, picked up a board book, and is "reading" it to her baby doll. Shelley's teacher has asked adult caregivers to jot down examples (two to five per week) of emergent reading behaviors. Just a simple sentence or two written by Nana in the literacy dialogue journal preserves the event and gives Shelley's teacher a glimpse into her literacy development at home. Further, Nana begins to be more focused in her observations of Shelley's emergent literacy behaviors and becomes an active partner with the teacher. Comments, suggestions, and questions flow back and forth between home and school, creating a shared accountability for supporting Shelley's literacy development. This exchange of information helps Nana become a more astute observer of Shelley's home literacy behaviors and realize that even seemingly insignificant behaviors are building blocks for future success in reading and writing.

Begin literacy dialogue journals by introducing the strategy at a family workshop. Have adults discuss what their children are currently doing—

scribble-writing, pretend-reading, attending to print, pointing to pictures when asked, and so on. Use their observations as a basis for discussion about emergent literacy and focused observations. Record their words in simple entries on an overhead transparency and talk about specific literacy skills. Model a few more entries and have adults discuss their significance. Provide a list of topics for observations depending on the ages and developmental stages of their children, such as vocalizing when adults point to pictures, responding to adults' requests to point to objects in books, or relating an object in a book to the real world. Supply journals (and writing materials, if necessary) and give parents a reasonable time frame to record entries and return the journals to you. As the process begins, decide how to manage your responses to each family's journal since you will need to balance the amount of time it takes you each week.

Be mindful of the families with whom you work and their unique orientations to literacy as you begin to use literacy dialogue journals. If you have a large population of Hispanic families, for example, you may want to respond in both English and Spanish. For caregivers who have limited literacy skills, you could provide simple checklists with symbols to record their observations and respond verbally to their entries. You may wish to make the journals optional to relieve the apprehension of some parents. Consider, too, that your request to write about their child's literacy development at home may be considered an invasion of privacy by a few of the families (Morningstar, 1999). Creative ways to fit the needs of all your families will ease the way and help make this strategy meaningful for all involved. Literacy dialogue journals present opportunities for teachers to explain literacy development in personalized ways, aid in parent–teacher conferences, help establish parallel practices, and create a shared and ongoing written conversation between home and school (Harding, 1996; Morningstar, 1999; Shockley, Michalove, & Allen, 1995).

Level Three: Volunteering

In the classic heart-warming story **What Mary Jo Shared** (Udry, 1966) Mary Jo has a dilemma about what to bring for show and tell. When she thinks she has something novel to share, it never seems to work out because other classmates have thought of it first. As it turns out, what Mary Jo shares is her father, who comes to school especially for show and tell. The way Mary Jo's dad donated his time to her class illustrates beautifully the notion that volunteering comes in many forms. Family members can become involved in their children's literate lives at preschool or child care by serving as resources, keeping records, donating and/or creating materials, sharing special talents, planning and/or supervising events, and engaging in classroom activities.

Depending on families' comfort levels, time constraints, and resources, plan volunteer opportunities that are most easily accomplished. Give options for both direct and indirect services to accommodate families. Examine program needs, identify volunteer services, recruit parents and caregivers, hold an

Please be a special storybook reader!

Dear Families,

We will send home a book and a cassette tape with your child every so often. Practice reading the book several times, then record yourself reading it aloud. Feel free to add any noises to make the story more enjoyable (animal sounds, music, a bell ringing to signal page turns, etc.).

On special days, we will play the tapes and guess whose family member recorded them. Let's try and keep this a secret (even from <u>your</u> child) so everyone can participate in guessing who our special storybook readers are. If you need a tape recorder, we have one for check-out.

Thanks for your help!

orientation if necessary, and maintain open lines of communication with volunteers concerning their efforts. Take time to celebrate their efforts in special ways to show your appreciation of their contributions (Rockwell et al., 1996).

Literacy Helpers

A simple way to ease parents and caregivers into volunteerism is to invite them to be Literacy Helpers (Butler, Liss, & Sterner, 1999). Indirect services such as making a flannel board and characters for a favorite story, creating games for the literacy center, donating writing materials, or typing dictation for documentation panels could be accomplished on the volunteers' own time table. In the Lucy Brock Child Development Center at Appalachian State University, the teachers planned a volunteer opportunity to alleviate the problem of separation anxiety. They sent home blank tapes and recorders for adult caregivers to record stories, songs, or poems. At naptime or center time, children played their caregiver's tape and were comforted. Another prekindergarten teacher sent home a book and a cassette tape occasionally, asking parents to secretly tape-record themselves reading it aloud and send it back. She used the tapes to surprise the preschoolers during story time, reporting that the children were excited and listened intently as they recognized their parents' voices.

Literacy helpers who wish to engage in direct services could sign up to read to children weekly, listen to children read, tell stories, share special hobbies, take dictation, use video or camera equipment to document literacy events, or invite children to their workplaces. One working mom enjoyed her volunteer job as "art lady." Once a month she researched a famous artist that would capture the interest of young children, brought in examples of paintings, gave a short talk on the artist, and helped direct a hands-on art project simulating the illustrative techniques used by the artist.

Family Stories

Family stories can be defined as "narratives in which the youngster or other relatives are the featured characters in simple home adventures of days gone by" (Buchoff, 1995, p. 230). Barton (1986) refers to stories as gifts that one generation gives another. Perhaps because of the mobility of today's families, genealogy has become a popular hobby. As parents or caregivers research family history, children become acquainted with family members they will never meet. Family stories breathe life into long-ago ancestors and vividly re-create a child's heritage. The oral nature of family storytelling allows young children to acquire and refine literacy skills, while establishing a close bond between adult and child (Buchoff, 1995).

Linda Winston (1997) has written an excellent book on using family stories at school. Winston's definition of family stories includes family sayings, keepsakes, photographs, celebrations, and customs. In child-care settings and preschool, family stories can become a part of the literacy curriculum in natural ways. Invite family members in to share their family stories and special keepsakes. Photographs tell stories that even very young children can appreciate. Informally displaying old family photos, along with keepsakes and family sayings, allows teachers to begin conversations about a child's family. Reading about family storytelling may also open the door to discussions. **Tell Me a Story, Mama** (Johnson, 1989) is a simple book to introduce family stories. As a young girl is tucked into bed, she requests favorite stories she has often heard from her mother's childhood. Gather stories from the families in your center or school. Focus on daily events and routines the adults enjoyed as children. Compile the stories into a book for children to take home and read with their families. Invite those who can come to share their stories with the children. Diaries, scrapbooks, and letters are additional ways to share events from a family's history and engage children in literacy experiences.

Family Albums

Documenting the lives of their children seems to be a passion for some families today. Cameras and video equipment are ubiquitous at most gatherings of children and families at home, school, or community events. Whether displayed with magnets on refrigerators, framed and grouped on tables, labeled and carefully put into albums, or stuffed into drawers, family photographs serve as visual documentation of a family's history, vividly reminding us of celebrations, holidays, reunions, recreational events, or significant developmental milestones (Winston, 1997).

The use of family albums as a literacy strategy at school capitalizes on a family hobby—photography—and provides opportunities for literacy learning and family participation on many levels. Both adults and children can orally tell stories about the pictures, write captions or narratives to accompany them, make a timeline of family history events, or create a photo essay of a special event in the family's life. Sequencing, storytelling, observing details, and "reading" the pictures are just a few of the facets of emergent literacy that can be supported by using family albums at home and school.

Children often wonder about their parents' childhoods. Two simple books to introduce the topic of family albums are **This Quiet Lady** (Zolotow, 1992) and **Me & You: A Mother–Daughter Album** (Thiesing, 1998). A young daughter describes her mother's childhood and early adult life in *This Quiet Lady,* as she looks at framed pictures and the family photo album. In *Me & You,* watercolor illustrations are arranged on the page like snapshots. The author/illustrator uses black and white for the mother's photos and color for her daughter's, to highlight the differences in decades. The text is simple and narrated by the mother as she shows her daughter the picture album. The illustrations are humorous and touching. For older preschoolers, Sandra Belton has written about the importance of family in **May'naise Sandwiches & Sunshine Tea** (1994). Big Mama tells Little Miss, her granddaughter, about her childhood memories while they look at Big Mama's scrapbook.

Remember, however, that not all families value pictures and may even object to their children being photographed, so a perceptive teacher will use a variation of family albums that allows children to use drawings or other memorabilia. For families who cannot afford cameras or film, consider writing a grant to buy disposable cameras or asking a local photography shop or studio to donate money, inexpensive cameras, or film. Digital cameras are available in some programs, eliminating the need for film. In early childhood programs based on the Reggio Emilia philosophy, photography is used regularly with accompanying descriptions in documentation panels to chronicle the children's learning. Perhaps families in Reggio-inspired programs could check out a school camera to use for a limited amount of time.

Level Four: Learning at Home

Infants, toddlers, and preschoolers are raised in diverse home settings, with myriad family routines and varying literacy backgrounds. Planning appropriate literacy activities to do at home requires that teachers become familiar with young children's lives outside of preschool or child care. Mutual trust and understanding between teachers and caregivers is built as teachers spend time with families in homes and neighborhoods. Keep in mind that adult caregivers differ in their perceptions about early literacy development and their ability to work with their children. It is important to encourage playful, enjoyable, and meaningful ways to engage in home literacy activities.

Home Visits

Home visits are one of the most basic ways to learn about the children and families in your preschool or child care. The children become acquainted with the teachers in a nonthreatening atmosphere—their own homes. Relationships with families start out on a positive, unhurried note and parents find that they can trust teachers. Learning about family structures, types of homes, and economic conditions of the children adds enormously to a teacher's understanding of the child's behaviors at school. By observing interactions between children and caregivers, teachers gain insight into family relationships. When a family is visited prior to the child's entering preschool or child care, both the adults and children feel special on the first day. Often, caregivers will participate more readily in their children's school experiences as a result of home visits.

Schedule the visit ahead of time to accommodate the work schedule of the caregiver(s). Go with a partner if you are concerned about the neighborhood or if you need a translator. Take along children's books to share and a camera to record the visit. With permission, take photographs of the child in his favorite places or with special toys. You can place the pictures at preschool on the children's cubbies to help them identify their own. The photos will give the comfort of a familiar scene when times at school are tough. In infant and toddler settings, the pictures can be used in a variety of ways to encourage language, literacy, and concept development.

Connie described her home visit experiences:

> The children enjoyed showing me favorite places in their homes and yards. I was able to informally observe types of literacy materials for both adults and children that were available in the homes, mentally noting the presence or absence of children's books, adult reading materials, magazines, and newspapers, and writ-

Home visits provide valuable opportunities to learn about children and families in the comfort of their own homes.

ing/drawing materials. When I was alone with the entering kindergarten child I pulled four or five books from my bag and asked which one he or she would like me to read. Many of the children were familiar with at least one of the books and enthusiastically chose a story to hear. I asked children where I should start reading and encouraged them to make predictions and talk about the pictures. While this was an informal experience, it gave me clues about the children's literacy experiences and the environment in which they were learning about reading and writing. It also provided an opportunity to introduce the literacy curriculum I would use in kindergarten.

Home Learning Activities

A mother and her young sons, ages 3 and 5, loved to read **The Very Hungry Caterpillar** (Carle, 1969). After reading it several times one day, they played with a related home-learning activity: a small bag that held a caterpillar-shaped piece of flannel and felt shapes of all the objects in the book. As their mother read the story again to them, the boys enjoyed following the story line by placing the felt shapes of different foods, chrysalis, and butterfly on the flannel. Then, each child took turns retelling the story on his own using the pieces. Later that afternoon the family took a walk around their yard to see if they could find any caterpillars or other insects. The mom reported later that they didn't see any caterpillars, but they did dig up some worms.

Whether shared on visits to families or placed in the classroom for check out, teachers can use home-learning activities to help families encourage early literacy development (Brock & Dodd, 1994). Home-learning activities are "simply designed experiences growing out of a child's interests and based on his physical, social, emotional, and intellectual needs" (Packer, Hoffman, Bozler, & Bear, 1976, p. 30) that give children and families a special time together to read, play, and learn. Tailored to the families' interests, lifestyles, and cultures, home-learning activities provide multiple opportunities to extend literacy learning from school to home.

Home-learning activities can be used as the basis for literacy activities such as role playing, story retellings, matching and sorting, letter recognition, early writing, rhyming words, listening skills, and language development. Many activities use objects already found in the home—for instance, sorting and matching socks or arranging pots and pans from smallest to largest. Others require simple materials prepared by the teacher and sent home in a lightweight bag or plastic shoebox. An easy and engaging way to make home-learning activities is to base them on a quality children's book. Figures 3.6 and 3.7 provide suggestions for home-learning activity kits and include a sample letter to families.

Home-learning activities that extend children's literacy learning are easy to develop when based on children's books. Suggestions follow for several books and related objects to use in home-learning activities. Literacy skills to be targeted could include understanding of story structure; sequencing; retelling; number, vocabulary, and concept development; and the conventions of print, among others. Adapt these ideas to make your own home-learning activities with other favorite children's books.

Book	Related Objects
1. *The Big Green Pocketbook* (Ransome, 1995)	pocketbook, items from story
2. *Bumblebee, Bumblebee Do You Know Me?* (Rockwell, 1999)	plastic flowers, flower pots
3. *Caps for Sale* (Slobodkina, 1947)	caps
4. *Chicka Chicka Boom Boom* (Martin & Archambault, 1989)	magnetic letters, cookie sheet
5. *Feast for Ten* (Falwell, 1993)	canvas or string grocery bag, plastic food, fabric numbers
6. *Is Your Mama a Llama?* (Guarino, 1989)	plastic animals
7. *Mrs. McNosh Hangs Out Her Wash* (Weeks, 1998)	clothesline, clothespins, selected items from book
8. *A Pair of Socks* (Murphy, 1996)	shoe box, colored socks
9. *Red, Blue, Yellow Shoe* (Hoban, 1986)	shoe box, familiar objects

FIGURE 3.6
Teacher to Teacher: Home-Learning Activity Kits

Dear Families:

We know you enjoy reading together with your child, so we've developed this home-learning activity for you to play after reading. In the bag you'll find a copy of *The Very Hungry Caterpillar,* a flannel caterpillar, and felt shapes of the objects in the book. As you read the book aloud with your child talk about the story and illustrations. Ask your child to tell which food is her favorite. Help her place her small finger in the cut-out holes and count the foods.

After reading, let your child retell the story by putting the felt shapes in order on the flannel caterpillar. Let her count and name the objects as they are put on the flannel caterpillar. She may want to make up her own story using the objects. If you have time this week, take a walk outdoors and see what insects you can find. Play counting games with objects around the house, like socks or spoons. Happy reading!

Sincerely,

[Teacher's Name]

FIGURE 3.7

Teacher to Teacher: Letter to Families About Home-Learning Activity

Diversity in your setting should be addressed by developing activities in the predominant home languages coupled with English translations. For families whose literacy levels are low, include tape-recorded stories and ideas for using the materials. Before giving the activities to families, find a time to introduce and model them, whether it is in a family night meeting at school or in the home. Teacher modeling plays a major role in the success and enjoyment of using home-learning activities. See Dodd & Brock (1994) for a full discussion of home-learning activities.

Family Lending Library

As teachers become comfortable making home visits and developing an assortment of home-learning activities, a Family Lending Library can be used to organize and store them. A Family Lending Library is a collection of books and materials for families to check out and use at home (Brock & Dodd, 1994). Through this system, teachers can provide families with materials and strategies to encourage their children's early literacy development. Considering family variances in available literacy materials, adult literacy levels, and knowledge about emergent literacy, a Family Lending Library allows teachers to help "level the playing field" of literacy development for young children.

The four main steps to planning and implementing a Family Lending Library are to (a) focus on families, (b) collect books and materials, (c) plan operational procedures, and (d) evaluate the effectiveness of the library

(Brock & Dodd, 1994). Using a family profile, home literacy questionnaires, conversations, conferences, and home visits, develop a literacy profile of the families you serve. Cultural and linguistic backgrounds, socioeconomic status, and family configurations are important factors in determining the contents of your Family Lending Library. Next, gather books and materials relevant to their needs and interests. Figure 3.8 offers some suggestions. Take into consideration the unique blend of families in your center or preschool and concentrate on furnishing relevant books and materials they would enjoy.

The third step involves investigating sources of funding the library. Additionally, you need to plan for location, hours of operation, check-out procedures, and advertisement. Finally, after the Family Lending Library has been in operation for three or four months, evaluate the success by collecting data from the families, formally and informally.

You may wish to start small—in a corner of your room, perhaps—with just a few items available for check-out. If space, personnel, and funding are not so limited, you may want to collaborate with other teachers to provide a separate room for the library. One kindergarten teacher focused her

---

- Children's books—a variety of genres, cultures, and languages
- Home-learning activities
- Toys (also a brochure on how to select toys for children)
- Games
- Children's magazines
- Audio- and videotapes (of children's books, field trips, special events at preschool)
- Cassette player
- Record player
- Storytelling information and props
- Puppets
- Cookbooks
- Books, magazines, brochures, and articles about parenting

Always make available English and non-English translations for linguistically diverse families.

FIGURE 3.8
Items to Include in a Family Lending Library

lending library on math and reading activities that matched the state curriculum objectives. Using towel rods mounted under wall cabinets, she hung plastic bags of home-learning activities so the lending library took up little space in her room. She had received a small grant from the county curriculum office to buy her supplies. In preschools or centers with plenty of funds, the lending library may be located in a large room overflowing with a huge assortment of books, games, videos, parenting materials, and home-learning activities. See Brock & Dodd, (1994) for a full discussion of a Family Lending Library.

FAMILY LITERACY PROGRAMS

Family literacy programs bring young children and their parents or caregivers together in an enjoyable and educational setting. Curricula that build on the strengths and needs of families may improve educational and employment opportunities for at least two generations (Paratore, 2001). The most successful family literacy programs include a four-prong approach: (a) adult literacy instruction, (b) emergent literacy experiences for children, (c) time for parents and children to be together, and (d) group discussions for parents (Barbara Bush Foundation, 2001). Programs that include a needs assessment and attempt to match the academic levels and interests of the participants have the highest rates of retention. Most family literacy programs also offer opportunities for families to learn English as an additional language.

Many parents are motivated to learn to read so they can read aloud to their children and help them with schoolwork. Reading aloud to children can bring parents great pleasure, and is often less intimidating than reading in front of other adults. Often, programs include a parent–child read-aloud time. The Intergenerational Literacy Project of Chelsea, Massachusetts, strives to support the literacy and academic success of children by improving the literacy of their parents (Paratore, 2001). As part of the program, parents maintain a log where they record literacy events in which they have engaged with their children, as well as their own literacy experiences. During the program segment that the parents and children spend together, they often engage in book extension activities, such as making a snowman after reading **The Snowy Day** *(Keats, 1962)*. As part of the program, fliers are sent home that feature the book of the week, including topics and activities related to the book.

Summary

Diversity in families contributes to rich literacy experiences and exchanges between home and school when teachers and families work together collaboratively. Children's literacy development blossoms most readily if the adults in their primary settings have consonant goals. Successful literacy partnerships are based on incorporating the multiple literacies that surround children at home, considering adult caregivers as partners in literacy, and providing a variety of family opportunities for inclusion in literacy.

Professional Development

1. Interview three teachers of infants and selected families whose child attends the program. Plan a family literacy workshop for families and infants, based on their needs, interests, and suggestions.
2. Choose a children's book and develop a home-learning activity to accompany it. Take it on a home visit, model how to use it, and leave it in the home about a week. Return to the home, collect it, and ask the caregivers for feedback about using it.
3. Select an age level (infant, toddler, pre-K, K) and create a literacy brochure for families that contains information on the following topics: the importance of reading to children, tips on reading aloud, selecting quality children's books, where to find good books, and a list of 10 age-appropriate books.
4. Develop a written plan for family involvement in a child-care center or preschool, using the Literacy Partnership Cycle described in Figure 3.1. Include a timeline for implementation, activities, and strategies for evaluation.

Internet Resources

http://pbskids.org/lions/index.html

"Between the Lions: Get Wild About Reading" is a Web site dedicated to reading funded by the Public Broadcasting System and the U.S. Department of Education. It is a wonderful Web site for families and teachers, featuring recommended books, games, songs, a newsletter, and videos about reading that can be viewed online.

http://www.famlit.org

The Web site for the National Center for Family Literacy features information on membership, programs (for example, Head Start, Even Start, Kentucky Institute for Family Literacy), conferences, policy and advocacy issues, and publications.

http://www.reading.org

The International Reading Association is a professional organization dedicated to the teaching of reading at all ages. There are many reading-related topics on the Web site, including teaching tips, book lists, family involvement, reading resources, grant funding, and conference information.

4

FAMILIES OF MANY CULTURES

Family units have been part of civilization since earliest times. Although the beliefs, composition, and functions of families have varied historically and from place to place, the institution has survived and continues to fulfill a basic need for connecting to one another. Each family develops unique characteristics depending on the community and the cultures, personalities, ages, and genders of the family members. Essentially all experiences we have as human beings can take place within families (Taylor, 1997). Feelings of love and hate, joy and sorrow, need and rejection are intermingled in family relationships. Our most poignant memories are usually recollections of our family experiences.

Within families our basic needs for food, shelter, clothing, love, and companionship are met. Families are also the basic economic unit in society, as the adults strive to provide for themselves and their children. While each family has the same fundamental needs, those needs are met in different ways depending on economic status, cultural beliefs or traditions, and individual preferences.

It is likely that you will be working with children who live in families that are similar in some ways and very different in other ways from the family in which you grew up. One of the most basic differences is linguistic diversity. Increasingly, teachers are working with children and families who speak multiple languages. Figure 4.1 describes one teacher's experience with multiple languages in the classroom.

Given the fact that more people are moving to the United States from other countries, and others relocate within this country, teachers are challenged to think of culturally compatible ways to work with young children and families (De Gaetano, Williams, & Volk, 1998). Our task is to affirm the strengths of all families as we help children assimilate into the rainbow of U.S. society.

Chapters 4 and 5 will introduce you to the diversity within U.S. homes and suggest ways that literacy connections can be made with families from different backgrounds. In this chapter you will learn about cultural differences among American families and children's literature that addresses this diversity. Chapter 5 focuses on the many configurations found in modern families and literature that can help children understand and appreciate these different structures.

FAMILIES, CHILDREN, AND CULTURE

Children grow and develop in ways that are uniquely influenced by the various contexts of family, neighborhood, school, community, and society. Families are the primary source of children's beliefs and attitudes about people and the world around them. As children become involved with more diverse populations outside the home such as playgroups, daycare, preschool, special activities, and community events, they may modify or adapt the practices and beliefs held by their own families.

As a first-year teacher, I was completely overwhelmed when, on the first day of school, my 16 preschoolers sat in front of me and half of them did not understand a word I was saying. I thought "My 'education' isn't going to help me when I can't understand them telling me they are thirsty." But we learned from each other and survived.

At the beginning of my second year, I was a little more prepared. With a little Spanish under my belt, we started off with "Five Little Monkeys Jumping on the Bed." We had a few puppets, body actions, funny voices for the characters, and lots of laughing. It worked! We did the same story for more than a week, and before long they were joining in with the words.

As a group, we also learned a few basic signs in sign language. By signing the words, "Please sit down, please stand up, friend, and I love you," at the same time I used the words in English, then Spanish, we quickly had an enjoyable way to communicate, even on the most basic level. Our class really enjoyed singing. Because most songs have repetitive phrases and a rhythmic beat, the children were singing along after a few days.

I realized that the children's confidence level played a large role in their willingness to try to communicate in English. My body language and facial expressions told them how willing I was to listen. I tried to not interrupt them, nodded my head in encouragement, and thanked them for trying when they were done. I also learned to appreciate the fact that everyone understands a smile. For the first few weeks of school, the most effective way I could communicate with the families and children was using a smile and giving a "thumbs-up."

Don't give up the first weeks of school. It's hard and stressful, but your kids are feeling anxious and scared, too. Smile, give lots of hugs, and speak kindly to everyone. They might not understand the stories you read yet, but they will know that you care about them and are glad they are there. The old saying is true: Your actions speak louder than your words.

FIGURE 4.1

Teacher to Teacher: Overcoming Language Challenges
Source: Elizabeth Childers, Asheboro City Schools, Early Childhood Development Center, Asheboro, North Carolina. Reprinted by permission.

The one construct that continuously serves as a core for developing communication and interactions with others is our family culture. Banks and Banks (1997) define *culture* as "the ideation, symbols, behaviors, values, and beliefs that are shared by a human group" (p. 434). Culture can be characterized simply as the roles we play, what we value, the ways we express ourselves, our goals for ourselves and our families, and our relationships with others (Springate & Stegelin, 1999). Families pass their culture to their offspring through *enculturation*—the process by which the next generation becomes socialized to live in a particular culture (York, 1991).

Brofenbrenner (1979) proposed an ecological model of human development based on children's families and culture. He emphasized the interrelated nature of the primary environments in which children live and interact—family, peer group, neighborhood, community, and school. Transitions among and between settings must be comfortable and supportive to young children for optimal development to occur. Adding the sociocultural view of Vygotsky (Bodrova & Leong, 1996) to our discussion, we recognize that children construct knowledge through physical manipulation and socially mediated interactions within their primary environments. Thus, social context not only influences our attitudes and beliefs, it also profoundly affects our cognitive processes. Language, based on culture, is the touchstone for helping us make sense of the world. Culture determines how children are socialized into literacy; however, families' daily uses of oral and written language may clash with mainstream expectations of literate behaviors. Mismatches between home and school expectations for literacy can delay or even halt the learning process if teachers are unaware of the myriad oral and written traditions children bring to school (Heath, 1983).

Carefully consider how culture contributes to your interactions with young children and their families. Responding positively to the cultural aspects of their lives will help you establish strong partnerships with families. Take a look at your own cultural heritage. Where is your family's country of origin? What customs, ceremonies, rituals, or holidays does your family observe? Do you speak a language other than English? Growing up, were there diverse families in your neighborhood?

PRINCIPLES FOR WORKING WITH CULTURALLY DIVERSE FAMILIES

All caregivers, regardless of their culture, need support, information, and encouragement to do the best they can for their children. How can teachers assist families as they strive to provide optimum experiences for their children, particularly in the area of literacy development?

Developing effective partnerships with families requires sensitivity, understanding, and clear communication. Helping young children feel a sense of pride about themselves and promoting respect for others should be paramount in any early childhood program. As you read and study the following principles, keep in mind that all families have strengths. Concentrate on developing a strengths-based foundation for working with children and families who bridge two cultures.

Principle 1: Become informed about the cultures of the families with whom you work

Educating yourself about the families with whom you work is an ongoing process involving changes in knowledge, attitudes, and skills. Teachers need accurate information about cultures to help them communicate effectively, understand different attitudes and values, and support young children and families as they adjust to new communities, child care, and school (York, 1992). Cultural knowledge includes understanding child rearing approaches, family literacy practices, gender roles, common values and beliefs, traditions, holidays, and family attitudes toward participating in child care. Take advantage of morning drop-off or afternoon pick-up times to chat with parents and care-givers. Informal conversations can reveal a lot about the language(s) used at home, daily routines, family roles, or expectations for literacy development.

Home visits can be invaluable sources of information about ethnically diverse family life. Not all families will accept home visitors—or even have a home to visit; however, teachers who respect cultural differences can use home visits effectively to learn about the family and community lives of their children. See Figure 4.2 for tips on home visits.

Teachers can also acquire knowledge about other cultures by asking caregivers to volunteer in the classroom by reading books, viewing films, perusing Web sites, and attending multicultural workshops and classes. Another enjoyable way to learn about families is by attending community events and celebrations sponsored by cultural groups, if outsiders are welcome. Such festivities provide educators with a glimpse into cultural practices and possibilities for participating in new traditions.

As you become informed about other cultures, it is important to simultaneously examine any biases you may have and work toward eliminating them.

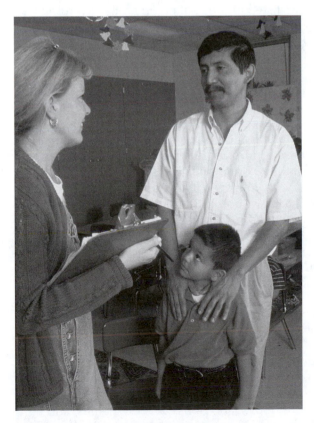

Informal conversations can reveal a lot about the languages used at home, daily routines, family roles, or expectations for literacy development.

Elizabeth Childers, a preschool teacher in an Even Start program, speaks very little Spanish, but her students are mostly Hispanic. As she visited the children's homes prior to the beginning of school, Elizabeth asked one of the mothers to accompany her on each visit and translate. Elizabeth took along her digital camera and some toys for the children. She took photographs of the families and turned them into matching cards for a memory game that the children played at preschool. She also used photos she took of the children to label their school "cubbies."

The parents are required to come into the classroom once a day as part of the Even Start program. Home visits helped Elizabeth form a bond with the families and eased the way for their participation. Additionally, as Elizabeth continues to do home visits, she learns more and more about language differences and cultural norms. When a class guinea pig was the feature in a newsletter sent to families, the Spanish words for "big rat" were used because "guinea pig" did not translate well. After visiting the classroom, parents were relieved to see that the "rat" was, in fact, a cuddly guinea pig!

FIGURE 4.2
Teacher to Teacher: Learning About Families

Having a positive attitude is the first step in the challenging and rewarding task of working with diverse families. Accepting and showing respect to all families; valuing ethnic pride; and being sensitive, flexible, and adaptable are professional qualities that all early childhood educators should possess (York, 1992).

Effective communication skills are based on knowledge of different cultural groups and ways they use verbal and nonverbal communication. A teacher's knowledge of a few key phrases in a family's native language may help newcomers feel welcome and accepted. It is equally important for educators to know how nonverbal communication, such as eye contact or physical proximity, is interpreted by different groups of people. When families see that you are making an effort to learn their communication style they will probably be more open in their exchanges with you. *Everybody Cooks Rice* (Dooley, 1991) and *Everybody Bakes Bread* (1996) are two books that depict similarities and differences among cultures. As the children in these stories go from house to house in their neighborhoods, they find that the families from various cultures are preparing the same basic foods—rice and bread—but in very different dishes. A few words in different languages and some unique traditions included in the text and illustrations help the reader gain knowledge of cultural differences.

Teachers need to acquire skills to help them select appropriate multicultural materials and remove any stereotypical items or parts of the curriculum. Derman-Sparks (1989) refers to this as an *antibias curriculum*—an approach to curriculum that challenges prejudice, stereotyping, and bias. Use of antibias "tool kits" (Kieff & Wellhousen, 2000) in early childhood settings will help children understand and learn about other cultures. A kit may contain resource books for adults; children's picture books; and dolls, puzzles, games, and consumable materials such as flesh-colored crayons and paints that promote cultural awareness and positive attitudes about a variety of cultures.

Children as young as 2 can begin to learn color names and apply them to the description of skin tones. Biases may emerge by 3 years of age if children adopt certain discriminatory attitudes of their families or society toward people of color (Derman-Sparks, 1989). The concept that people come in many different shades of brown is presented in ***The Colors of Us*** (Katz, 1999), as Sonia and her artist mother take a walk to observe the beautiful skin tones of their neighbors and relatives. Friends and family are described as "creamy peanut butter," "cocoa brown," "the color of pizza crust," and "tan like coconuts and coffee toffee." Sonia returns home to blend her mother's paints and create pictures of everyone they saw on their walk. This would be a great book to recommend to families who live in diverse neighborhoods. The language and illustrations could help children learn to celebrate differences and recognize similarities among all people. In classrooms, teachers could read the book to introduce activities where children compare their skin colors and use skin-tone paints to explore the concept that people come in all different colors.

In one school district where in-service training in multicultural education was offered, teachers developed action plans for applying what they had learned in workshops. More than half of the action plans involved developing bibliographies of culturally diverse books to supplement the curriculum (Tatum, 2000). Adults as well as children can learn a great deal about other cultures by examining the artwork and text of high-quality literature for children.

Principle 2: Become "culturally responsive" (York, 1991, p. 177) toward family relationships and values as you work with diverse families

Families have culturally derived goals and expectations for their children that will influence their adaptation to early childhood settings (Okagaki & Diamond, 2000). For example, all families do not hold the same beliefs and practices about children's development, family relationships, parental involvement, education, literacy, or home/school communication. In some cultures parents believe that the role of the family is to nurture their children, while it is the teacher's responsibility to educate them. Other cultures assume that the school is responsible for academic as well as moral education. One preschool teacher found during her home visits to Mexican American families that parents' first question was, "How is my child's behavior?" rather than an inquiry about cognitive development. Family involvement in preschool or day care may be sparse because it is a new cultural concept (Eastern Stream Center on Resources and Training, 1998). Ignoring variances among families will lead to cultural discontinuity between home and child-care settings, negatively affecting young children's development and adjustment (Ramsey, 1998).

Parents and caregivers vary in their desire to emulate a "typical" American family (York, 1991). Some who have just arrived in the United States may want their children to learn American ways but not lose their home language and customs. Other families may desire that their children blend in more readily with the dominant culture so that they will feel at home and be accepted by their neighbors and playmates. Whatever the circumstances, becoming culturally responsive in your program means that you have begun to learn about the families with whom you work, identified potential sources of discontinuity, and developed ways to consider and honor families' cultures while retaining the integrity of your professional training. Becoming sensitive to families' cultural standards and children's home experiences will help reduce conflicting and contradictory child-care strategies and support complementary practices.

Avoid a "tourist approach" to including diverse families in your early childhood curriculum (Derman-Sparks, 1989). Such an approach is characterized by having children participate in a few selected activities or experiences related to different cultures, then moving on to the regular curriculum. Holidays, foods, and customs become trivialized and stereotyped when the focus is on exotic differences between cultures. Learning about celebration and traditions of other cultures, however, can broaden children's awareness of others' experiences and promote respect for differences. Thoughtful inclusion of cultural celebrations can enhance the curriculum and increase children's sense of self-worth. The questionnaire in Figure 4.3 will help you learn about family celebrations.

Appreciation for diversity in families should be integrated daily throughout the year (Beaty, 1997; Boutte & McCormick, 1992). Everyday experiences, infused into the curriculum, will promote children's understanding, acceptance, and support for others. Regularly including experiences in the curriculum that feature different cultures will reduce children's misconceptions about others. Boutte (1999) states that two basic complementary concepts should guide a multicultural curriculum: (a) all people have similar basic needs such as water, food, shelter, respect, and love, and (b) people may fulfill these needs in diverse ways (e.g., housing, clothing, food) because they are different. Using diverse children's literature, such as that listed in Figure 4.4, will support a curriculum that celebrates the diversity of all children while focusing on commonalities in every culture (e.g., families, neighborhoods, language, toys, games, music, and friends) (Beaty, 1997).

Principle 3: Honor the language and literacy backgrounds of families from all cultures

Children come to early childhood programs and schools having been exposed since birth to the language and communication styles of their families. The talk they hear at home is an important part of children's self-image and family identity. All cultural groups have rich, complex linguistic systems, which often vary from standard English in unique and interesting ways. When teachers and caregivers respond to children's home language or dialect in positive ways, show an honest appreciation for the language, and try to understand the speech patterns, they are building connections with both children and families.

In the past decade, approximately 20% of U.S. school-age children lived in homes where languages other than English were spoken (Waggoner, 1994). Teachers of children whose primary language is not English have the responsibility of learning about bilingual and bicultural development to support the learning of their students. It is important to remember that while children may pick

Family Celebrations

Name _____ Child's Name_____

1. What special cultural events or holidays are celebrated in your family?

2. How could our program be involved in and support your celebrations?

3. What ways could we include everyone's special days in our center, since our families represent many cultures?

4. How do you feel about occasions we celebrate at the center that are not part of your family's traditions?

5. What suggestions do you have to make our celebrations inclusive of all families?

6. Would you be available to share special customs or celebrations with the children in our center? If so, what would you like to share and when would be a convenient time for you?

FIGURE 4.3

Teacher to Family: Learning About Family Celebrations

Source: Adapted from "Rethinking Celebrations," by B. Neugebaurer, 1994, *Child Care Exchange, 100,* pp. 40–41.

It is important for children to understand that we are all special, unique individuals who have a common need to be loved and accepted. Helping children develop positive self-esteem is integral in their ability to accept others. Incorporate culturally diverse picture books naturally into the curriculum, on a daily basis, to encourage children to value themselves and accept others. Involve family members in the book sharing and related activities.

Title	Culture	Ideas for Sharing
1. *Whoever You Are* (Fox, 1997)	All	Make a classroom display of the children's photos, using the idea of the jeweled picture frame featured in the book. Have each child or a family member dictate a caption for the photo.
2. *Margaret and Margarita* (Reiser, 1993)	Hispanic	Discuss ways the children can learn other languages.
Jambo Means Hello: Swahili Alphabet Book (Feelings & Feelings, 1974)	African	Ask a family member to teach the class phrases or songs in other languages.
3. *The Name Jar* (Yangsook, 2001)	Korean	Learn the "story" of each child's name. Put the stories in a book and have the children illustrate their "name story."
Tikki Tikki Tembo (Mosel, 1968)	Chinese	
4. *I Want to Be* (Moss, 1998)	African American	Help the children list their positive qualities.
Amazing Grace (Hoffman, 1991)	African American	Take photos of the children and use captions.
5. *Jamaica Tag-Along* (Havill, 1989)	African American/ Hispanic	Talk about ways to include others in play. Make a chart of caring behaviors and let the children illustrate it.

FIGURE 4.4

Teacher to Teacher: Valuing Ourselves and Accepting Others

up basic conversational skills in a new language rather quickly, it takes longer to acquire more abstract language and literacy concepts (National Association of the Education of Young Children, 1996). Maintaining one's home language while acquiring a new language helps children preserve their connections to family and community. Verbal storytelling is an important literacy event in cultures where traditional folktales and family stories are passed from one generation to the next. Inviting family members to share stories, art, or music from their home cultures will help children feel more at home in child care or preschool.

Home literacy is informal, woven into the daily fabric of life and family culture (Voss, 1996). The literacy activities of families are based on their history and habits, exposing boys and girls to the rich patterns of their homes and cultures.

In every culture, a range of literacy events occurs in the context of daily living: reading newspapers, magazines, or religious writings; writing letters to family or friends; making lists; recording family histories; reading novels or children's books; reading recipes; filling out forms; drawing or painting; and reading instruction manuals. The literacy materials in homes of bilingual or multilingual families may be in several languages. In some households, neighbors and friends may be called on to help translate letters and forms that arrive from school (Heath, 1983). Educators who understand the language, reading, and writing experiences of families strengthen the links between home and school literacy.

Principle 4: Incorporate culturally diverse literature and experiences to help link home, school, and community settings

Multicultural literature reflects the unique diversity of cultures within the United States. Sometimes called *culturally diverse literature,* this body of literature reflects the racial, religious, or language microcultures outside the mainstream, portraying an accurate view of the variety of individual cultures (Cullinan & Galda, 1998; Tomlinson & Lynch-Brown, 1996). As the enrollment in early childhood programs becomes increasingly diverse, multicultural literature should be shared regularly with young children. Books that contain sensitive, accurate, and positive stories and information about cultures outside the mainstream offer unique messages to all children, regardless of their cultural background. Teachers who make a concerted effort to bring multicultural literature into their programs demonstrate respect for the richly diversified cultural heritages represented in their children's families.

Reading literature about minority cultures has been characterized by a "mirrors and windows" metaphor (Sims Bishop, 1992). If the literature reflects one's own culture, it is comparable to looking in a mirror. Books that allow a glimpse into a culture different from one's own give us new visions, as in looking through a window. Hearing stories about different cultures is an easy and enjoyable way for young children to learn about themselves and others. In addition, a teacher's presentation of culturally diverse literature can promote sensitivity to other cultures, instill a sense of pride in one's heritage, and encourage appreciation of diverse literary traditions (Marshall, 1998; Temple, Martinez, Yokota, & Naylor, 1998).

There is a limited amount of quality literature available about certain minority groups, so teachers need to read, reflect, and select carefully to offer the best range of culturally diverse books. Teachers who recommend outstanding books to families model respect for the culture and provide a high standard of book selection that families can adopt. Keep in mind that all children's literature, regardless of the type, needs to adhere to high literary and artistic quality and have a worthy theme, strong plot, and well-rounded characters. Figure 4.5 presents questions to ask when evaluating culturally diverse literature.

Reading to children who are not speakers of English requires special attention. One prekindergarten teacher found that some of the non-English speaking children in her class were not familiar with books and just carried them around during the first month of school. When she began to read aloud,

- Are stereotypes that distort or misrepresent the culture avoided so that the characters are authentically and sensitively portrayed?
- Are the cultural details, language, and values accurately presented?
- Is the author someone who is from within the culture or one who has an outsider perspective? If the book is written by someone outside the culture, is it accurate and respectful?
- Do the illustrations enhance the quality of the text and depict accurate and authentic representations of the people and culture?
- Have you included books that represent the culture historically, as well as those that illustrate today's children and families?
- Is there a balanced selection of books that represent the wide variety of cultural groups in the United States?

FIGURE 4.5

Evaluating Culturally Diverse Literature

they would become bored and restless. Storytelling, acting out the books, and giving the children books to look at quietly during rest time helped them learn about books and engaged them in interesting activities based on stories. Although no money was available for the teacher to buy children's books in other languages, she began investigating possible funding sources and donors for books. Figure 4.6 offers suggestions for reading with children who are learning English as an additional language.

High-quality children's literature about diverse cultures should be readily available in any early childhood program. Including multicultural literature from all genres and sharing appropriate titles with families will further a sense of community, enrich young children's understanding of and identification with diverse cultures and families, and provide considerable enjoyment of a mosaic of literary heritages. In the following sections, information will be provided on diverse families, and a short selection of the quality literature available within each group will be discussed.

AFRICAN AMERICANS

African American families have been shaped by a long legacy of involuntary immigration and slavery. Suffering indignities that tore apart their families and forced them to learn survival and adaptation strategies, African Americans have had "one of the most unfortunate family life histories from which to build a viable ethnic American culture" (Hildebrand, Phenice, Gray, & Hines, 1996, p. 54).

Compared with families from European descent, African American families have been characterized as being outside the norm, deficient, and lacking

1. Begin with short read-aloud times. Children may be inattentive because they are unfamiliar with English and do not comprehend the story. In addition, the content of the pictures and the act of listening to a story may be new to children who have recently immigrated. Try starting with books that can be completed in a few minutes and gradually increase the time of reading aloud.

2. Read to small groups. Sharing books with several children at a time increases opportunities for conversation. Plan occasions to share books with only the children who are second-language learners to emphasize vocabulary, syntax, and other language skills. On other occasions, read to heterogeneous groups of children to allow non-native English speakers to learn from children who are fluent in English.

3. Be selective about books. Choose literature that meets the needs and interests of the children in your class. For those just beginning to learn English, picture dictionaries, concept books, and ABC books are good choices. As children develop their language, predictable books and those with repetitive phrases can be used to scaffold language learning. Be sure to include books in the children's home languages, if available, as well as those depicting children from many different cultures.

4. Tell stories. Use puppets, flannel-board figures, stuffed toys, or other props. Include book-related dramatic play. Also, try telling parts of the stories while showing the pictures.

5. Read stories again and again. Repeated readings builds vocabulary and comprehension. Each time children hear a story read they understand more about story schema and character development. Discuss different aspects of the story with each re-reading.

6. Support retelling and "independent" reading. Encourage second language learners to retell stories based on the pictures and their memory of the language and storyline of the book. Wordless picture books are particularly helpful for children acquiring English as an additional language. Encourage English retellings, but allow retellings in their native language as well on occasion.

FIGURE 4.6

Teacher to Teacher: Ideas for Reading with Children Who Are Learning English as an Additional Language

Source: Adapted from *One Child, Two Languages,* by P. O. Tabors, 1997, Baltimore, MD: Brookes.

family traditions (Belton-Owens, 1999). Segregation, discrimination, and stereotyping have been daily barriers in the struggle of African American families to forge a positive American identity and retain their pride in their heritage.

Picture books about African American culture and history can affirm children's sense of heritage, enlighten children of other cultures, and help combat stereotypes often promoted by the television or print media. In ***Our People*** (Medearis, 1994) a father helps his young daughter use dramatic play to act out the history and contributions of African Americans. From the ancient pyramids to the inventions of George Washington Carver, the father explains the "glorious past" of African Americans and gives his daughter hope for a "glorious future." The illustrations depict a playful and loving father–daughter relationship and the informative text is easy for young children to understand.

The symbolic colors and patterns of kente cloth are the subject of **Kente Colors** (Chocolate, 1996). A rhythmical text and boldly colored illustrations combine to acquaint young readers about the making of kente cloth by the Ashanti and Ewe people of Ghana. Indigenous animals, African landscapes, and cultural traditions are introduced as the colors and uses of the kente cloth are described in beautiful two-page spreads. Capturing the essence of the African continent, **Jaha and Jamil Went Down the Hill** (Kroll, 1995) is an African Mother Goose that adapts traditional Mother Goose rhymes. Many diverse areas of Africa are represented in the lyrical rhymes and colorful illustrations that blend traditional and modern-day African life.

Faraway Home (Kurtz, 2000) is a touching story about an African American father who must return to Ethiopia to care for his ailing mother. His young daughter does not want him to go, for fear he will not return. The father consoles her with descriptions of growing up in Ethiopia and assures her he will come back to her. Beautiful watercolor illustrations depict the Ethiopian landscape, wildlife, and traditional customs in his stories while showing the strong bond between father and daughter.

Until 2002, African Americans were the largest ethnic minority group in the United States, making up 12.8% of the population in 1998 (U.S. Census Bureau, 2000). In 1995, 10.1% of American children were Black (Washington & Andrews, 1998). Married couples constitute 47.1% of African American families; 45% of African American households are headed by a female with no spouse present; and only 7.8% are headed by a male (U.S. Census Bureau, 2000). Eighty-four percent of African Americans live in poor inner-city communities, where material and human resources have become marginalized as middle-class African Americans have migrated to the suburbs (Hildebrand et al., 1996). Living below the poverty line is a reality for 26.1% of African American families (U.S. Census Bureau, 2000).

Despite the statistics, the strategies of endurance and survival have combined to bring positive strengths to African American families. Parenting practices are usually dominated by mothers, are child-centered, and involve close physical contact. Interaction styles may be more authoritative, as children are taught respect for their elders within the family unit (Springate & Stegelin, 1999). Family relationships are emphasized, extended social networks of relatives and friends are cultivated, and children are encouraged to value loyalty in personal relationships (Barbour & Barbour, 1997; DeFlorimonte, Boutte, & LaPoint, 1999; Hildebrand et al., 1996).

Emphasizing the importance of extended families, **On the Day I Was Born** (Chocolate, 1995) combines traditional African customs surrounding a baby's birth with newfound family rituals. Relatives gather to name and bless the baby, who is surrounded with love and gifts throughout the celebration. An-

Many African American families emphasize the importance of family relationships and cultivate extended networks of relatives and friends.

other book that presents a lively look at an extended African American family is **So Much** (Cooke, 1994). The main character is a baby, whose relatives come to visit throughout the day. Aunts, uncles, cousins, and grandparents interact in loving ways with the baby until Daddy comes home. The relatives yell, "Surprise," and begin to celebrate Daddy's birthday. Baby is finally put to bed, where he falls asleep knowing that everyone loves him "so much." Repetitive phrases, the large format of the book, and energetic gouache illustrations contribute to the appeal of the story and make it a wonderful read-aloud. Two other noteworthy books about African American extended families are **Bigmama's** (Crews, 1991) and **Quinnie Blue** (Johnson, 2000).

Talking, singing, and storytelling are often used to transmit social and cultural values to young children, based on a long history of oral communication (Hale, 1991). In **Cornrows** (Yarbrough, 1979), for example, songs, poetry, history, and culture are woven into the story as a young girl and her brother have their hair braided by Mama and Great-Gammaw.

In many African American families, the church plays a vital role in shaping young children's lives and views of the world (Hildebrand et al., 1996). **Sunday Week** (Johnson, 1999) warmly portrays a young girl eagerly awaiting Sunday as she goes about everyday life in her family and community. The phrase "Sunday week," familiar to many Southern families in its definition, "a week from Sunday," takes on a personal meaning when seen through the eyes and experiences of the young girl as she anticipates her favorite day. Each day of the week

MORE FAVORITES

African American Children's Books

Amazing Grace (Hoffman, 1991)

Baby Says (Steptoe, 1988)

Feast for 10 (Falwel, 1993)

Girls Together (Williams, 1999)

Honey, I Love and Other Love Poems (Greenfield, 1978)

I Love My Hair (Tarpley, 1997)

I Smell Honey (Pinkney & Pinkney, 1997)

Just Right Stew (English, 1998)

The Magic Moonberry Jump Ropes (Hru, 1996)

One of Three (Johnson, 1991)

Our People (Medearis, 1994)

Saturday at the New You (Barber, 1994)

Yo! Yes? (Raschka, 1993)

brings feelings, events, and chores unique to the contexts and people of her home and neighborhood, such as Thursday story time with Miss Augusta or Saturday work time when floors are waxed and clothes are hung out to dry. Finally, the long-anticipated Sunday arrives with its routines of sunrise church bells, worship at Lovely Hill, Sunday dinner, and a drive with the family.

Hale (1991) contends that African American children's literature is central to developing positive self-images in young children. Establishment of an ethnic self-identity contributes to feelings of self-worth and gives children a sense of belonging to their culture. ***Bright Eyes, Brown Skin*** (Hudson & Ford, 1990) features African American children in their daily routines at preschool. Through simple, descriptive text, the author celebrates the physical characteristics of children of color. ***Nappy Hair*** (Herron, 1997) is another book that sends positive messages of pride about appearance to young African American children.

HISPANIC AMERICANS

Hispanics comprise the fastest growing and youngest ethnic group in the United States. They numbered 32.8 million in 2000 and make up approximately 12% of the U.S. population (U.S. Census Bureau, 2000). The numbers are expected to exceed 41 million by 2010 (Washington & Andrews, 1998). The youth population (younger than 18) is expected to grow by 30% between 1995 and 2005. The three major subgroups of Hispanic Americans are Mexican Americans, Cuban Americans, and Puerto Rican Americans.

Mexican Americans, who make up 66% of the Hispanic population in the United States, came to this country as a result of territorial conquest and immigration over many years. Some are recent immigrants, while ancestors of others have resided in the United States for many generations, primarily in the southwest (Bennett, 1999). One-third of Mexican Americans live below the poverty line in substandard rental housing. Approximately 10% are farmworkers, mostly migratory, who follow the planting and harvesting season north and south on both coasts. Many Mexican adults who come to the United States to work send money back to Mexico to support family members there.

The Spanish language has been said to be the glue that holds various Hispanic groups together. However, teachers of newly immigrated Mexican children should be aware that not all Mexicans speak Spanish. Approximately 8% of Mexicans speak one of 288 American Indian languages (Grimes, 2002). Before the Bilingual Education Act of 1968, most schools forced Spanish-surnamed children to speak English and offered little or no instruction in Spanish. Children were encouraged to take on American names and assimilate into the new culture as rapidly as possible. In losing their mother tongue, children also lost self-esteem and family roots (Garcia, 1997; Hildebrand et al., 1996).

The common Spanish proverb "a strong tree has strong roots" underscores the power of family and heritage (Garcia, 1997). Unfortunately, when people are stripped of their culture and language or economically, socially, or educationally impoverished, they are unable to maintain the strong roots needed for healthy families. Those who have assimilated too quickly, according to Garcia, often become rootless, losing their identity, and "falling down."

A clever book that focuses on Hispanic foods and family traditions is *Too Many Tamales* (Soto, 1993). An extended family has gathered to celebrate Christmas, which includes making tamales together. Thinking she has dropped her mother's ring in the batter, Maria and her cousins eat an entire batch of tamales in their quest to find it. The ring is discovered on Mother's finger, and everyone gathers in the kitchen to prepare another batch of the favorite holiday food.

The roles of family members and cultural and religious traditions are humorously portrayed in *Snapshots of a Wedding* (Soto, 1997). Illustrator Stephanie Garcia creatively combined sculpty clay, fabric, and found objects in diorama format to relate the experiences of the flower girl at a family wedding.

Most Hispanic Americans honor the sanctity of the family, and look to family members for advice and support. Although many Mexican American men have been economically forced to leave their homes and seek work in the United States, they do so reluctantly. The traditional Hispanic family accepts Biblical male–female roles with the father as breadwinner and protector, and the mother as nurturer of the children and helper to her husband. Most Hispanic women do not want to leave their children to work outside the home, but today many do so out of economic necessity.

Three values Hispanic Americans would probably agree they hold in common are respect, responsibility, and the importance of personal relationships. Respect means showing love and affection and giving and receiving protection. The youngest and oldest family members are usually the most valued in Hispanic families. Adults and older children celebrate births through christenings and indulge the babies and preschoolers in the household.

Spending time with and caring for the extended family takes priority for most Hispanic Americans. Grandparents are sought out for advice and respected for their wisdom. Human relationships, "people before things," are valued above material possessions.

The importance of close relationships with extended family is expressed in many Hispanic books. **In My Family/En Mi Familia,** written and illustrated by the well-known Mexican American painter Carmen Lomas Garza (1996), depicts the author's childhood experiences in Texas. Family celebrations, religious beliefs, traditional foods, and stories are shown through detailed paintings, accompanied by Spanish and English text. On one page Garza tells of her aunt and uncle making empanadas, sweet turnovers filled with fresh squash and sweet potatoes; on another she recalls her mother telling about the Mexican legend of the weeping woman.

Although education is highly regarded in Hispanic families, it does not come between a person and his or her family loyalty. A trip to visit an ill family member would come before a class project for Hispanic students. Formal education should be kept in its place and not used to show off or set one apart from the culture.

For many years there was a dearth of Hispanic literature for children, and that which existed was wrought with stereotypes, such as children wearing sombreros and men taking siestas (Nieto, 1992). However, during the past decade there has been a substantial increase in the number and quality of books by Hispanic American authors that authentically portray cultural experiences.

Hispanic literature can expose young children to the many contributions of Spanish-speaking people, encourage self-acceptance among Hispanic children, and promote an understanding of the many ethnic groups within the culture (Isom & Casteel, 1997/1998). Non-Hispanic children can also develop understanding and appreciation of differences and similarities between their own culture and Hispanic culture. The many bilingual books available today promote familiarity with and respect for the Spanish language and heritage (Smolen & Ortiz-Castro, 2000).

When selecting Hispanic literature, be sure that the text and illustrations accurately depict the specific Hispanic culture and the people, time, and place of the story. When stories are written in Spanish and English, it is important that the language is rich and natural, and that the dialogue is natural for the particular Hispanic culture and region.

Four generations of women are shown making tortillas, gathering flowers, washing clothes, and singing lullabies in **Tortillas and Lullabies/Tortillas y cancioncitas** (Reiser, 1998). Written in both Spanish and English, the book illustrates the values of love and respect shown through kind deeds. Six women artists from Costa Rica created the bright acrylic paintings. Another multigenerational book, **Abuela** (Dorros, 1991), is the story of a little girl and her grandmother having an imaginative adventure of flying over New York City. Through colorful collage illustrations and a mixture of Spanish and English text the author and illustrator depict a close relationship between grandmother and granddaughter and celebrate the rich diversity of city life.

Hispanic literature can expose young children to the many contributions of Spanish-speaking people, promote self-esteem, and support pride in their cultural heritage.

The stunning artwork in **Market Day** (Ehlert, 2000) is a visual treat. The illustrations of a Hispanic family's trip to the farmer's market were created almost entirely from the author's collection of folk art, primarily from Central and South America. The illustrations include a painted clay truck from Mexico carrying cloth dolls from Bolivia, Guatemala, and Mexico. Other pictures are of a mola butterfly from Panama and mouse dolls from Indonesia. The vivid colors and textures, along with the familiar topic and rhythmic language make the book appealing to children ages 2 to 5, as well as to their parents. This visual smorgasbord will help children become familiar with the tradition of buying and selling food at an open market common to many Latin American countries.

Two animal folktales, written in both languages, convey much cultural information through pictures and story. **The Bossy Gallito** (Gonzales, 1994), the Cuban version of an old cumulative tale from Spain, tells of a rooster's adventures on his way to his uncle's wedding. Illustrator Lulu Delcre found the models for her depictions of birds, plants, and buildings in the Little Havana section of Miami. In the Hispanic folktale tradition of the southwest, **A Spoon for Every Bite** (Hayes, 1996) is a retelling of an old story of wit overcoming greed. When a poor couple have their first child, they ask a wealthy neighbor to become the *compadre* (godfather). At a dinner together the rich man laughs because the couple has only three spoons, boasting that he has so many spoons at his house he could use a different one for each day of the year. The

MORE FAVORITES

Hispanic Children's Books

Bakery Lady (Mora, 2001)

A Birthday Basket for Tia (Mora, 1992)

Carlos and the Squash Plant/Carlos y la Planta de Calabaza (Stevens, 1993)

Chato and the Party Animals (Soto, 2000)

Cuckoo/Cucu (Ehlert, 1997)

Gathering the Sun: An Alphabet in Spanish and English (Ada, 1997)

Mama Provi and the Pot of Rice (Rosa-Casanova, 1997)

New Shoes for Silvia (Hurwitz, 1993)

Pablo's Tree (Mora, 1994)

Sol a Sol (Carlson, 1998)

Vejigante/Masquerader (Delacre, 1993)

wife replies that they have other neighbors who use a different spoon for each bite of a meal. In the end, the wealthy man has spent all of his riches on silver spoons, while the "poor" neighbors have outsmarted him by using tortillas as eating utensils. Young children will delight in the humor and might also enjoy eating a Mexican dish with tortilla chips.

Mediopollito/Half-Chicken (Ada, 1995), a folktale originally from Spain, has Latin American, Cuban, and Mexican interpretations, as well. The bright, whimsical illustrations of Mexican villages painted by Kim Howard set the tone for this adventurous tale. Young children will delight in the character of Half-Chicken, who is rewarded for his kindness to others by being chosen to be a weather vane. The story shows that being different can mean being special.

ASIAN AMERICANS

Covering a wide variety of national, cultural, and religious heritages, the term *Asian Americans* refers to four major subgroups from approximately 29 countries (Feng, 1994). Diverse in origins, ecological adaptations, and histories, the major groups and several representative countries of each are East Asians (China, Japan, and Korea), Pacific Islanders (Hawaii, Samoa, and Guam), Southeast Asians (Thailand, Vietnam, Cambodia, Laos, Burma, and the Philippines), and South Asian (India and Pakistan) (Feng, 1994; Huang, 1993). Often the term *Asian American/Pacific Islanders* is used to refer to this population.

Teachers need to be culturally sensitive to the wide range of heritages in Asian American families, recognizing the distinct nature of each of the groups

(Hildebrand et al., 1996). Use of children's literature can highlight the diversity of Asian Americans and give insight into traditions and customs that are unique to certain populations. The majority of books about Asian Americans reflect characters from Chinese and Japanese cultures (Aoki, 1981; Cullinan & Galda, 1998). Excellent examples of two traditional tales are ***The Boy of the Three-Year Nap*** (Snyder, 1988) and ***Lon Po Po*** (Young, 1989). Both books have been honored for the illustrations, the former winning a Caldecott Honor Medal and the latter winning the Caldecott Medal.

In addition to including books about the dominant Asian cultures, it is important to locate and use books that portray groups of Asian Americans that are underrepresented, such as the Hmong. Needlework is a treasured skill in the Hmong culture, and subgroups identify themselves through differently embroidered and appliquéd clothing. A form of narrative stitchery, story cloths, has emerged as a way to transmit the Hmong culture to future generations. ***Nine-in-One, Grr! Grr!*** (Xiong, 1989) is a folktale in which the illustrations are modeled on the technique of appliquéd story cloths. Through the rhythmical text and colorful illustrations, preschoolers will be introduced to traditional Hmong folk beliefs and wildlife.

Immigrating to the United States for disparate reasons, Asian Americans represent myriad cultural and historical backgrounds. Some immigrants came from Asia to escape the ravages of war or oppressive governments; others migrated to fulfill personal dreams or pursue further education. Socioeconomic status, educational attainment in their native countries, and reception by the dominant culture vary greatly for Asian American families (Huang, 1993; Cheng, 1998; Feng, 1994). The Asian American population is one of the fastest growing minority groups in the United States (Cheng, 1998; Feng, 1994; Hildebrand et al., 1996). According to the U.S. Census Bureau (2000), 4% of the population is Asian American. In 1995, 2.5% of children in the United States were Asian American (Washington & Andrews, 1998). Although there are more affluent Asian American families than poor, the poverty rate is approximately 8% (Hildebrand et al., 1996).

Children's books that accurately represent the modern lives of Asian American cultures may help children move beyond the stereotypical "chopsticks and dragons" view of the people and lifestyles (Pang, Colvin, Tran, & Barba, 1992). Contemporary Asian American families should be represented in the literature you share with young children, to balance the overabundance of folktales that depict traditional times and customs. A classic story is ***Umbrella*** (Yashima, 1958), about Momo, a young Japanese girl who is born and lives in New York. She receives an umbrella and red rubber boots for her third birthday and is impatient to use them. When a rainy day finally comes, she walks to nursery school and back using her new presents. Children will enjoy the language play used to describe the raindrops on Momo's umbrella and may relate to her desire for independence and responsibility. ***Emma's Rug*** (Say, 1996) tells the story of a young girl of Asian descent who is inspired artistically by staring at an old rug she was given as a baby. When her mother washes it without her daughter's knowledge, Emma feels as if she has lost the ability to cre-

MORE FAVORITES

Asian American Children's Books

Angel Child, Dragon Child (Surat, 1983)

Chinatown (Low, 1997)

Cleversticks (Ashley, 1991)

Grandfather Tang's Story (Tompert, 1990)

Halmoni and the Picnic (Choi, 1993)

Hoang Breaks the Lucky Teapot (Breckler, 1992)

I Am Vietnamese American (Blanc, 1997)

Konnichiwa! I Am a Japanese-American Girl (Brown, 1995)

Korean Cinderella (Climo, 1993)

Lao-Lao of Dragon Mountain (Bateson-Hill, 1996)

Little Oh (Melmed, 1997)

Luka's Quilt (Guback, 1994)

A River Dream (Say, 1988)

The Squiggle (Schaefer, 1996)

Where Is Gah-Ning? (Munsch, 1994)

ate the award-winning paintings that have made her a local celebrity. She eventually discovers, however, that creativity comes from within.

An addition to the literature on Korean Americans, **Father's Rubber Shoes** (Heo, 1995) describes the loneliness of a young boy, Yungsu, who has recently moved with his family to the United States. When his father explains that the move allowed the family to have a better life, Yungsu tries to become more positive about his new life.

In many Asian American families, parents make great sacrifices for their children and expect that children will respond by bringing honor to the family (Shen & Mo, 1990). A book that illustrates family honor is **Sam and the Lucky Money** (Chinn, 1995). In accordance with a Chinese New Year tradition, his grandparents have given Sam *leisees*. Leisees are small red envelopes that contain money; in Sam's case, four dollars. As Sam and his mother navigate the streets of New York on their way to see the New Year's parade, he must decide how to spend his money. He realizes he needs more money to buy some of the items he wants, and begins to be ungrateful for the small gift. Although Sam wants to honor his family, he gives his money to a homeless man.

The importance of cross-cultural bonds in a family is evident in **Dumpling Soup** (Rattigan, 1993). Set in the islands of Hawaii, the story celebrates the tradition of making dumpling soup on New Year's Eve and features a family composed of Korean, Japanese, Chinese, Hawaiian, and *haole* (Hawaiian for foreigner or white people) members. A glossary is provided at the beginning of the book that contains English, Hawaiian, Japanese, and Korean terms found in the story. Told from a young girl's point of view, the story shares the richness of diverse traditions in a multiracial community.

Some Asian American parents hesitate to become involved in their children's education because of their beliefs about adult roles. They believe it is the responsibility of teachers and school administrators to educate and discipline children at school. The parents' responsibilities at home include supervising homework and supporting their children's academic progress (Cheng, 1998; Lee, 1995; Shen & Mo, 1990). In addition, the language barrier may make it difficult to form immediate partnerships with Asian American families, especially with those who have no written language or educational system such as the Hmong population (Huang, 1993; Lee, 1995). It is important, then, not to characterize some families' lack of involvement in early childhood programs as indifference, but to look further, consider cultural beliefs, and learn ways to comfortably and effectively include parents and caregivers.

NATIVE AMERICANS

The people native to North America comprise a diverse population of Indians, Alaska Natives, Aleuts, Eskimos, and Metis (mixed bloods). Rather than identifying themselves as individuals in a family or community, some Native Americans prefer membership in a certain tribe as their identification (Hildebrand et al., 1996). More than 500 tribes are grouped regionally, with the Navajo reservation representing the largest (Hodgkinson, 1992). In our discussion we will use the term *Native Americans* unless referring to a specific tribe, although fully recognizing and respecting the individuality of each distinct group.

Children's literature that accurately portrays the different Native American populations and their history will promote appreciation and understanding of the many groups. Native American folktales are rich in cultural details and provide a starting point for discussions about different customs, dress, geographic regions, housing, language, and food. Consider the comparison of **Two Bad Boys** (Haley, 1996) and **Raven** (McDermott, 1993), two tales of trickery emerging from the Cherokee and Pacific Northwest nations. *Two Bad Boys* is an ancient Cherokee legend about a lonely boy who finds a playmate beneath the surface of the river water. The "Wild Boy" leads him into adventures that forever affect the ways the Cherokee people hunt, plant, and work for their food. Haley's carefully researched gesso illustrations capture the essence of traditional Cherokee life in North Carolina.

A trickster tale set in the Pacific Northwest, *Raven* has distinctive artwork representing the native culture of that area. The story is an explanation of how the sun came to be in the sky, and celebrates Raven, a figure central to the tales and artwork of the region. The illustrations, done in gouache, colored pencil, and pastel, have unique designs often seen in Pacific Northwest art.

Initial comparisons of the illustrations in the two books could help children begin to see that native tribes differ in many ways. Collecting books that portray similar artwork, such as the Cherokee tale **How Turtle's Back Was Cracked**

(Ross, 1995) and ***There Was an Old Lady Who Swallowed a Trout!*** (Sloat, 1998) would further confirm the distinct differences in these two tribes and regions.

Less than 1% of the population classify themselves as American Indian, Eskimo, or Aleut (U.S. Census Bureau, 2000). Perhaps due to the high rate of unemployment found on or near reservations, the majority of Native Americans live in or around major urban cities (Hildebrand et al., 1996). In 1990, more than half of the population lived in six states: Oklahoma, Arizona, New Mexico, California, Washington, and Alaska (Hodgkinson, 1992). The median income in 1990 was $19,866 compared with $30,056 for all races, and 47.3% of Native American families lived below the poverty line. Approximately one-half of the population is younger than 20 (Joe & Malach, 1998).

Many Native Americans live bicultural lives, having moved to cities from the reservations for economic and other reasons. Adapting to the modern world while retaining elements of tribal traditions, families may celebrate a child's naming ceremony in addition to engaging in mainstream childhood customs and lore such as birthdays or believing in the tooth fairy (Joe & Malach, 1998). Certain customs, such as the use of a cradle board, may appear to teachers to conflict with Euro-American ways of thinking about children's development.

Teachers of very young children need to be aware of Native American customs, ceremonies, and tribal traditions to help support families while easing the child's transition into daycare or preschool settings (Okagaki & Diamond, 2000). ***Navajo ABC*** (Tapahonso & Schick, 1995) is a Dine (Navajo) alphabet book that could be used to help teachers and children learn about native artifacts and the traditions of the largest tribe in the United States. A glossary is provided to help translate and more clearly define the alphabet words. A contemporary look at a native tradition is seen in ***Where Did You Get Your Moccasins?*** (Wheeler, 1986). When a young boy proudly brings his new

MORE FAVORITES

Native American Children's Books

Dreamcatcher (Osofsky, 1992)

Green Snake Ceremony (Watkins, 1995)

Many Nations: An Alphabet of Native America (Bruchac, 1997)

The Night the Grandfathers Danced (Raczek, 1998)

On Mother's Lap (Scott, 1992)

Rainy's Powwow (Raczek, 1999)

Red Bird (Mitchell, 1996)

The Rough-Face Girl (Martin, 1992)

Sootface: An Ojibwa Cinderella Story (San Souci, 1994)

Very Last First Time (Andrews, 2002)

Family members can share stories, artifacts, or traditions from their culture to help children value diversity.

moccasins to an urban, multicultural school, his classmates ask questions about them. He answers in a cumulative text, as the children learn a traditional way of making moccasins. The surprise ending could be used as a discussion prompt to clarify traditional and modern life of native people.

In Native American families, extended family members may be responsible for some childrearing practices, such as discipline. Parents often seek advice from the elder members based on their age and life experiences. A child's documented developmental milestones may vary from those of the mainstream culture. For example, instead of recording a child's first words, Native American parents may celebrate the first laugh. Early mastery of self-care skills allows children to become self-reliant and autonomous, two characteristics valued in most Native American families (Joe & Malach, 1998). *Mama Do You Love Me?* (Joosse, 1991), is a warm story about a young Inuit (Eskimo) girl verbally testing her independent spirit and learning about her mother's unconditional love. The colorful illustrations—including Arctic animals and native clothing—combine with a detailed glossary to make it a wonderful read-aloud. A companion book set in Alaska that demonstrates a mother's love is *On Mother's Lap* (Scott, 1992).

Songs, storytelling, and ceremonial activities remain central in the lives of many families. Children often partake in rituals and ceremonies as soon as they can sing or dance. *My Navajo Sister* (Schick, 1996) was written as a letter from a non-Native girl to her Native American friend, Genni. Throughout the story, as the two girls participate in modern life on a reservation, they become close friends as Genni shares the spirit of Navajo life.

Native Americans believe that all living creatures and things in the natural world are connected and should be treated as sacred (Hildebrand et al., 1996).

Northern Lullaby (Carlstrom, 1992), set in Alaska, beautifully illustrates the Native American tenets of harmony with nature and respect for creatures in the living world. Airbrush and watercolor illustrations by Leo and Diane Dillon depict a child's fantasy view of the natural world at bedtime. Native American beliefs about the moon's spiritual powers are presented in *Moonsong Lullaby* (Highwater, 1981). Photographs represent the text, which is a rhythmic poem spoken by elders around the campfire. Comparison of the two lullabies could lead to a discussion of the significant role that nature plays in Native American life.

ARAB AMERICANS

The first Arab Americans immigrated to the United States from Syria and Lebanon about the end of the 19th century. Settling in the Midwest, many became peddlers and merchants. After World War II a second wave of Arab immigrants arrived from Lebanon, Palestine, Syria, Turkey, and Albania, fleeing political unrest. Another group of immigrants arrived in the 1960s from North Africa, Pakistan, and India (Bennett, 1999). The largest groups of Arab Americans currently live in Detroit and Dearborn, Michigan.

Both immigration and political unrest are addressed in *The Silence in the Mountains* (Rosenberg, 1999), the story of young Iskander and his family's move to the United States. When war breaks out in their homeland, the grandparents, parents, and child immigrate, first to a city, then to a country home. Missing the peaceful mountains of his native land, Iskander does not feel at home until his grandfather takes him for a quiet walk in the woods. There he finds a new kind of contentment among the "twitterings and rustlings" of the trees and birds. A silver teapot, a decorative rug, and other cultural artifacts shown in the illustrations add to the authenticity of the story.

It is important for professionals working with Arab American families to note the common characteristics of close family ties, hard work, submission of individual ambition to the welfare of the family, personal honor (keeping one's word), and hospitality to those in need (Ashabranner, 1991). Kinship is the basis of strong economic and political units within communities. Families are patrilinial (traced through male descendants), patrilocal (newly married couples reside with the husband's family), and patriarchal (the father has complete authority over the wife and children) (Hildebrand et al., 1996). Religious rules and traditions provide guidelines for interactions and roles within families (Lynch & Hanson, 1998). In many cases girls have fewer freedoms than their brothers and more responsibility for household chores, such as washing dishes and cleaning. As families become more acculturated, women and girls are becoming more independent, making more personal decisions, and taking on careers outside the home.

Among newly arrived Arab Americans, the father is likely to be the decision maker and should be consulted regarding educational issues. Educators need to be sensitive to the culture shock and language difficulties newly arrived Arab Americans may experience. It is important that children and families not "lose face" or bring any dishonor upon themselves or their families (Schwartz, 1999).

Within Arab American communities, families are responsible for developing religious and moral values in the young. Children are expected to obey their parents, be polite to their elders, and demonstrate generosity, cooperation, humility, and helpfulness toward others (Hildebrand et al., 1996). Children are taught to work hard, respect their teachers, and refrain from gossip, lying, or quarreling. Problem solving typically is a group, rather than an individual, process; therefore Arab American children may work more effectively in groups than individually.

Teachers should also be aware of the following possible differences between American and Arab cultures. Very conservative Arab men and women may not sit next to individuals of the other gender and might not even shake hands with someone of the opposite sex (Jackson, 1995). Also, some Arabs consider it impolite to say "no" in conversations, so they nod and appear to agree. Teachers may think that parents have concurred with them; then, when they do not follow through, they may mistakenly be perceived as unreliable (Wilson, 1996).

A study by Moosa and Adams (2001) illuminates key points for teachers to consider when working with recent immigrants from Arab nations. From extensive interviews with Arab American mothers, the researchers found that the mothers preferred personal contact, including face-to-face meetings and phone calls, over notes and newsletters. Also, large families and lack of funding for transportation might limit children's participation in after-school activities. The mothers in this study were interested in parent education workshops, but they wanted to be involved in selecting topics that were relevant to them. What could look like lack of interest to teachers might actually be a reflection of feelings of alienation on the part of the mothers.

Children's literature can serve as a springboard for families to discuss their roots and many contributions to U.S. culture. **Sitti's Secrets** (Nye, 1994) and **The Stars in My Geddoh's Sky** (Matze, 1999) contrast Arab and American culture through stories of visits between grandparents and grandchildren. In *Sitti's Secret* a little girl and her father travel to Palestine to visit her sitti (grandmother), who dresses and lives in the traditional way. They eat yogurt and cucumber for breakfast, bake flat bread in an outdoor oven, and greet each day by saying good morning to the lemons on the tree. In *The Stars in My Geddoh's Sky*, the geddoh (grandfather) flies to the United States to visit his grandson, bringing gifts of a camel saddle, jewelry, and a brass gong. The grandfather teaches Alex to cook middle-eastern foods and write his name in Arabic. Pictures by Bill Farnsworth depict city and rural life in a Mediterranean country and the ritual Muslim prayers. Both books teach much about Arab lifestyle, including strong intergenerational ties.

The Armenian folktale **A Drop of Honey** (Bider, 1989) tells of Anayida's dream about going to the market to buy ingredients for baklava, a sweet pastry. The dream begins with a drop of honey falling from a clay pot and evolves into a cumulative tale with animal characters knocking down stalls in the market.

The moral of the story is that small quarrels can lead to big problems. A recipe for baklava is included.

Sadly, some Arab Americans have suffered from being stereotyped as religious fanatics or terrorists, particularly in the months following the World Trade Center tragedy of September 11, 2001. In one family the father (a professional with Arab ancestors) received threatening messages. A neighbor refused to take the family's 5-year-old child to a birthday party, and an older son said that he guessed he "would have to be better" (so that other children would stop treating him unkindly). Others of Arab descent reported receiving outpourings of love and support from friends and strangers.

As a consequence of this stereotyping and negative portrayal of Arab-looking people in the media, Arab American children may suffer from racism more than African American and Native American children. Parents and teachers may be unaware of the stereotypes children are exposed to in the media or at school. Teachers can work toward eliminating these false ideas by seeking out successful Arab Americans to participate in class projects and serve as role models in child-care centers and schools. They can also display and discuss pictures of Arabs and Arab Americans at work or carrying on daily tasks. Through personal contacts teachers can encourage mothers, fathers, and other family members to take on a visible role by volunteering in the classroom. By working together we can begin to build positive images of all people in our communities.

SUMMARY

The face of the United States is changing. We are no longer a nation of Black and White, but a blending of many nationalities and colors. Children born at the end of the 20th century and the beginning of the 21st century will come of age in a new era of U.S. history, where they will attend school and work with individuals from many ethnic backgrounds. Teachers will need to hone their interpersonal skills, and increase their knowledge and understanding of diverse cultures to successfully work with families who subscribe to a range of values and cultural practices. Educators can find support in their task of developing acceptance by sharing culturally diverse literature with young children and the adults who care for them.

FOR PROFESSIONAL DEVELOPMENT

1. Select several culturally diverse books and evaluate them according to the criteria presented in Figure 4.5. Plan ways to use the books to help children learn about similarities and differences between cultural groups.
2. Take a "cultural walk" with a friend or ride around the neighborhood in which your students live. Observe people, shops, restaurants, places of worship, and public play areas for ethnic diversity. Are there signs or advertisements in lan-

guages other than English? What seems to be the most predominant culture represented in the community? How will you use this information to plan literacy experiences for the children and their families?

3. Develop an antibias "tool kit" that would be appropriate for 3- to 5-year-olds. Include resources for adults, children's picture books, dolls, games, and activities to promote understanding and knowledge of a variety of cultures. See Kieff and Wellhousen (2000) for a description of antibias tool kits.

4. After reading the suggested books on Arab Americans and related information in the chapter, develop a plan for working with a 4-year-old boy from Lebanon. What information might be helpful in preparing for your first home visit? What home literacy activities would you suggest for his family?

5. Invite family members into your class to read aloud a favorite children's book from their culture. If a visit to class is not possible, send a tape recorder home and have the adult tape a read-aloud session with the child. Put it in the listening center for all the children to enjoy. Telling a story, instead of reading aloud, may be a better option for some adults.

6. Send home a newsletter containing a list of high-quality picture books about diverse cultures. If the families' home language is other than English, make sure to have some copies printed in their language(s). You may want to include culturally diverse fingerplays, nursery rhymes, or songs. See Beaty (1997) for suggestions.

7. Develop a list of bilingual books to include in a child-care or preschool classroom library.

INTERNET RESOURCES

http://www.multiculturalchildrenslit.com

"Celebrating Cultural Diversity through Children's Literature." This is an excellent Web site for annotated bibliographies categorized by genre and grade level. Related links provide lots of information on the featured cultural groups.

http://falcon.jmu.edu/~ramseyil/multipub.htm

"Multicultural Resources for Children." This Web site is offered by the Internet School Library Media Center. It contains general resources for multicultural children's books as well as specific bibliographies.

http://www.teachingtolerance.org

"Teaching Tolerance." This is a project of the Southern Poverty Law Center in Montgomery, Alabama. Although many of the lesson plans and topics for discussion may relate more to elementary children, there are good suggestions that can be adapted for younger children. Their book, *Starting Small: Teaching Tolerance in Preschool and the Early Grades* is right on target for preschool teachers. They also publish a newsletter for teachers of young children.

http://www.bilingualbooks.com

Bilingual Books for Kids, Inc. sponsors this Website, which contains a large selection of books written in side-by-side text of English and Spanish. Links to categories (e.g., nursery tales, myths, counting and ABC books) make selection easy. Games, music, and learning tapes are also offered on the Web site.

All Types of Families

In the middle of the 20th century the average family had a father who was employed in the community, a mother who worked within the home, and one or more children. Although other family structures existed, they were not as common as the nuclear family, and were rarely depicted in books or other forms of media. As we enter the 21st century, it is obvious even to the most casual observer that families are much more diverse than they were 50 years ago. Our country is made up of a kaleidoscope of families from different races, cultures, and religions. Today's parents may be single adults, grandparents, teenagers, gay or lesbian couples, or interracial couples. Fortunately, the evolving structure of American families is increasingly represented in children's literature, affirming for children that their home life is acceptable.

With so many types of families represented in our schools and child care centers, it may be difficult to find agreement on the meaning of *family*. Before reading on, try writing your own definition of *family*, then see how it compares with the definitions that follow.

Students in a class on family involvement taught by one of the authors wrote:

> A family is made up of both adults and children who love, respect, trust, and share with one another. Usually the adults provide for the children and they do their best to meet each other's needs.
>
> A family is a unit of people who share common goals, lifestyles, and responsibilities. They are committed to each other and rely upon each other for emotional and physical support.

The following definitions were written by professionals who work with and study families:

> We define families in an inclusive sense to be composed not only of persons related by blood, marriage, or adoption, but also sets of interdependent but independent persons who share some common goals, resources, and commitment to each other over time. (Bubolz & Sontag, 1995, p. 435)
>
> Family is a collection of people who pool resources and help each other over the long haul. Families love one another even when that requires sacrifice. Family means that if you disagree, you still stay together. (Pipher, 1996, p. 21)

Discuss these examples with your classmates. Do you agree with one of the definitions over the others? Are there parts of the definitions with which you disagree?

PRINCIPLES FOR WORKING WITH DIFFERENT TYPES OF FAMILIES

Think about what you have read thus far about building partnerships with families and the diverse cultures that shape childrearing and literacy practices. As you work with different types of families, it is important to set goals for your own learning and development. We hope you will use the following two principles to guide your thinking and actions.

Principle 1: Support families as they strive to meet their children's needs

From experts in psychology, education, and sociology, as well as the news media, we hear that modern families are in crisis (Elkind, 1994; Pipher, 1996; Children's Defense Fund, 2000). Young couples and single people raising children in the 21st century often live apart from their families of origin. As a result of their mobility, it is difficult for some families to establish social connections before it is time for them to relocate again. Extended families, which once provided encouragement to new parents and support in times of crisis and stress, may be too far away to assist young families in need.

With more than half of all mothers of young children in the workforce, and the majority of fathers employed outside the home, many families are hurried and stressed both morning and evening, as adults prepare meals and tend to household tasks. Modern advertising entices people to desire more goods, thus many adults think that they need to work more hours to provide their families with material possessions. Other families, who work at minimum-wage jobs, must struggle to provide the basic necessities.

Another issue is the prevalence of media in homes and society. Television and computer games isolate family members and provide poor role models for children. The media have replaced community for many people, with more being known about TV stars than about the family next door. According to psychologist Mary Pipher (1996) these vicarious relationships breed a new kind of loneliness and limit interactions with real people and the diversity of our communities. Children who watch violent shows on television become desensitized to violence and often use verbal and physical aggression as a way to solve problems.

Violence pervades impoverished urban communities. In some neighborhoods children rarely leave their apartments and spend almost no time in open, outdoor spaces. When families feel threatened by violence, their interactions with each other become anxious and negative. The aggression and isolation in our culture has bred a crisis that transcends class boundaries (Pipher, 1996).

All families need encouragement and support, regardless of their income or educational level. With the complexities of modern life, no family has the ability to meet the needs of all their members at all times (Allen, Brown, & Finlay, 1995). Although the vast majority of parents are working hard to do what they believe is right, rearing children is still a difficult task (Elkind, 1994). What types of assistance do families need? Consult Figure 5.1 for information on services that family support programs can provide.

Principle 2: Base your work with families on the values of respect, affirmation, and validation

The "typical" nuclear family composed of a mother who stays home, a father who is the breadwinner, and one or more children, is no longer the norm. In fact, according to the 1993 census, only 26% of families in the United States had that configuration (Barbour & Barbour, 1997). Family formations changed

Teachers and early interventionists are not expected to provide all of the following services themselves; however they should become knowledgeable about the services in their communities. Agencies such as family resource centers, parent education programs, and social services may provide needed assistance. Teachers *can* listen with understanding, encourage, and respect parents as they face the challenges of rearing young children in the 21st century. Families of young children may need:

- Support and encouragement for families overwhelmed by child-care and household responsibilities (Allen et al., 1995)
- Advice on how to help children cope with violence in their communities
- Information for developing parenting skills, including approaches to nurturing and interacting with children in positive ways
- Adult education for developing their own literacy skills
- Health care and nutritional information
- Counseling and special services
- Respect and acknowledgment of their strengths

FIGURE 5.1
Support Services for Families

dramatically during the last quarter of the 20th century. Children today may go through several different family clusters in their growing up years. For example, a child might be born into a nuclear family, live with one parent after a divorce, and then become a member of a blended family when parents remarry.

Early childhood educators may find that some family configurations conflict with their personal values and beliefs. Professionals who work with young children and their families need to clarify in their heads and hearts how they view family structures and how they might respond to families that are very different from their own (Burke, 1999). It is important to keep in mind that many types of families can provide the loving and supportive care children need for healthy development (Teaching Tolerance, 1997). Developing an awareness of any subtle or overt prejudices one holds toward nontraditional families can be an important first step in working effectively with all caregivers (Barbour & Barbour, 1997).

All families deserve respect, affirmation, and validation of their strengths. Actively listening to a mother express her fears about her child, her frustrations with some service agencies, or her feelings of inadequacy over not finishing high school is one way teachers can show respect. Asking parents, grandparents, and other caregivers to share time and knowledge about their child, skills, language, and culture with the class is another way we can affirm families and build bridges between home and school. What skills and experiences do you bring to your work with young children and families that will enhance your effectiveness in working with families that have diverse configurations?

All families deserve respect and affirmation and validation of their strengths.

SINGLE-PARENT FAMILIES

Single-parent families have become increasingly prevalent as a family structure. Children living with a single mother or father constituted more than 25% of U.S. families in 1999 (Kleist, 1999). Barbour and Barbour (2001) describe four variations of single-parent families:

1. Single mothers, divorced, widowed, or never married, living alone with their biological children.
2. Single fathers, divorced or widowed, living alone with their biological children.
3. Single parents (male or female) divorced or never married living alone with adopted children.
4. Male or female parent living alone with children and spouse incarcerated, deserted, or moved away. (p. 57)

Mothers head 87% of the population of single-parent households; however, the number of fathers raising children alone is on the rise (Barbour & Barbour, 2001). The Children's Defense Fund (2000) reports that because single mothers often do not receive full child support, they are three times more likely to be poor than other adults. Low wages and unstable arrangements for child care combine to make it difficult for mothers to pay for child care and reduce the number of hours they can work. In 1999, 30% of all mothers in the labor force who had children younger than 6 were single parents.

Regardless of the type of single-parent household, there are likely to be adjustments and stress-related issues due to only one person shouldering the tasks of parenting and managing a household. While many adults make a conscious decision to become part of a one-parent family, financial burdens, lack of child care, housekeeping chores, and absence of emotional support and companionship often overload the single parent (Rockwell, Andre, & Hawley, 1996; Gestwicki, 1987). It is important to note, however, that social class, racial or ethnic origin, family history, age, educational level, parenting styles, and parental values are all significant factors in the success of single parenting (Hildebrand, Phenice, Gray, & Hines, 1996; Rockwell et al., 1996).

One population of single parents that merits special attention is teenage mothers. According to the Children's Defense Fund (2000), approximately a million teenage girls become pregnant each year. Teen moms are less likely to go to college than their peers and 83% are from low-income families. Frequently they choose not to identify or marry the father because of his inability to pay child support (Berger, 2000; Hildebrand et al., 1996). Adolescent unmarried mothers commonly live in multigenerational households and rely extensively on kinship networks for fiscal, physical, and emotional support (Hildebrand et al., 1996). Teachers who work with single teen moms need to be especially sensitive to teens' developmental level of parenting skills, the changing roles faced by new teen moms, and the financial constraints with which they must cope. Find out about programs that support teen moms in the community (DeJong & Cottrell, 1999) and share this information with families at your center. If young moms participate in experiences that aid their own personal growth and knowledge of child development, the quality of family life and interactions with their children will be enhanced greatly.

Mainstream society's view of single parents is often negative and uncomplimentary; thus, teachers and families must work together to ensure that such attitudes do not affect young children. In a family-supportive daycare or preschool, teachers will respectfully gather pertinent information about single-parent families and plan appropriately to establish secure and positive home/school relationships. Figure 5.2 lists ways to accomplish this.

Single-parent households are fast becoming the most common family grouping in the United States (Barbour & Barbour, 2001). Picture books for young children featuring single-parent families are not as prevalent as chapter books, but most realistically portray the range of emotions and situations that these families encounter. A classic story about a single working mother and her daughter is Vera B. Williams' (1982) *A Chair for My Mother.* Saving up tips from her job as a waitress, the mother hopes to buy a chair, "A wonderful, beautiful, fat, soft armchair" (Williams, 1982, unpaged). When a fire destroys their apartment and belongings, they stay with family members until they are able to relocate and finally buy the chair. Sharon, an early childhood student

1. Do not assume that the child's last name is the same as that of the single parent. Be sensitive in your efforts to find out any differences and always use the appropriate surname for child and parent.

2. Offer alternate times for conferences. Single parents often have heavy work schedules, transportation problems, or child-care issues. Find out the best time for the parent to attend and work it into your schedule.

3. Some parents' work schedules may not allow for involvement at school. Suggest possibilities for involvement in center or preschool activities that allow for at-home contributions. For example, parents could develop materials for the classroom (that you have supplied), record stories (send home a tape recorder and book), or make items for the class that are their specialty or hobby.

4. Social activities and informal opportunities to mingle with other single parents are important. Provide information about organizations that sponsor gatherings and/or support groups for single parents.

5. Family finances are often strained to the limit in single-parent households. Help families locate cooperatives that share child care, clothing, or service exchanges.

6. Parents may not know the range of community services that are available to them such as public parks, libraries, health and social service agencies, GED or literacy programs, and public transportation. Acquaint them with needed services.

7. Teachers must be respectful of single parents' relationships with other adults. If appropriate, encourage parents to bring significant friends or family members to gatherings, conferences, and celebrations at school (Berger, 2000; Hildebrand et al., 1996; Rockwell et al., 1996).

FIGURE 5.2
Teacher to Teacher: Involving and Supporting Single Parents

and single mom, borrowed the book from Elizabeth to read to her 4-year-old daughter, Christin. When the book was returned, Sharon had included the following in a thank-you note: "Christin loved it. She had me read it to her several times in the past two days. Last year when Christin was three, as a result of divorce, we were left with very little furniture. I'm a waitress and I save my change for items we want. One of those items was a chair. My daughter Christin went with me to buy it. She recognized all the similarities in the book. Now she wants me to get her that book."

In ***Silver Rain Brown*** (Helldorfer, 1999), a young boy waits with his pregnant mother throughout the hot summer drought for her baby's birth. Longing

MORE FAVORITES

Single-Parent Families

Always My Dad (Wyeth, 1995)

Good-Bye, Daddy! (Weninger, 1995)

A House by the River (Miller, 1997)

Read for Me, Mama (Rahaman, 1997)

Totally Uncool (Levy, 1999)

for rain and wishing his father would return, he keeps busy playing with friends and helping his mother. When at last the cool, silver rain arrives one night the baby is born. They decide to call her Silver Rain Brown. The book realistically presents a single-parent family's hard times and hope for the future.

A book for younger audiences, **Jonathan and His Mommy** (Smalls, 1992) is a short, upbeat story about a mother and son taking a walk around their neighborhood. The descriptive language makes it a perfect book to combine with movement activities. Additionally, the loving relationship between Jonathan and his mommy will bring comfort to children from any type of family. Also for younger children, **Everett Anderson's Christmas Coming** (Clifton, 1991) gently presents a young boy's Christmas without his father. In poetic form, the story begins on December 20 and counts down the days until Christmas, describing the sights, sounds, and activities of the season.

FAMILIES WITH GAY OR LESBIAN PARENTS

> "The most important thing about a family is that
> all the people in it love each other."
> *(Newman, 2000)**

Early childhood professionals are committed to creating classroom environments that welcome all children. Most educators today are accepting of children from various cultural, ethnic, and religious backgrounds, as well as children from single-parent homes. Other family backgrounds and structures may not be as visible to child-care providers and teachers. Gay and lesbian families constitute a lifestyle that may not be initially obvious to teachers (Clay, 1990; Wickens, 1993).

*From Newman, L. (2000). *Heather has two mommies*. (Ill. D. Souza). Los Angeles: Alyson Wonderland. Used by permission.

Most educators believe it is their professional and ethical responsibility to provide a nurturing educational environment for all children, regardless of their family background. The same teachers who work effectively with young children may have strong religious or ethical beliefs that are intolerant of gays and lesbians. The goal for educators should be to respect all parents and respond to them in supportive and caring ways.

While gay and lesbian couples have been part of most societies for thousands of years, only recently has there been strong interest in these couples forming families (Stacey, 1998). Most gay and lesbian parents had their children while they were part of a heterosexual marriage or relationship. Other couples adopt children or take advantage of new reproductive technologies, including artificial insemination and in-vitro fertilization. It is estimated that there are between 8 million and 10 million children living in more than 3 million gay and lesbian families in the United States (Wickens, 1993).

Research shows that there is no measurable difference in the parenting ability of gay and lesbian parents compared with heterosexual parents. The two groups are much more similar than they are different in their parenting styles (Clay, 1990). Most gay and lesbian couples report that they try to make their children's home life as normal as possible, while protecting children from possible prejudice.

Some simple strategies can help children and their gay or lesbian parents feel more at home in your center or classroom:

1. Begin forms with Parent's name/Parent's name, instead of Mother's name/Father's name.

2. Avoid specific Mother's Day or Father's Day activities. You might try making things for special grown-ups in the children's lives.

3. Have pictures, puzzles and books that portray many different types of families.

4. Answer children's questions about same-gender relationships and marriages clearly and honestly. Try to understand the meaning behind children's questions (Cahill & Theilheimer, 1999).

There are a limited number of books on gay and lesbian families available for young children. The authors hope that this area of family literature will expand in coming years as these family structures become more visible and accepted in our society.

Through colorful, full-page illustrations and one line of text per page, Michael Willhoite tells the story of a young boy's weekend visits with his father and his father's partner in *Daddy's Roommate* (1990). The two men are pictured at home eating, cleaning, shaving, and sleeping together. It also shows how both men interact with the little boy, helping him catch bugs, reading to him, and chasing away monsters. The book emphasizes the ordinary aspects of their living arrangement and parenting activities. When it was published in 1990, *Daddy's Roommate* became one of the most controversial children's books in recent years. It was the subject of an editorial in *The New York Times*, and many conservative groups have tried to have it banned from libraries.

Five years later Willhoite wrote **Daddy's Wedding** (1995), depicting the commitment ceremony of the same boy's father and long-term partner. The book brims with the excitement of the gay couple, their friends, and relatives (including the ex-wife and her husband). Like the earlier book, this one shows acceptance of gay couples and the normality of their experiences, and reflects the trend toward gay and lesbian marriages.

Heather, a preschooler, is proud of her two mommies: Mommy Kate, a doctor, and Mommy Jane, a carpenter (**Heather Has Two Mommies,** Newman, 2000). She loves her new preschool, but becomes confused when some of the children talk about having daddies. Heather has never thought about having a daddy. Her wonderful teacher reassures her that she is special because she has two mommies. All the children draw and tell about their diverse families. Like Willhoite's books, *Heather Has Two Mommies* was extremely controversial after it was first published in 1989. The new addition has fewer words per page, making it accessible to even 3-year-olds.

Prejudice against gays, even within families, is discussed in **My Two Uncles** (Vigna, 1995). Elly enjoys going with her father to visit her Uncle Ned and his partner, Phil. With Gran and Grampy's 50th anniversary approaching, Elly and her uncles prepare a diorama to celebrate the occasion. But when Grampy does not allow Phil to attend the party, Ned refuses to come. Elly's dad explains what it means to be gay: "Sometimes a man loves another man in the way a married couple loves each other" (Vigna, 1995, unpaged). Although the relationship the father has with his son and his son's partner is not completely happy at the end of the story, there is a hint that the older man is trying to understand his son.

The books above may bring up a number of issues about prejudice toward gay and lesbian couples that is prevalent in our society. As teachers preparing to work with gay and lesbian families it is important for us to examine our own experiences and fears. By working through any apprehensions,

MORE FAVORITES

Gay and Lesbian Families

1,2,3: A Family Counting Book (Combs, 2001)

ABC: A Family Alphabet Book (Combs, 2001)

The Best of Colors/Los Mejores Colores (Hoffman, 1999)

Lucy Goes to the Country (Kennedy & Canemaker, 1998)

we will be able to show families how much we value them (Springate & Steglin, 1999). Try asking yourself the following questions and discuss your responses with your classmates:

- What have been my experiences with gay and/or lesbian families?
- How can I learn more about the home lives of the children in my classroom?
- How would I greet a mother who has a female partner?
- How would I handle two boys in the dramatic play area pretending that they are gay fathers?
- How would I handle one child teasing another about having two moms or two dads?

MULTIGENERATIONAL FAMILIES

Dequavious, a lively 5-year-old, noticed there was an older visitor in his K–1 classroom. He ran over to her and said in his loudest voice, "Whose grandma are you?" Without waiting for a reply, he ran off to the block center. Although our visitor wasn't offended—and was in fact *nobody's* grandma—his question brings to mind the diverse roles older family members often play in young children's lives today.

The days are long gone when grandparents had lots of wrinkles and white hair, used canes, had false teeth, and sat around in rocking chairs regaling younger generations with stories from their childhood. Today's grandparents are often active, productive, interesting adults. Many, however, are becoming grandparents earlier and are sometimes required to raise another family—their grandchildren (Smith, Dannison, & Vach-Hasse, 1998).

Families in which the grandparents are the primary caretakers are referred to as "multigenerational," "intergenerational," and "skipped-generation" families (Franklin, 1999). Grandparents who assume responsibility for their grandchildren do so because of family circumstances, including death (of one or both parents), divorce, drug addiction, unmarried teen mothers, desertion by the parent(s), mental illness, AIDS, or parental imprisonment (Rothenberg, 1996; Smith et al., 1998). The number of grandparents caring for grandchildren is increasing, in part due to recent legislation.

In 1997, the Census Bureau reported that 7.7% of all children in the United States lived with a grandparent, which translated into approximately 5.5 million youngsters. The same year, it was reported that about two-thirds of the children in grandmother-headed homes with no parents present lived in poverty (U.S. Department of Commerce News, 1999). African American children are more likely to live in grandparent-headed homes than either Caucasian or Hispanic children (Jendrek, 1994; Rothenberg, 1996). In a study of custodial grandparents whose adult children were addicted to crack cocaine, the grandparents ranged in age from 41 to 71, with a median age of 53 (Minkler & Roe, 1993).

Grandparents who are raising their grandchildren strive to provide safe and stable environments.

As grandparents strive to provide safe and stable environments for their grandchildren, complex emotional, social, physical, and financial issues often arise. Guilt or embarrassment may surface concerning the failure of their own adult children to become successful parents. There may be ongoing emotional conflicts in their relationships with adult children that add to the burden of raising grandchildren (Franklin, 1999; Smith et al., 1998). When grandparents assume responsibility for young children, routines are altered, roles are redefined, and personal pursuits are delayed, all requiring extensive and long-term life changes and adjustments. Financial strains are common, stretching retirement or limited incomes to the maximum (Smith et al., 1998).

Children who live with their grandparents deal with a range of feelings. They may express grief and loss over the absence of their parent(s) and guilt because they mistakenly believe themselves to be the cause of the change. Fear of the unknown and present inconsistencies in their lives may be coupled with embarrassment about their family composition, which is different from the norm of their peers. Children living with grandparents may exhibit anger that results from the feeling that they have no control over their lives (Smith et al., 1998). Counseling and/or therapy for both grandchildren and their grandparents may be required to ease the transition into grandparent-headed households.

Supporting families in which the grandparents play parental roles requires special attention and strategies. Teachers need to understand their unique situations, keep in constant communication with the primary caregiver(s), and employ home/school involvement techniques that equally enrich the lives of the children as well as their grandparents. Table 5.1 offers suggestions for working with grandparents who are raising their grandchildren.

There are many books about the relationship between a grandparent and grandchild and others about grandparents living with their adult children and families. Children's books about grandparents as parents, however, are hard to locate. One beautiful, bittersweet book about this family structure is ***Sweet, Sweet Memory*** (Woodson, 2000). Illustrations by Floyd Cooper combine with a simple, lyrical text to describe a young girl's memory of her grandpa, who has just died. When she begins to feel overwhelmed by the loss, she remembers things he used to say to her when they were in the garden. Thinking of their conversations, she is comforted by his belief that "everyone and everything goes on and on."

Amazing Grace (Hoffman, 1991) presents an extended family in which the mother, grandmother, and child live together. The grandmother plays a pivotal role in helping Grace realize her potential and develop her self-concept as a young black girl. Caroline Binch's expressive and realistic watercolor illustrations beautifully capture the love between Grace and her grandmother. Descriptions of nonstereotypical grandparents can be found in ***Our Granny*** (Wild, 1993) and ***Kevin's Grandma*** (Williams, 1975). A delightful and witty book about a multigenerational family, *Our Granny* celebrates all kinds of grannies with af-

TABLE 5.1

Assisting Grandparent-Headed Families

Grandparents	Children
1. Provide a resource list of social services agencies that aid grandparents raising a second family.	1. Consistent access to caring adults should be available. Placing the child with an experienced and empathetic teacher will ease adjustment.
2. Respite care is usually at the top of the list for these families. Make available opportunities for grandparents to have some time alone.	2. Design lessons and experiences that build confidence and trust, and allow for children's self-expression.
3. Schedule extra time for conferences, keeping in mind that schools are much different places now than when grandparents attended.	3. Make diversity a daily theme in your classroom. Plan ways that grandparents can contribute, either directly or indirectly.
4. Revise home/school materials so that they are "family-friendly." Use inclusive language, find out who will be signing important forms and reading notices, and accurately acknowledge the name given by the child to the grandparents.	4. Read and discuss books about grandparent–grandchild relationships.

Sources: *Grandparents as Parents: A Primer for Schools,* 1996, Urbana, IL: ERIC Clearinghouse on Elementary and Early Childhood Education. (ERIC Document Reproduction Service No. ED401 044), and "When 'Grandma' Is 'Mom': What Today's Teachers Need to Know, by A.B. Smith, L.L. Dannison, and T. Vach-Hasse, 1998, *Childhood Education, 75*(1), pp. 12–16.

MORE FAVORITES

Multigenerational Families

Dear Annie (Caseley, 1991)

Dear Juno (Pak, 1999)

Fireflies for Nathan (Oppenheim, 1994)

Grandma and Grandpa (Oxenbury, 1984)

Shoes from Grandpa (Fox, 1989)

Stina (Anderson, 1988)

The Two of Them (Aliki, 1979)

Watch Out for the Chicken Feet in Your Soup (dePaola, 1985)

When I Was Young in the Mountains (Rylant, 1982)

fectionate and comical illustrations by Julie Vivas. Coupled with lively, descriptive language that shows the range of hobbies, jobs, and passions of today's grandmothers, *Our Granny* makes a wonderful read-aloud. An older book, but equally enjoyable, is *Kevin's Grandma*. A young boy narrates the story, comparing his rather traditional grandmother with Kevin's Honda-riding, yoga-practicing, and judo-trained grandma.

Grandfather and I (Buckley, 1994) is a warm story about the love between a grandfather and preschool boy. Everyone else in the family hurries about, but the grandfather and grandson leisurely enjoy each other's company, taking a long walk and ending the day by reading a book together.

FAMILIES WITHOUT HOMES

Waking up in shelters, cars, tent cities, or on the streets, children and families who are homeless face complex and challenging problems each day that require special attention and understanding from teachers. Although there is no typical profile of a homeless family, 9 out of 10 are headed by females whose median age is in the late twenties. Racial and ethnic minority groups constitute three quarters of the families (Anderson & Koblinsky, 1995). The fastest growing segment of the homeless population is children (National Coalition for the Homeless, 1999). In 1997, it was reported that there were 216,391 preschoolers with no home to call their own (Children's Defense Fund, 2000).

Why are families homeless? Frequently living from month to month and struggling to pay their bills, families most often become homeless because of economic problems (Anderson & Koblinsky, 1995). Minimum-wage jobs that provide no health benefits, the decreasing availability of low-income housing, rising food prices, child-care expenses and availability, and the high cost of transportation often combine to push families to the margins of society and into homelessness (Eddowes & Hranitz, 1989). Other contributing factors are neighborhood violence, limited access to medical and social services, and isolation from family support networks.

The effects of homelessness on children are numerous and far-reaching, frequently including one or more of the following: developmental delays, anger, helplessness, fear, aggressive behavior, short attention span, sleep disorders, and separation anxiety. Homeless children experience a higher incidence of illness, infection, and poor dental hygiene (McCormick & Holden, 1992; Klein, Bittel, & Molnar, 1993; Koblinsky & Anderson, 1993). Parents are consumed by daily survival tasks, allowing them limited time and personal resources to support their children emotionally, socially, or cognitively. Infant and toddler care for homeless families is rarely available. Living in shelters, in cars, or on the streets is dangerous and may engender mistrust, apathy, and despair in children. Transience inhibits children's ability to form lasting relationships with peers or adults, allows them no privacy and few personal belongings, and most important, denies them ready access to education (Eddowes & Hranitz, 1989; Klein, Bittel, & Molnar, 1993).

The McKinney Act, passed by Congress in 1987, established the Education of Homeless Children and Youth program to alleviate the problem of limited educational access. It provides funding to state educational agencies to ensure free, appropriate education to all homeless children and youth, including preschool children (National Coalition for the Homeless, 1999). Gains have been made through the funding and implementation of state policies, however barriers remain that make it difficult for homeless children to attend preschool regularly or at all. Common roadblocks are (a) missing or inadequate health care and immunization records, (b) lack of transportation, (c) half-day child-care or preschool programs that do not offer extended day care, (d) residency requirements, (e) lack of proof of the child's age, (f) questions about guardianship, and (g) lack of funding for programs that serve homeless children (Eddowes & Hranitz, 1989; Koblinsky & Anderson, 1993; National Coalition for the Homeless, 1999; Nunez & Collignon, 1997).

Families who are forced to live in temporary or emergency housing cope daily with extremely stressful and sometimes overwhelming problems. Parent involvement should not become another burden, in addition to daily survival struggles. Figure 5.3 provides suggestions for supporting homeless families.

Reading stories to young children about people who do not have homes can increase awareness of others' feelings, help them understand the ways that people help each other, and encourage them to value other people. Lamme and McKinley (1992) assert that sharing picture books that feature considerate and thoughtful characters helps children vicariously experience caring behaviors, thus building a foundation for empathy and altruism. When choosing books about homeless people or families, a primary concern should be the developmental appropriateness of concepts, vocabulary, narrative, and illustra-

1. *Link families with needed services and information.* Establish collaborative networks with health, employment, and social-service agencies. Work with churches, service clubs, food banks, nonprofit organizations, and area businesses to help provide families with basic needs. Arrange assistance with transportation to centers and preschools. Cooperate with shelter directors to share information and resources for families with children in your program and to obtain referrals when new families move in.

2. *Help parents appreciate and understand their children.* Families that are homeless are not necessarily dysfunctional. Although distracted by daily survival needs, family members care about their children. Provide information about children's developmental levels and ways to encourage learning. Share photos and/or artifacts that document children's talents, play patterns, behaviors, and language development. If possible, include parents in making decisions related to their child's development and learning. Plan special programs or classes designed for homeless parents and caregivers. Support groups or mentors may be helpful. Propose realistic alternatives to the usual family involvement strategies. Suggest appropriate ways that parents can help their children at preschool and in the temporary places they live.

3. *Provide a stable, predictable, and nurturing environment for children.* An early childhood center or preschool classroom may be the only refuge from a chaotic world for young children, making it imperative to structure the environment to optimally support the diverse and comprehensive needs of homeless children (Klein et al., 1993). Keep routines and activities consistent to minimize adjustment difficulties for transient children. Furnish quiet spaces in the center or classroom for privacy and personal possessions. Provide opportunities for play—most homeless children have no play spaces where they live. Give careful attention to daily menus and nutrition—children who live on the streets or in shelters do not have daily access to fresh fruits, vegetables, or dairy products. Keep extra clothes and food for emergencies and provide toys and books that children can check out. Develop a routine for children preparing to move to lessen the feelings of loss for them, as well as the grief their playmates and teachers may feel. As part of the routine, make a photograph book of favorite activities, people, and experiences at school to give to children when they leave (Klein et al., 1993; Koblinsky & Anderson, 1993; McCormick & Holden, 1992; Nunez & Collignon, 1997; Somerindyke, 2000).

FIGURE 5.3
Teacher to Teacher: Working with Homeless Families

tions. Other qualities to look for are a positive tone, a problem-solving approach, respect for the homeless characters, and evidence of cooperation and caring within a community (Hoffbauer & Prenn, 1996).

A book that meets many of these criteria is **Fly Away Home** (Bunting, 1991), the story of Andrew and his father, who live in a community of homeless people in an airport. The realities of homelessness—being careful not to get caught by airport authorities, sleeping in a different area each night, and washing up each morning in the airport bathroom—are presented in simple language and illustrations that respect the dignity of the characters. When a bird that is trapped in the airport finds a way to escape, young children will be heartened by Andrew's optimism that he will one day be able to "fly away" to his own home, like the trapped bird.

The Lady in the Box (McGovern, 1997) and **Mr. Bow Tie** (Barbour, 1991) illustrate how children, families, and community members work together to help improve the lives of homeless people. In the first story, Ben and Lizzie notice a lady who sleeps in a box in their neighborhood. Although their mother has warned them not to talk to strangers, they supply the "lady in the box" with crackers, peanut butter, soup, and a scarf from home. When Mom discovers their activities, Ben and Lizzie receive her help in befriending the homeless woman and learn the value of people working together to care for one another.

Mr. Bow Tie is based on the true story of a homeless man who finds his family through the help of two children and their parents. Offering a look at the close, personal involvement of a family in one homeless man's life, *Mr. Bow Tie* demonstrates unique compassion, especially when the family takes him into their home to bathe and change clothes. Vibrant gouache and watercolor illustrations are combined with simple text to show the positive changes in Mr. Bow Tie's life as he prepares to be reunited with his family.

MORE FAVORITES

Families Without Homes

December (Bunting, 1997)

Home Is Where We Live (Groth, 1995)

The Homeless Hibernating Bear (Kids Livin' Life, 1993)

I Can Hear the Sun (Polacco, 1996)

Uncle Willie and the Soup Kitchen (DiSalvo-Ryan, 1991)

MULTIRACIAL FAMILIES

My face? I look like both of them—a little dark,
a little light. Mama and Papa say, 'Just right!'
Davol, 1993*

During the preschool and kindergarten years children are interested in who they are. They strengthen their physical abilities, identify with their families, make new friends, and compare themselves with others (Wardle, 1998). As they inquire about their identities, young children observe their own skin tone and the colors of their friends and classmates. Part of children's inquiry into their identity is based on the color of their skin and other ethnic characteristics (Morrison & Borders, 2001).

Today's multicultural society is also very multiracial. There are more than 2 million multiracial children, and the numbers are rising (Morrison & Borders, 2001). Definitions of race and ethnicity must be fluid today, as many children and adults have three, four, or more ethnic identities (*Meacham,* 2000, September 18). An early childhood consultant observed, "We look at the continuum of skin tones and hair textures in the room and it's obvious that a world full of people have been mixing it up for a long time now" (Lutton, 1998, p. 49).

In reflecting on his childhood as the son of a black father and a white mother, author James McBride observed, "I myself had no idea who I was. I loved my mother yet looked nothing like her" (McBride, 1996, p. 70). His stepfather, godparents, and other relatives who lived nearby were black, further complicating his childhood perspective of his dual heritage.

Some young multiracial children will not be aware of their "differences" until they enter an early childhood program or school. They may become curious about their identity when other children ask them questions such as, "Are you black or white?" The early childhood and adolescent years are critical times in the development of racial identity (Wardle, 1992).

Children ages 3 to 7 are in the process of forming their identities and initiating social contacts in their neighborhoods and schools. The degrees to which others accept them and any labels they may acquire have a strong impact on children's developing self-image. Acceptance of one's own physical characteristics, including skin color, is an important part of developing an identity. Children as young as 2 or 3 can recognize color difference and can apply that knowledge to skin color (Derman-Sparks, 1989). Teachers can provide positive support to biracial or multiracial children as they attempt to join their dual heritage without compromising either background (Morrison & Borders, 2001).

At an early point in your relationship with multiracial families, ask how the parents support their child's racial awareness and identity. How do they handle negative comments directed toward their child? How do they instruct

---

**From Davol, M. W. (1993). *Black, White, Just Right*. (Ill. I. Trivas). Morton Grove, Il: Albert Whitman & Co. Used by permission.*

their child to respond to these comments? How do they hope their child's racial identity will be upheld at school? Teachers may be able to answer parents' questions about children's development and how development relates to their evolving self-concept and understanding of race. See Figure 5.4 for classroom activities to help children build awareness of diversity.

Children's books about multiracial and biracial children and their families provide an easy way to begin the conversation about diversity. Written in verse, ***Black, White, Just Right!*** (Davol, 1993) tells the identity story of a little girl whose mother's face is "chestnut brown" and whose father's face "turns pink in the sun." Using the child's voice, the author goes on to describe types of exercise, foods, pets, and art the parents and child like, so that skin color is seen as only a small part of each person's character.

A child's growing awareness of racial identity is the theme of ***You Be Me, I'll Be You*** (Mandelbaum, 1990). Little Anna admits to her father that she is unhappy because she believes she is not pretty. When she tells her father that she

---

1. Display pictures that represent the variety of family configurations and ethnic backgrounds of American families. Invite as many families as possible to visit your classroom and share family traditions.

2. Provide many art activities where children can mix "people paints" to match their skin tones, hair color, and eye color (Derman-Sparks, 1989; Teaching Tolerance, 1991; Wardle, 1992). Other art materials that come in skin tones include construction paper, crayons, markers, and tissue paper. Children enjoy experimenting with individual characteristics when they create with a variety of art media.

3. Children might make hand prints from one of the materials mentioned above, cut them out, and arrange them from darkest to lightest.

4. With the consent of the children and parents, snip small bunches of hair from each child and paste on separate index cards. Have the children match the hair swatches to photographs (Derman-Sparks, 1989). In one preschool classroom where children became interested in each other's hair, an African American parent invited her hairdresser to the class to demonstrate hairstyles and products she used with her customers.

5. Kindergarten children might develop a graph of the different eye colors represented in the classroom.

6. Read books about children with various skin tones and ethnic characteristics, such as *Whoever You Are* (Fox, 1997), *Families Are Different* (Pellegrini, 1991), and *The Colors of Us* (Katz, 1999).

FIGURE 5.4
Teacher to Teacher: Building Respect for Diversity

Teachers can support children's growing awareness of their racial identity.

wants light skin like his, Father devises a plan for them to look like each other. First Anna smears damp coffee grounds on her father's face to darken it, then arranges his hair in little braids like her own. They smear Anna's face with flour, dress her in Father's hat and tie, and walk downtown to meet Mom on her way home from work. Charming splatter paint and collage illustrations help to convey this story with warmth and sensitivity.

When Pablo, a child of dual heritage, tells his parents he needs to bring a food from his culture to school for international food day his mother suggests that he choose something from the family *panaderia* (bakery). Early Sunday morning he joins his parents as they open the bakery and prepare both Mexican and Jewish baked goods. He decides on jalapeno bagels, which represent both of the family's cultures. Mouth-watering recipes for several of the foods mentioned in the book are provided at the end of **Jalapeno Bagels** (Wing, 1996).

Two Mrs. Gibsons (Igus, 1996) is a loving story of the author's childhood with the two most significant women in her life—her mother, a Japanese immigrant, and her grandmother, an African American minister. Throughout the book, the two Mrs. Gibsons' personalities, styles of child care, cooking, and approaches to life are contrasted. In the end, Igus explains that these very different women are alike in their love for her father and her. Paintings by Daryl Wells enhance this heartwarming story of the joining of two diverse cultures.

MORE FAVORITES

Multiracial Families

Billy and Belle (Garland, 1992)

Black is Brown is Tan (Adoff, 1973)

Grandfather Counts (Cheng, 2000)

"More, More, More," Said the Baby (Williams, 1990)

IMMIGRANT FAMILIES

No matter how long it takes us, we are going to America.
Bierman, 1998

The United States is a country of immigrants. With the exception of Native Americans, everyone in this country is either an immigrant or the descendant of one. The United States has the highest immigration rate over the longest period of time of any country in the world, with about 20% of the population being either first- or second-generation immigrants (Rong & Preissle, 1998). Since 1965, the United States has experienced substantial demographic changes resulting from immigration, changing the cultural makeup of many cities and schools. For example, since 1980, Atlanta has seen a 113% increase in the number of students who speak a home language other than English. The majority of immigrant children today are from either Mexico or Asia.

Children whose families came to the United States voluntarily have an easier time adapting to a new language and culture than those from families that face starvation or political threat if they remain in their country of origin. Although not forced to immigrate, these families have not come under completely voluntary conditions.

One teacher told of a Hmong family who, upon arriving in their new home in western North Carolina, was taken to their apartment by a sponsoring church member. Since it was late, the American man showed the family where things were in the apartment then left. Later, the family members told their child's teacher that they had slept with the lights on all night. They had never had a home with electricity, and did not know how it worked.

While it is essential for children to learn English and the features of U.S. culture, it is also important for them to maintain their home language and cultural identity and practices. Children and their families can learn the tools of the new "discourse community" without rejecting their own community or totally assimilating U.S. culture (Gee, 1990; Hones & Cha, 1999). It is imperative that teachers learn about the funds of knowledge, or resources for daily life that children bring with them from their home cultures (Moll & Greenberg, 1990). Eating and toileting routines, exchanging greetings, and the ways children show respect to adults are aspects of culture important to interactions with preschool and kindergarten children.

How My Family Lives in America (Kuklin, 1992) contains the stories of three young children: Sanu, whose father immigrated from Senegal; Eric, whose father immigrated from Puerto Rico; and April, whose parents were born in Taiwan. Each short story, accompanied by photos, describes how the family maintains cultural practices through cooking, dance, hair styling, playing games, or learning the written and oral language of the country of origin. Recipes for foods described in the book are provided. Suggestions for working with immigrant families can be found in Figure 5.5.

When the World Was New (Figueredo, 1999) depicts a Spanish-speaking family moving from a warm island to a cold northern city. The author portrays the obstacles faced by many newly immigrating families—learning a new language, finding work, locating schools and medical care, and adjusting to a different climate. The air seems cleansed and life renewed when the first snowfall seems to bring the family hope and calm.

Children can become acquainted with the concept of immigration by learning about their own family's origins. Family members could visit your classroom or center to share their own or their ancestors' stories of coming to America. Encouraging families to bring props or visual aids will help young children understand some of the concepts that might be introduced through the stories. Children could then retell the immigration stories through drama, puppetry, dictated stories, or art. In one classroom where there were several Hmong children, the teacher read *Dia's Story Cloth* (Cha, 1996) and invited sev-

---

- Modify the curriculum and adjust materials to make them more meaningful to immigrant children.
- Inform children about U.S. society and help them cope with unfamiliar institutions, such as school and health care.
- If feasible, hire staff members who are fluent in the languages of the families in your program, or provide language workshops.
- Provide opportunities for caregivers to improve their language and marketable skills, which in turn will improve their economic status.
- Help immigrant families and native families learn about each other (McDonnell & Hill, 1993).

FIGURE 5.5
Teacher to Teacher: Working with Immigrant Families

MORE FAVORITES

Immigrant Families

Celebrating Families (Hausherr, 1997)

Home at Last (Elya, 2002)

Journey to Ellis Island: How My Father Came to America (Bierman & Hehmer, 1998)

Painted Memories, Painted Words (Aliki, 1998)

The Trip Back Home (Wong, 2000)

eral Hmong parents to describe their journeys to this country. Mothers of some of the children helped these second-graders make story cloths of their own with glued fabric and embroidery.

MIGRANT FAMILIES

Migrant farmworkers and their children spend parts of each year in different communities throughout the United States, following the crops they help plant and harvest. The majority of migrant farmworkers—90% to 94%—are Hispanic, including 80% born in Mexico (Martin, 1994). Many families move back and forth between schools in Mexico and the United States. The children of migrant workers are sometimes called "invisible," alluding to the willingness of some educators and social workers to ignore them and let them move on to become someone else's problem. It is difficult to keep school records for the more than 2.8 million children who travel with their families in the migrant stream (Duarte & Rafanello, 2001; Velasquez, 1994).

Migrant farmworkers are the lowest paid occupational group in the United States, with the typical family of five earning less than $5,000 a year (Rothenberg, 1998). The lifestyle of children of migrant farmworkers is often characterized by a cycle of poverty, poor health and nutrition, irregular school attendance, social isolation, low self-esteem, limited English proficiency, and high drop-out rates (even among upper elementary students) (Menchana & Ruiz-Escalante, n.d.). If children are needed to work in the fields for the family to survive, that takes precedence over schooling or other activities (Prewitt-Diaz, Trotter, & Rivera, 1990).

Migrant children may also suffer adverse effects from frequent moves, sometimes due to ridicule by classmates and school personnel. They often live in substandard housing, with entire families occupying one or two rooms. Even though they often live close to migrant labor camps, migrant families can experience a sense of isolation. Frequent moves do not allow time for building close connections with other families, schools, or communities. "The constant dislocation precludes any real connection to the society around them" (Duarte & Rafanello, 2001, p. 27).

The Office of Migrant Education is a federal organization that oversees and supports educational programs for migrating children. Each state has special funds set aside to provide education and services for migrant children from preschool through grade 12. There is also a national tracking system to assist with the transfer of records between schools to ease the transition for children. The Migrant Head Start program provides services to children from 6 weeks to 5 years old for 12 hours or more a day. With migrant families sometimes beginning work as early as 4 A.M., some programs run from 4 A.M. until midnight, with parents sometimes attending meetings as late as 9 P.M. (Duarte & Rafanello, 2001).

In communities with high numbers of migrant farmworkers radio stations sometimes broadcast in both Spanish and English. Some radio stations are designed specifically for this population, and have a call-in service where people can leave messages for other farmworkers. Diego has the nickname **Radio Man** (Dorros, 1993) because he is always listening to the radio—when he wakes up in the morning, as he helps in the fields, and on late-night drives when the family is looking for work. The book shows the family following the crops north, from cabbages in Texas to cherries in California and apples in Washington. Diego misses his friend, Dave, whom he left behind in Texas, but through a radio station in Washington the two friends are able to connect again.

My Very Own Room (2000) is based on Amada Irma Perez's own family story. Amanda, her parents, and five younger brothers immigrated to the United States when she was very young. Like many migrant farmworkers, the parents in this story are able to provide only a small home with one bedroom for their six children. The little girl begins to play behind a curtain in a storage closet and dreams of making it into her own room. With help from her mother and other relatives, she transforms the tiny space into a place where she can sleep, read books, and write in her diary.

MORE FAVORITES

Migrant Families

Gathering the Sun: An Alphabet in Spanish and English (Ada, 1997)

Going Home (Bunting, 1996)

La Mariposa (Jimenez, 2000)

Today Is the Day (Riecken, 1996)

Working Cotton (Williams, 1997)

1. Create a positive classroom atmosphere and model respect. Eliminate teasing and ridicule by demonstrating respect for all students and proactively teaching children to care about other children and treat them with kindness. Invite mature students in your group to serve as "buddies" for newcomers.

2. Build on strengths of students from migrant families. Even young migratory children are well-traveled and may have interesting experiences to share from their time on the road and living in different communities. They may also have the advantage of being bilingual and bicultural.

3. Provide an atmosphere and learning situations that enhance self-concept. Ensure that children can be successful at most activities they attempt. Children also feel better about themselves when other children and adults value them. Reading and discussing books such as *Amazing Grace* (Hoffman, 1991) can help children realize that they can be anything they want to be.

4. Build on children's travel, language, and agricultural experiences as you develop curriculum. Units on weather, food preparation, crops, climate, and storytelling are usually relevant to children of migrant farmworkers.

5. Include culturally relevant curriculum by reading books in Spanish and English and books about migrant farmworkers. Have pictures and puzzles that show people from many backgrounds engaged in different types of work (Menchana & Ruiz-Escalante, n.d.; Duarte & Rafanello, 2001).

FIGURE 5.6

Teacher to Teacher: Educational Approaches for Working with Migrant Children

Figure 5.6 lists several educational approaches to working with migrant children.

CHILDREN OF INCARCERATED PARENTS

It is estimated that 200,000 children in the United States have an imprisoned mother, and 1.6 million have an imprisoned father (U.S. Department of Justice, 1997). With the prison population increasing by 6.5% yearly, it is probable that the number of children with parents in prison will increase as well. The number of women in prison has tripled since 1985. Among those entering prison, 6% are pregnant (Seymour, 1998). Children of color are disproportionately affected.

Children who have a parent in prison are invariably poor before, during, and after the imprisonment. Children whose mothers are in prison often experience multiple placements with relatives and within the foster care system (Seymour, 1998). Twenty percent of children whose mothers are imprisoned observed the arrest, and those who did not witness it directly often imagine it in their minds (Child Welfare League of America, n.d.). Even infants are affected, as most are separated from their mothers soon after birth. As of 1993, only three states maintained prison nurseries (Bourdouris, 1996).

The lives of children with incarcerated parents are profoundly disrupted. They usually have complex needs resulting from poverty, domestic violence, parental substance abuse, and inadequate housing. In school or child care these children may exhibit difficulties such as acting out, antisocial behavior, and learning problems. They will probably try to hide their parent's imprisonment from classmates and be embarrassed if others learn of it.

The emotional trauma of parental incarceration can include fear, anxiety, guilt, sadness, depression, and emotional withdrawal. The emotional and financial stability of the remaining parent or new caregiver; the child's age and health; the length of the incarceration; and the amount of support from family, school, and community will affect the extent of the negative consequences each child experiences. Many children experience abuse or neglect before their parents go to prison, and the risk continues when the parent is released, due to the stress associated with re-entering the community and workforce (Seymour, 1998).

Very young children will have a difficult time understanding why the parent left, and why he or she does not visit or return. Since half of all incarcerated parents do not receive visits from their children, and the rest receive infrequent visits, it is almost impossible to maintain an ongoing relationship (Snell, 1994).

Visiting Day (Woodson, 2002) portrays the sequence of events on the day a young girl and her grandmother travel by bus to a prison to visit the child's father. The story is related from the child's point of view, in a straightforward manner, with no details given about the reasons her father is in prison. In the grandmother's words, her son is "doing a little time" (unpaged). James Ransome's sensitive paintings depict warm and respectful relationships among neighbors, friends, and family, while revealing the range of emotions they experienced that day. This book would be appropriate to use in a conversation with a child as young as 4 who is experiencing the incarceration of a family member.

In *A Visit to the Big House* (Butterworth, 1993) 5-year-old Willy is reluctant to visit his father in prison. Mother reminds Willy that he once stole gum and that didn't make him bad, but he did have to return the gum to the store and apologize. Being in prison, she continues, is a way his father is making up for what he stole. Mother, Willy, and 7-year-old Rose go on their first visit to their father in prison. The stark, ominous building with guard towers and barbed wire makes Rose wonder if they will be allowed to come out. The mood lightens when they are allowed to see their father, who is sad but smiling. Susan Avishai's pencil drawings convey the range of emotions the children and their parents experience on their first visiting day at a prison.

Several noteworthy programs in the United States and Great Britain involve prisoners in literacy activities designed to connect them with their children. With a small grant for materials, Pauline M. Geraci, an Adult Basic Education literacy teacher in Minnesota, developed a program titled Reaching Out the Write Way (Geraci, 2000). Male prisoners who participate in the program are first introduced to children's literature and the bookmaking process, then construct books and write stories for their children or other family members. The computer program Storybook Weaver was used to facilitate the writing process. "Writing this way provided inmates a non-threatening way to open their hearts and share their thoughts" (p. 633). Responses from families declared the success of the program. Children were thrilled to have something concrete from their fathers, and read the books over and over. One child memorized the book and took it to bed each night.

Breaking Barriers with Books is a program using children's literature to build and maintain positive experiences between incarcerated fathers and their children (Genisio, 1996). The program is composed of three parts: (a) instruction about children's literature, storytelling, and the reading/writing connection; (b) parent/child visits during which fathers read books aloud, engage children in conversations related to the books, and write or draw pictures in journals together; and (c) parent support groups focusing on journal writing, setting personal goals, and discussing their children's reading interests and

MOTHEREAD, INCORPORATED

Motheread, Incorporated, is a private, nonprofit organization that teaches adults how to develop the literacy skills of young children using quality literature. The organization focuses on groups that are typically hard to reach, such as prison inmates, grandparents, compensatory education students, and families with at-risk children. Family members attend workshops with a three-prong purpose: (a) to improve adult literacy skills, (b) to teach methods for effectively reading to young children, helping them develop thinking and literacy skills, and (c) to enhance communication within the family. Classes may be held in schools, churches, libraries, correctional facilities, child abuse prevention agencies, or public housing facilities. Trainers receive 24 hours of instruction before they work with families using this program. In addition to the basic program designed for families of preschoolers, the organization also offers B.A.B.Y. (Birth and Beginning Years), a program that promotes health care, appropriate parenting, and literacy strategies for new and expectant parents.

Source: "Between the Lines," 2002. http://www.motheread.org

visitation experiences. The instructor responded to journal entries written by the inmates, adding anecdotes about parenting and conveying approval for their work. In addition, seven of the fathers produced an in-house publication of poetry and essays written for their children, expressing appreciation, love, and concern.

Children who have had a parent in jail are much more likely than other children to become part of the juvenile justice or adult criminal systems themselves. Parenting classes, family literacy programs, and regular visits are beneficial for bonding between parents and children. There is also new evidence that it can lower the rates of re-arrest for parents and build relationships that may break family cycles of imprisonment.

SUMMARY

American families have undergone radical changes in recent decades, yet they remain a stable force in society and in the lives of children. It is important for teachers to have a broad, inclusive definition of *family* and be prepared to work with diverse home configurations. When educators accept and collaborate with families, children will be more likely to feel secure and ready to learn. It is the responsibility of child-care programs and schools to shape successful, evolving programs that involve all types of families.

The family is an important part of each child's identity. Teachers can facilitate positive dispositions toward different structures by using the children's books and activities recommended in this chapter and by keeping abreast of societal trends and new children's literature addressing family diversity.

FOR PROFESSIONAL DEVELOPMENT

1. Reflect on your experiences within your family today or your family of origin. Think about times that seemed special to your family and what made them so. Write a two-page paper about one incident in your life that shows insight into your family dynamics and values. If you are willing, share the paper with your classmates.
2. Interview a single parent. Ask this mother or father about experiences raising a child alone. What are the benefits, disadvantages, hardships, and joys? What advice would he or she give people who are new to single parenting? What advice would he or she give to teachers about working with single-parent families?
3. Develop a book list about families tailored to the unique family structures represented in your classroom. Write an accompanying newsletter with tips for reading the books aloud and having discussions about different types of families (both their own and families of the children's friends).
4. Invite adult family members to your class to share activities their family enjoys doing together, such as singing, playing an instrument, crafts, or games. You

might also ask them to tell a story about their family or read a book depicting a family that is similar to theirs in some way.

5. Interview a preschool or kindergarten teacher about the different types of families within her classroom. Ask her what strategies she has developed to effectively involve families, particularly in the area of literacy.

INTERNET RESOURCES

http://www.singleparentcentral.com

"Single Parent Central" is a Web site dedicated to single parenting. The information addresses issues such as positive discipline, selecting quality child care, government resources, a career corner, and money management.

http://www.aarp.org/confacts/programs/grandraising.html

"Grandparents raising grandchildren: Where to find help" is a Web site sponsored by the American Association of Retired Persons (AARP). It contains a wealth of information and resources on legal matters, finances, insurance, and quality child care. Links to special topics are useful, such as traveling with grandchildren, playground safety, and financial assistance.

http://www.pta.org

The National PTA Web site has a link to parent involvement, which gives information on many ways to help involve families. Other topics include current issues such as raising children who are tolerant of others, nutrition, literacy development, television viewing, Head Start initiatives, and more.

FAMILY TRANSITIONS

The family is a dynamic, ever-changing group of individuals in relationship with one another. According to family systems theory, each relationship within a family affects every other relationship (Jaffe, 1997). The relationship between the parents has an especially powerful influence on children. If families generally have strong, positive ties, children can weather temporary discord or crisis with little or no long-term effects. Strong intergenerational family connections can provide a healthy social environment for young children.

Changes in the family—brought about by moving, divorce, or death—may be misunderstood by young children. Parents and teachers often find it helpful to locate developmentally appropriate books on emotion-laden topics to help children learn that others have the same experiences and feelings they have. Books can also provide a model of coping strategies and concrete information about difficult topics.

Bibliotherapy—using books to help people with emotional issues—can assist children informally as they sort out their thoughts and emotions about family situations. The arrival of a new baby, for example, is a natural occasion to offer parents a few books to read with big sister or brother. In addition, questions or activities can be proposed to help stimulate discussion with the older sibling and work through new behaviors that may occur. Clinical uses of bibliotherapy should be left to professionals, but sensitive teachers can recommend and/or read aloud books that promote understanding and insight about transitions within families. Figure 6.1 provides more detail about bibliotherapy.

NEW BABY

> "Hi new baby!" you whispered.
> And the baby looked up at you—
> And stopped crying.
> *Harris, 2000**

When his baby brother was a few weeks old, 2½-year-old Tommy decided he had had enough of this fussy, smelly visitor. He found a small suitcase, filled it with some of the baby's clothes, set it by the front door, and informed his mother that it was time for the baby to go!

The arrival of a new brother or sister, either by birth or by adoption, represents an important transition for young children. Emotions may vary between pride, excitement, anger, and jealousy. Those who have been "only" children soon discover that they no longer have the exclusive attention of their parents. A 9-year-old boy, reflecting on the birth of his sister three years previously, commented, "I felt like a king until she was born." It is important for early childhood educators and caregivers to recognize that a variety of feelings

Bibliotherapy is the use of books to help sort out emotional issues. It is a strategy that can be used informally to assist children as they examine, discuss, and work through their thoughts and emotions about difficult situations that occur within families. All families undergo transitions and experience stressful times. Children's behaviors at school are often active indicators of troubles or transitions at home. Build positive relationships with parents and caregivers early in the year so that if problems occur within families the adults and children will feel comfortable sharing them with you. Some common family transitions that may be eased by the use of bibliotherapy are:

- new baby
- adoption
- children with special needs
- divorce
- remarriage
- moving
- death

Bibliotherapy can be used with an individual, a small group, or the entire class, depending on the topic to be discussed. It is a powerful strategy for helping children work through their feelings about events in their lives, so be careful, perceptive, and responsive in the ways you interact with the individuals involved. There are three components to bibliotherapy: identification, catharsis, and insight. Following are guidelines for informally using bibliotherapy.

Identification

1. Identify the family issue, situation, or problem.
2. Discuss the child's feelings and behaviors with the parents or caregivers.
3. Select appropriate books to use.

Catharsis

4. Choose the most appropriate setting to read aloud—either home or school.
5. Read one-on-one or in a small group.
6. Talk with the child(ren) to help elicit emotions and reactions.
7. Provide opportunities for the child(ren) to express themselves through creative strategies (e.g., writing, drawing, painting, role-playing, puppetry, music, play dough).

Insight

8. Engage the child(ren) in follow-up conversations to help clarify their new insights about how and why their feelings may have changed.
9. Accept all feelings as valid and focus on productive ways to cope.

FIGURE 6.1
Teacher to Teacher: Learning About Bibliotherapy

So you are having a new baby! How exciting! You may be wondering what you should tell your toddler or preschooler about becoming a big brother/sister. How should you introduce the idea of a new baby? What are some ways to help your child prepare for this life-changing event? How can you prevent sibling rivalry? While there are no set answers to these questions, the following tips might help:

How should I introduce the idea of a new baby?

- Avoid breaking the news to your child too early. Seven or eight months is a long time for a preschooler to wait. Try telling your child three or four months before the baby's arrival.

- Make your explanations very simple for your toddler or preschooler. Explain that a new baby is growing in a special place inside Mommy called a womb. (Using the terms *tummy* or *stomach* can confuse children into thinking that you ate something that made the baby.)

- Answer questions in a concrete way when they are asked. Don't go overboard with scientific data!

What are some ways to help my child prepare for a new sibling?

- Explain what babies are like in realistic terms—they are not playmates for quite a while. They usually sleep, eat, and cry at first.

- Show your child his or her own baby pictures as a springboard for a discussion of babies. Also, read books about new babies and their behavior so your child will have an idea of what to expect (such as *And After That* by Jeanne Ashbé, 2002).

- If your doctor, midwife, or hospital has an age-appropriate program for siblings, think about enrolling your child.

- Bring your youngster along on shopping trips for the new baby and let him pick out a special gift.

How can I prevent sibling rivalry?

- Encourage big brother/sister to talk to the new baby while it is still in the womb.

- Emphasize that this is his or her baby, too.

- Spend as much one-on-one time with your older child as possible. Perhaps Mom and Dad can take turns with the new baby so that each can have more time with the older sibling.

- Avoid having the baby in your arms the first time your child sees it. If the baby is in a bassinette or next to Mom, it may not be as threatening the first time. Invite big brother or sister to hold the baby right away.

FIGURE 6.2

Teacher to Family: Welcoming a New Baby

- Engage the help of the older sister or brother in diapering, burping, and feeding.
- Give lots of encouragement to your older child for all of his or her "grown-up" accomplishments.

Even when the best preventive measures are taken, most children show some signs of rivalry. Your consistence, patience, and love will show your child that you still love him the same as always.

Suggested Web sites:
www.aboutourkids.org/articles/siblingtips.html
www.parallexweb.com/parenting/sibriv.html

FIGURE 6.2 (Continued)

are normal and appropriate for a young child. The adult's task is to help the older brother or sister find ways to appropriately share feelings and become comfortable with his or her new place in the family. Figure 6.2 provides information to families expecting a new baby.

In ***The New Baby at Your House*** (1998) author Joanna Cole and photographer Margaret Miller capture the experiences of four families with new babies. Through narrative, questions, and pictures, they acknowledge the complexity of feelings children have when a new sibling arrives. When Molly wishes she could be the baby and get all the attention, the question is posed, "Do you ever feel that way?" opening an opportunity for children and caregivers reading the book to discuss similar reactions. A lengthy note to parents at the beginning of the book provides hints to prepare young children for the birth of a new baby. The author suggests minimizing other transitions around the time the new baby arrives, such as starting a new day care or toilet training.

The big sister in ***Hi New Baby*** (Harris, 2000) reveals the range of emotions older siblings frequently experience—anger, disgust, jealousy, and finally, love. The story is the father's retelling of the day his 2-year-old daughter meets her new baby brother. Charming pencil and pastel illustrations by Michael Emberly show the wrinkled newborn gazing at his sister, grandfather changing a diaper, and mother nursing. The sister enumerates all the things she can do that the baby is unable to do, and expresses why she doesn't like him. "Your baby's soooo boring! I wish it would DO something!" (Harris, 2000, unpaged). On the last page the baby stops crying while she holds him and gives him a kiss.

Elizabeti's Doll (Stuve-Bodeen, 1998) and ***Mama Elizabeti*** (Stuve-Bodeen, 2000) provide glimpses into the ways a child from another culture—in this case, Tanzania—might experience the birth of a new sibling. When her mother has a new baby, Elizabeti wants a baby of her own. She searches outside for something that would be the right size to hold and care for and love. Eventually she finds a smooth rock that she names Eva. Mama helps Elizabeti tie Eva to her back with a cloth called a kanga, and the little girl continues to do her chores and gather water from the town well. In the sequel, *Mama Elizabeti*, another new baby is born, and Elizabeti becomes the caretaker for Obedi, now

MORE FAVORITES

New Baby

Darcy and Gram Don't Like Babies (Cutler, 1993)

Frog Face; My Little Sister and Me (Schindel, 1998)

I'm a Big Brother (Cole, 1997)

I'm a Big Sister (Cole, 1997)

Just Like a Baby (Bond, 2001)

McDuff and the Baby (Wells, 1997)

My Big Brother (Fisher, 2002)

Pushkin Minds the Bundle (Ziefert, 2000)

Rosie's Babies (Waddell, 1990)

Silver Rain Brown (Helldorfer, 1999)

This New Baby (Jam, 1998)

Waiting for Baby (Ziefert, 1998)

We'll Paint the Octopus Red (Stuve-Bodeen, 1998)

What's Inside? (Ashbe, 2000)

an active toddler. She watches her brother while sifting rice, washing clothes, and sweeping the dirt floor of her family's home. When Obedi wanders off, Elizabeti develops a creative solution by tying him to her waist with the kanga.

ADOPTION

> I was so happy to see you that I
> Cried the moment I took you in my arms…
> You cried, too.
> I had been waiting for you my whole life.
> *Lewis, 2000**

For many generations adults have taken responsibility for children not born into their family. In the United States tens of thousands of children are adopted each year. In families formed by adoption, parents and children develop a deep love that Yoest (1990) compares to the relationship of husband and wife, who are not biologically related yet form a lasting bond. "[Adoption] illustrates the infinite ability of the human heart to love" (Yoest, 1990, p. 13). What is important in adoptive households is not how a child became part of the family, but the connections that are developed within the family unit (Giardini, 1990).

Families experiencing the transition of adoption are similar in most ways to those experiencing the birth of a child. Each family member must make

*From I Love You Like Crazy Cakes *by Rose Lewis. Copyright © 2000 by Rose A. Lewis (Text); Copyright © 2000 by Jane Dyer. By permission of Little, Brown and Company, (Inc.).*

accommodations for the new child as the structure of the family changes. When families adopt children who are beyond infancy, the new siblings will need to bend to each other's personalities and needs. The older sister in *Emma's Yucky Brother* (Little, 2001) has always wanted a little brother; however, when her 4-year-old brother moves into their home he does not smile at Emma and rejects the cookies she made. With some help from their parents, Max and Emma begin to understand each other's feelings.

Those who work with adoptive families believe that parents should help children learn about adoption from a very early age. As they develop cognitively, children grow in their understanding of the meaning of adoption. Some adoptive parents overestimate their children's knowledge and understanding of adoption, thinking the child comprehends more than she really does (Keeler, 1996). Because children come to new understandings gradually and conceptualize differently at each stage of development, it is important to revisit important issues again and again as children mature. Children's books that portray adoption as a normal experience and use correct terminology can open the door for dialogue and provide children with vocabulary and concepts to talk about their feelings. It is important to be aware of how much children can understand about adoption at different ages:

1. Children younger than 2 cannot fully conceptualize what it means to be adopted. The idea can be introduced with pictures and simple stories.

2. Children between 2 and 5 can begin to understand that there are different ways of becoming part of a family.

3. Children ages 6 to 8 can grasp the difference between birth and adoption and know that adoption is permanent (Giardini, 1990).

Young adopted children sometimes think birth and adoption are mutually exclusive—if they are adopted they were not born. Therefore, books on adoption should address the concept of relinquishment in clear, simple terms. In *Tell Me Again About the Night I Was Born*, Curtis (1996) uses a child's voice to explain this concept. "You couldn't grow a baby in your tummy, so another woman who was too young to take care of me was growing me and she would be my birth mother, and you would adopt me and be my parents" (Curtis, 1996).* The child narrator in Curtis' book goes on to describe her parents' airplane trip to a distant city where they saw their little girl in the hospital for the first time. The flight home and first night together are poignantly described and accompanied by delightful pictures of a cozy home littered with baby manuals, bottles, diapers, and toys. Curtis based the book on her own experiences as a mother of several adopted children.

In *The Mulberry Bird* (Brodzinsky, 1996), the father bird flew away long before the baby bird was born and the young mother bird is unable to protect her infant from storms and predators. With the help of a wise owl, the mother bird chooses a family of shore birds to become her baby's new family. The message in *The Mulberry Bird* assures children that their birth mothers think of them and love them. "Mother Bird loved Baby Bird all of her life" (p. 43). Although this book is somewhat lengthy for young children to listen to all at one time, it could be read in segments or adapted for individual attention spans.

It is important for all children, whether adopted or not, to understand the following "truths" about adoption:

1. Adopted children are born the same way all children are born.
2. Children are adopted *after* they are born.
3. Birth parents choose adoption because they are not able to care for children.
4. Adoption is a legal process in which the adoptive parents and child(ren) become a family forever.
5. Children and adults in adoptive families love each other just like people in all families (Sharkey, 1998).

Teachers and parents should take care to select books that convey positive concepts about adoption and avoid books that introduce children to inappropriate ideas and language, and books that do not mention birth parents.

Internationally adopted children make up a growing segment of the population of adopted children in the United States. In 1998, more than 15,000 children were adopted from other countries (Adoptive Families, 1999). For these children, awareness of adoption comes early because of the obvious physical differences between themselves and their parents. Although some children may be uncertain about their race or birth culture, most adoptive parents encourage biculturalism and create ties with students or adults from the child's birth culture (Friedlander, Larney, Skau, Hotaling, Cutting, & Schwam, 2000). One parent shared with the authors how important *cultural mediators* were in helping her learn the customs and social behaviors of her child's birth country. Cultural mediators may be community members who have emigrated from the same country as the adopted child and are willing to share their stories and cultural backgrounds with the adoptive families. Some parents also attend support groups with other families whose children are adopted from the same country, and children may attend "cultural camps" or language classes.

Children who are adopted from different countries may enjoy hearing stories about their arrival day over and over. Maya, a 9-year-old child who was adopted from India, wrote the story of the day she arrived:

> My mother was in the shower and the phone rang. She jumped out, ran to the phone, and got the message that I was born. She got excited, she screamed and called at least thirty people. Finally, after four and a half months, I came. My mother was so happy she was crying and I was sound asleep. When I woke up, I wondered where I was. I turned around, looked up and saw my mom and smiled, then fell back asleep.

MORE FAVORITES

Adoption

The Coffee Can Kid (Czech, 2002)

Happy Adoption Day! (Paschkis, 2001)

Horace (Keller, 1991)

A Koala for Katie (London, 1993)

Our Baby from China: An Adoption Story (D'Antonio, 1997)

Over the Moon: An Adoption Tale (Katz, 2001)

Allison (Say, 1997) is a touching story of an Asian child adopted by American parents. When Allison's grandmother sends her a kimono, the little girl realizes that she resembles her Chinese doll more than she resembles her parents. She notices the similarities between her friends at daycare and their families. The facial expressions in Say's paintings of Allison and her parents illuminate the sadness, confusion, and love they feel as Allison first rejects her parents, then comes to a new understanding of her adoption. At the end of the story, Allison asks if they can adopt a stray cat, thus expanding the family to include a new member who needs a home.

Rose Lewis tells the moving story of the adoption of her daughter in *I Love You Like Crazy Cakes* (2000). The story begins in a Chinese nursery, with nannies caring for a room full of baby girls, two in each crib. A world away, a woman who has no child writes to the Chinese for permission to adopt one of the babies. Rose flies to China to be united with her child, and immediately knows that she and her daughter are a perfect match. "When you looked at me with those big brown eyes, I knew we belonged together" (unpaged). The exquisite watercolors by Jane Dyer are a perfect complement in this tender story.

DIVORCE

Each year more than 1 million American children will experience the end of their parents' marriage (Pedro-Carroll, Sutton, & Wyman, 1999). Divorce, and the conflicts before and after it occurs, precipitate myriad adjustments in the lives of children and families. The multiple stresses resulting from divorce combine with other risk factors and protective factors to shape the child's emotional life and long-term psychological well-being. For many children the stress experienced during a divorce is comparable to that of having a parent die; divorce is an extremely painful and traumatic process for children. "The lives of children of separation and divorce are profoundly changed psychologically, socially, and economically. They must adjust to new roles and relationships in conjunction with changes in the family's economic status, neighborhood, schools, and friends" (Pardeck, 1996, p. 233).

Young children are highly dependent on their families for their physical and psychological well-being. Divorce exposes them to enormous crisis and change that they do not fully understand. Toddlers, prekindergarten, and kindergarten children generally lack the cognitive skills to understand what is happening during a divorce and may lack the emotional and verbal skills to express their feelings and seek the help they need.

When parents divorce, children are confronted with complex and often conflicting feelings. They are told that their parents love them, and yet one of them is leaving. They may have believed that their parents loved each other, yet now they are no longer living together. Children between 3 and 6 are ill-equipped cognitively to deal with these complex emotions and may develop irrational or dichotomous beliefs (Cohen & Ronen, 1999). Because of their fear of abandonment, young children may worry that the custodial parent will leave, particularly if they have misbehaved. Some children may believe that they have caused the break-up or may react angrily toward the parent they believe has caused the separation. Other youngsters do not comprehend the permanence of divorce and may try to reunite their parents. Lacking the verbal skills to express their emotions well, preschool children often respond behaviorally to a parental divorce. They may show symptoms of physical illness (such as stomachaches or diarrhea), fits of anger, periods of crying, violent outburst, or withdrawal.

Experts disagree as to the most difficult time, psychologically, for a child to experience divorce. Some say young children are more vulnerable for the reasons just cited. Others believe that younger children are more resilient and accepting of changes in family structure. Regardless of the time in their lives when children experience a divorce, it can have implications for emotional, social, cognitive, and physical well-being. These symptoms usually abate with time and support, as family members adjust to the changes that have occurred.

Teachers need to be cautious not to blame the divorce if a child from a single-parent home is having problems. Children living in intact homes can have behavioral and cognitive problems as well. There can be many reasons for emotional, physical, and learning difficulties other than parental separation (Munger & Morse, 1992). Remember to look at all relevant influences when assessing a child's behavior and learning.

Each child responds differently to divorce depending on age, gender, personality, and factors of resilience. Children will be more resilient if some of the following protective factors are present in their lives: good relationships with both parents, frequent visits with the noncustodial parent, positive self-esteem, an easygoing temperament, role models for positive coping, a supportive child-care or school atmosphere, and friends or relatives who offer warmth and guidance.

How can schools and child-care programs help children develop resilience and support families through the trauma of divorce? Sammons and Lewis (2000), two behavioral pediatricians, provide several suggestions, which we have adapted in Figure 6.3.

The following paragraphs will introduce some books that might be used for bibliotherapy to help children name and cope with their feelings or solve their problems. As they move through the stages of the grieving process—denial, anger, depression, and acceptance—hearing stories about children in situations similar to their own can be very reassuring (Kramer & Smith, 1998).

It's Not Your Fault, Koko Bear (Lansky, 1998) tells the story of a little bear whose parents are getting a divorce. Like many young children, Koko feels sad and confused, especially when his father moves out of the house. Papa Bear makes it clear that the divorce is not Koko's fault and that he does not want to leave his son. Koko's parents have what some would call an "ideal" divorce; they share parenting and talk with each other amicably. In addition to the story line, each page contains questions parents and children can discuss together, such as "Do you ever have feelings like Koko?" Suggestions are provided to assist parents in talking about divorce with their young children.

Often teachers are the most stable adults in a child's life during a divorce. Here are some suggestions for communicating with children and their parents during this time.

1. Be consistent in discipline. While it is important to understand the reasons that children may be acting out, it is reassuring for children to know that certain expectations do not change. Children will feel more secure if they have routines and know what to expect.

2. Help children feel successful. Provide opportunities for young children to help out in the classroom, ensure success in activities, and provide authentic praise and encouragement. "It really helped me when you cleaned up all the dress-up clothes."

3. Encourage children to express their feelings and ask questions. A listening ear may be the secure, safe haven children need during the transition of divorce. Children may be grieving for an absent parent, or feeling angry or confused. Drawing, painting, playing with puppets or dolls and a dollhouse may help less verbal children act out their emotions and come to understand how they feel.

4. Be on the child's side, not on the side of either parent. If possible, help parents focus on the welfare of the child as well.

5. Communicate with both parents and keep them involved in your program. This might include duplicate newsletters, phone calls, or notes about their child's progress. Provide information, such as books about divorce to help them communicate openly with their child. (A good resource for parents is *Vicki Lansky's Divorce Book for Parents*, Lansky, 2000.)

FIGURE 6.3
Teacher to Teacher: Helping Children Cope with Divorce

Good-Bye Daddy (Weninger, 1995) begins as the story of a little boy who is unhappily returning from a visit with his father. As he cries and hugs his teddy bear, the bear begins to tell him the story of his own visits with Father Bear and the confusion of having parents who live apart. The teddy bear's story addresses the topics of mother working hard and having little time for play, adventures, and rough and tumble play with Father on their visits, and the difficulty of transitions after visits with father. This sensitive story told within a story is easily accessible to 3- to 5-year-olds who are undergoing parental separation or divorce.

When Janey's mommy and daddy get a divorce, preschool-age Janey goes with her mother and Funny, the dog, to live with Grandma. In the classic book about divorce for young children, ***Where's Daddy?***, Goff (1969) addresses the fears and issues confronting a very young child in crisis. Fearing that her daddy went away because she was bad and that her mommy might not return from work, Janey acts out her anger by hitting Funny. She begins to cope when her father comes to visit, her mother takes her to see her office, and her grandmother begins spending more time with her during the day. Though somewhat dated (the mother has sole custody), *Where's Daddy* is still an accurate emotional portrayal of a child going through a divorce. Children as young as 2 could benefit from hearing this story read by a supportive adult.

A more contemporary scenario for a child of divorce is portrayed in ***My Mother's House, My Father's House*** (Christiansen, 1989). Cheerful watercolor illustrations accompany the story of a little girl who spends Monday through Thursday at her mom's house and Friday through Sunday at her dad's home. Throughout the book she compares her two homes. Mom's house has seven rooms and many photographs; Father's house has three large rooms and lots of books. When she sleeps on the sofa bed at her father's house she dreams of one day owning a home of her own and living in it every day of the week. Unlike characters in the other books, these parents do not meet, but drop off the child in the other parent's driveway. While the story is positive in that the child tells what she likes about each home, there is also sadness about having two homes. Many children who are part of joint custody agreements could relate

MORE FAVORITES

Divorce

Gracie (Ballard, 1993)

Let's Talk About Divorce (Rogers, 1996)

A New Room for William (Grindley, 2002)

to the situation depicted in the story and might want to share what they like and don't like about each parent's home.

REMARRIAGE

Most children of divorce will also experience the remarriage of one or both parents. It is estimated that one out of three children will be part of a stepfamily before they reach the age of 18 (Jaffe, 1997). Little research has been conducted on children whose parents remarry, probably due to the assumption that children from reconstituted families fair better academically and behaviorally than children living in single-parent families. However, it might surprise those unfamiliar with stepfamilies just how much adjustment is required for the new family to function smoothly. First, the parents must adapt to a new relationship. At the same time, the stepparent may be learning the skills of parenting (possibly for the first time) and trying to care for a child who may resent him or her.

Relationships within stepfamilies are less stable in general than relationships within biological families. However, children younger than 9 are more likely to develop a loving relationship with a stepparent (Jaffe, 1997), making the outlook for stepfamilies with younger children more promising than for families with adolescents. The following books touch on some of the issues, such as loyalty to the biological parent and territorial disputes, common in reconstituted families.

Children as well as adults must adapt to new relationships when parents remarry.

MORE FAVORITES

Remarriage

My Stepfamily (Johnson, 1997)   *Stepfamilies* (Rogers, 1997)

Anna Grossnickle Hines describes her own family's experiences with re-marriage through the eyes of her younger daughter in **When We Married Gary** (Hines, 1996). While some picture books on this topic ignore the children's father, Hines addresses the absent parent in this way: "Mama said he had problems and wasn't ready for a family. She said it was too bad, and he didn't know what he was missing because we are her treasures."* Gary invites the children to call him "Papa," since they already have a daddy. When Gary comes into their lives, the four seem to fit together like pieces in a puzzle, working and playing together, and fitting around each side of the table for supper.

When Cynthia's mom, Inky, marries Harry the shoe store man, the new situation requires adjustments for everyone in the family. **Getting Used to Harry** (Best, 1996) is a light-hearted look at the accommodations children and adults must make when a parent marries. Things just aren't the same for Cynthia—the spaghetti sauce has too much garlic, Harry takes over the bathroom when he shaves, and Cynthia and her mom no longer go out for ice cream together or dance barefoot ballet. When both Inky and Harry start spending time with Cynthia alone, as well as together, the new family seems to come into balance.

In **When I Am a Sister**, Robin Ballard (1998) tells the story of a little girl whose father and stepmother are expecting a new baby. The child asks how things will change when she comes back to visit: "When I come back, will I still have my same room right next to yours?" She is reassured that most things will be the same, except she will be a big sister. Having a new stepsibling is not an unusual experience for children today. This book provides reassurance to the young child in this situation.

MOVING

Learning how to make new friends, and losing friends through separation, are among the major challenges of the early childhood years. Modern families are on the move. Six million U.S. families relocate each year, challenging parents

*From *When We Married Gary* by Anna Grossnickle Hines. Used by permission of HarperCollins Publishers.

and teachers to help children adjust to new living and learning environments (Jalongo, 1994/1995; Olkowski & Parker, 1992). Whatever the reason for the move, and regardless of the distance, changing homes and communities is a stressful event that may require adaptive behaviors. It is widely known that children fear separation and abandonment above all else. Therefore, it seems evident that all children, even those who look forward to moving, may experience some anxiety. It may be that prekindergarten and kindergarten children have the most difficult adjustment to relocation, because they are starting school at the same time (Jalongo, 1985).

Young children view moving as a loss of their home and everything they know, including friends and the people in their neighborhoods. For 3- to 5-year-olds, ***The Leaving Morning*** (Johnson, 1992) expresses the sadness children feel as they say goodbye to their homes and the people they know. Paintings by David Soman show the empty rooms of an apartment and the sad faces of a brother and sister, as well as the fond expressions of well-wishers, neighbors, and cousins, when the family says its final farewell.

Another book appropriate for preschoolers is ***Moving Molly*** (Hughes, 1988). Hughes's knack for telling stories from a young child's perspective allows the reader to see what Molly saw from her basement apartment window, as well as her view of the delightful playthings in the corner of the garden, which her parents call a junk heap. The book comes full circle when Molly, who has been lonely in her new house, sees another moving van arrive; this time bringing new neighbors with twins her age.

Children's resistance to moving is depicted in ***Maggie Doesn't Want to Move*** (O'Donnell, 1987) and ***Alexander, Who's Not (Do You Hear Me? I Mean It!) Going to Move*** (Viorst, 1995). While his parents cheerfully pack and discuss the advantages of their future home, Alexander remembers the people and places he loves and refuses to move by saying, "Never. Not ever. No way. Uh uh. N. O." Simon, the older brother in *Maggie Doesn't Want to Move*, projects his distaste for moving on his 2-year-old sister, Maggie. While Mother packs, Simon takes his little sister to the playground and visits places and people he will miss, telling them all that *Maggie* doesn't want to move. Both Alexander and Simon contemplate the idea of moving in with favorite neighbors and staying on in their old neighborhoods. While Viorst leaves her character still resistant on the final page, O'Donnell's book ends with Simon, Maggie, and their mother learning about the advantages of their new location.

Children are affected by a move whether they move themselves or they are they are the friends who are left behind (Brodkin, 1996). It may take several months or a year for children to adjust to the loss of a friend. ***Annie Bananie*** (Komaiko, 1987) illustrates the emotions experienced by a child whose best friend is moving away. While the book is comically positive and reassuring overall, the ending acknowledges that the child who is moving will make other friends, and possibly another "best friend." Reading this book to a child who is anticipating the departure of a playmate might open the door for a discussion of feelings and encourage a creative recollection of pastimes the children enjoyed together.

To ease the transition of moving, consider these suggestions. First, provide honest answers to questions and concerns. When taken on a tour of her new house, one child showed little interest. Later, when she asked where she would sleep and what she would play with, her parents realized that she did not understand that they would move their furniture and toys into the new home (Jalongo, 1994/1995). Children wonder if all their family members are moving with them and whether they will like their new child care centers or schools, make friends, and have teachers who will be nice to them.

Second, teach children coping strategies and information about the moving process. Early childhood teachers might develop a project or set up a "moving center," complete with boxes for packing and a vehicle that can be transformed into a moving van. Brochures from moving companies, maps, books about moving, and travel games might stimulate creative play and help children express their feelings about their own move or that of a friend.

Third, welcome families who are new to your child care center, school, and/or community. Encourage them to visit your program, provide answers to their questions, and offer assistance as they adjust to the new surroundings. Plan periodic events, such as a class breakfast, to welcome new families. One of the authors remembers asking her daughter's preschool teachers for a referral to a pediatrician and suggestions for painters and carpenters to help in their new home.

Finally, provide a warm send-off to children who are moving away. One family child-care provider took all the children in her home center to a pizza restaurant with an indoor playground to say farewell to a child who was moving across the country. Your plans need not be as elaborate, but rituals that honor children's transitions will help them adjust to changes. Children might make cards or draw pictures for the friend who is leaving and the teacher might send along a few photographs of class activities. These suggestions, along with sharing the books in the bibliography can support both children and families before and after the transition of moving.

MORE FAVORITES

Moving

Good-Bye House (Banks & Evans, 1994)

Ira Says Good-Bye (Waber, 1988)

My Best Friend Moved Away (Carlson, 2001)

SPECIAL CHALLENGES

When a child with special challenges is born, the family not only faces adjustment to having a new member, they also may be grieving for the loss of the child they had imagined. Parents may react to the news of a special child with fear, frustration, guilt, hurt, or disappointment (Berger, 2000). They may face medical procedures for the child, health or adaptive equipment, support professionals who visit their homes, and many years of working with the special education system. Children with severe disabilities require a great deal of time, attention, and patience that can tire even the most caring and dedicated parents. If there are other siblings in the home, they may feel that they are not receiving a fair amount of attention from their parents. Teachers who are sensitive to these issues can assist families in finding respite care and locating programs such as Parent to Parent (www.fsnnc.med.unc.edu) that match families who have children with similar challenges. They can also guide brothers and sisters to support groups for siblings of children with disabilities.

We'll Paint the Octopus Red (Stuve-Bodeen, 1998) is a beautiful example of a family's acceptance and understanding of their newest member, a baby born with a disability. Big sister Emma makes elaborate plans for what she will do with her new sibling before he is born. They will visit Grandfather's farm and feed cows, go on an African safari, and paint a red octopus at an art fair. When

Props enliven the enjoyment of book sharing for children who have hearing impairments.

Father comes home, sad and upset, he tells Emma that her little brother has Down syndrome. She goes through her list of activities to do with the baby and father agrees that Isaac will be able to do them all, with extra help and patience.

A Screaming Kind of Day (Gilmore, 1999) is a fine example of a book that demonstrates that a child with a disability is more like, than unlike, her peers. In the morning Scully wakes to her brother yanking her braids and her mother's impatience. The rainy day at home, viewed from a little girl's perspective, is filled with all-too-realistic behaviors, frustrations, and punishments. After a long, peaceful nap, Scully awakens to the aroma of her dad's spaghetti, a grin from her brother, and a hand held out in love from her mom. The fact that Scully is told by her mom to put in her hearing aids, and that later she yanks them out as a form of rebellion, seems almost incidental to the story. Gordon Sauve's striking acrylic paintings lend credibility to this family story. Figure 6.4 offers suggestions for reading with children who are deaf or have hearing impairments.

Children with decreased hearing ability function across a wide spectrum of mild to profound challenges. Increasing numbers of children with hearing loss can listen to stories using hearing aids or cochlear implants. Sitting on an adult's lap allows for good listening conditions, as the caregiver's voice is near the little one's ear. The lap position allows for best listening and shared attention to pictures.

   One option is to place the child on the adult's lap at a slight angle to give the child a view of the book and the adult's facial expression, gestures, and signs or cues (if these are used). Creative pillow arrangements can maintain a cozy environment, allowing for comfort and visual access. Cookbook stands or similar devices free the adult's hands for signing. Placing the child on the adult's lap allows the reader to reach one or both arms around the child to sign words or phrases in front of the child.

   Styles of book reading should vary according to the child's ability to process information through hearing. There is no need to talk loudly if amplification is appropriate. Naturally expressive reading styles can build interest and meaning as it does for all children. Reducing background noise, good maintenance of hearing aids, use of FM listening systems, and proximity to the child will enhance the story reading experience.

   Books can provide the caregiver who is using signs or cues an opportunity to practice new communication skills. Some books have signs pictured with the object or action they represent. The conceptual signs of American Sign Language are rich in visual expression. Cued speech offers support for phonemic awareness. Rhyming patterns can be perceived and enjoyed visually by fluently cuing the phonemes of poems or phonetically patterned language in books. Props and related experiences enliven the enjoyment and learning of book sharing using either method of communication. Additionally, enactments, mime, gestures, and facial expressions can add to the enjoyment of story reading.

FIGURE 6.4

Teacher to Teacher: Reading to Children Who Are Deaf or Hearing Impaired
Source: Theresa M. Barrett, Office of Education, North Carolina Department of Health and Human Resources

Maria Diaz Strom, a former teacher of art for children with visual impairments, has written and illustrated a charming, vibrant book called **Rainbow Joe and Me** (1999). Young Eloise tells her neighbor Joe about the pictures she paints in bold, swirling colors. Joe replies that he can mix colors, too, in his own special way, even though he can't see. Their friendship progresses until, one day, Joe pulls out a saxophone and makes colors for Eloise with his music—"Long, lazy green. Then violet. Pretty violet that blends back into blue" (Strom, 1999, unpaged).

Where's Chimpy? (Rabe, 1988) and **Russ and the Apple Tree Surprise** (Ricker, 1999) are two outstanding inclusion books about children with Down syndrome. In both books the preschool-age children are sensitively photographed in daily activities with their families. In the first book, Misty has lost her toy monkey, Chimpy. As she and her father search the back yard, the house, and the car, she recalls the routine events of her playful day. In the second book, Russ wishes for a swing set, but all he has in his back yard is an apple tree. He and his family pick apples together and make an apple pie for dessert. After the pie is eaten, Grandpa takes Russ into the yard to see a surprise—a swing hanging from the apple tree. Both books demonstrate that children with Down syndrome are more like other children than they are different.

Another noteworthy book picturing children with Down syndrome is **ABC for You and Me** (Girnis, 2000). The children are shown engaging in activi-

MORE FAVORITES

Special Challenges

Be Good to Eddie Lee (Fleming, 1993)

Handtalk Birthday (Charlip, Beth, & Acona, 1987)

Lucy's Picture (Moon, 1997)

Mama Zooms (Cowan-Fletcher, 1993)

Moses Goes to a Concert (Millman, 1998)

Moses Goes to School (Millman, 2000)

Our Brother has Down Syndrome: An Introduction for Children (Cairo, 1997)

A Place for Grace (Okimoto, 1993)

Russ and the Almost Perfect Day (Ricker, 2000)

Silent Lotus (Lee, 1991)

Songs in Sign (Collins, 1995)

We Can Do It! (Dwight, 1997)

1. Choose books that sensitively portray the child, not the disability, showing him/her in a variety of settings, among a variety of children.

2. The facts about the disability should be correct and integrated into the story line in such a way as to not romanticize the disability or misinform the reader.

3. The book should promote acceptance of and empathy, not sympathy, for the character who is disabled.

4. The illustrations should be clear and realistic, encouraging children to interact and identify with the plot and characters to the fullest extent possible.

5. The plot should be interesting and realistic enough to answer children's questions about the disability and/or promote discussion of the disability. Positive, as well as negative emotions should be included in the story line to present a realistic view of the disability.

6. The book should emphasize that the child who is disabled is more like than unlike his/her peers.

FIGURE 6.5

Teacher to Teacher: Choosing Books to Use in Inclusive Classrooms
Sources: "Using Books About Handicapped Children," J. Greenbaum, M. Varas, and G. Markel, 1980, *The Reading Teacher, 33*(4), pp. 16–19; and "Books About Children with Special Needs: An Annotated Bibliography," B. Lass, and M. Bromfield, 1981, *The Reading Teacher, 34*(5), pp. 30–38.

ties with objects corresponding to each letter of the alphabet. For "C" two girls pet a cat, "S" shows sand play, and "Y" is one child twisting yarn around another. This is a colorful, happy, and inclusive alphabet book. For some helpful suggestions on choosing books to use in inclusive classrooms, see Figure 6.5.

DEATH

> The teacher said, "Maybe Jim needs time to feel sad."
> *Cohen, 1984*

Several generations ago children were exposed to death as a natural part of life. Grandparents lived with the younger generation, and illness and death occurred in the home. Today, people are living longer, but the older generations often live apart from their families. The final stage of life may take place in nursing facilities or hospitals. See Figure 6.6 for a list of books that deal with aging and illness.

In the recent past children were hidden and protected from death. They were rarely taken to funerals, and adults used terms such as *passed*

Changes within extended families also affect young children, whether or not those individuals live in the child's home. The aging and illnesses of older friends, grandparents, or great-grandparents are sensitively expressed in a number of books designed for preschool and kindergarten:

- *Now One Foot, Now the Other* (dePaola, 1981)
- *The Sunsets of Miss Olivia Wiggins* (Laminack, 1998)
- *The Sunshine Home* (Bunting, 1994)
- *When Grandpa Came to Stay* (Caseley, 1986)
- *Wilfrid Gordon McDonald Partridge* (Fox, 1985)

FIGURE 6.6
Teacher to Teacher: Aging and Illness

away to soften any discussion of the deceased. Today most experts agree that it is healthy for children to be involved in the death and grief process (Christian, 1997). It was once thought that children did not grieve. Now we know that because of their immature thinking processes and limited understanding of death, children's grief takes a different form than that of adults.

Children younger than age 5 cannot conceive of the finality and irreversibility of death. They may expect the person who has died to return or simply "wake up." Their limited understanding of cause and effect may lead young children to think that the death was brought about by something they did or some unrelated factor. One child thought that cancer was caused by a person's hair falling out (Christian, 1997). When adults try to protect children from death by not telling them the truth, or telling them very little, children may make up their own fantasies.

Sometimes adults think children are too young to know a person has died and keep the information from them. Charlotte Zolotow's poignant classic, **My Grandson Lew** (1974), tells of a young boy awakening one night to tell his mother that he missed his grandpa. Because Lewis was only 2 when his grandfather died, and the grandfather lived far away and visited only occasionally, the mother thought her little boy would not miss him. But Lewis had been waiting for a long time for his grandfather to come back.

Children ages 5 to 10 are very interested in the physical aspects of death, events that occur during a funeral, and the concrete facts about death. At this stage they are coming to understand that death is irreversible and final. They want to know what caused the death and where the person is now. After the family shares their memories of the grandfather who has just died, the young narrator in **Where Is Grandpa?** (Barron, 2000) asks his father, "All right. Can anybody tell me....Where is Grandpa now?" Children seek answers to their important questions.

Because of their increased understanding of death, kindergarten and elementary children may feel the loss of a loved one very strongly, and may become concerned about their own and others' immortality. An informational book such as **Talking About Death** (Bryant-Mole, 1999) can provide factual answers to children's questions about death and the rituals that surround it.

You Hold Me and I'll Hold You (Carson, 1992) describes a child's experiences at the funeral of her great aunt. Since her great aunt was a distant relative, the occasion became more of a learning experience about the process of death, participating in a funeral, and observing the grief of others. The mixed-media illustrations by Annie Cannon show a family mourning together and a young girl grappling with her understanding of death. Interestingly, the two sisters in this book live in a single-parent home with their father.

One of the favorite things Sam and Douglas did when they visited their grandparents was to watch **Grandpa's Slide Show** (Gould, 1987). Grandpa would set up the projector and focus the slides and Grandma would tell about each slide. Grandpa would say, "Next slide, please," when he was ready to continue. The children respond to the news of the grandfather's death in ways that would be expected for their ages. "Douglas acted silly. He couldn't believe it. Sam didn't want to believe it, but he knew it was true." The text and illustrations provide a succinct description of a funeral that kindergarten children could comprehend. In the last pages of the book the slide show continues, with Mom working the projector and Grandma and the boys discussing the slides. This is a touching book that would surely stimulate discussion of similar events in a child's life.

Often children's first, and sometimes most profound, encounter with death takes place when a pet dies. **The Accident** (Carrick, 1976) is a masterful representation of the phases children pass through following a tragedy, such as the death of a pet (Spitz, 1999). Christopher sees his dog, Bodger, killed when the animal runs across the road to meet him and is hit by a truck. The illustration on the following page shows the driver touching Bodger with one hand and raising the other hand, as if to keep the boy away. When his parents arrive, Christopher hopes that "somehow his dad would take care of things." But not even his father has the power to reverse death. The morning after the accident Christopher learns that his father, acting quickly and using his best judgment, has buried Bodger. The boy responds with anger, but eventually goes with his father to find a stone to mark the grave. As father and son share their memories of the dog, we can see that Christopher has come to terms with and accepted the death. For suggestions on helping children understand death, see Figure 6.7.

Experts in early childhood education and death education have a number of suggestions about helping children understand death (Charkow, 1998; Christian, 1997; Goldman, 1996; Staley, 2000):

1. Keeping in mind their developmental levels, be truthful with children about the death. Be patient; death is a difficult concept to understand and children may need you to explain it to them again and again.

2. Reassure the child that the adults who remain will take care of them. Children are totally dependent on the adults who care for them. When caregivers die, children may think there is no one to care for them.

3. Children grieve in their own way. Young children, especially, are very physical and may react to death by not sleeping or eating, becoming restless, experiencing separation anxiety, or having angry outbursts. If children's questions are answered and adults provide patience and security, these symptoms will diminish in time.

4. Express your own feelings to children. Let them know it is okay to be sad and cry. Model appropriate ways to cope and deal with stress. Joshua's mother was killed in an automobile accident a few days before he began kindergarten. Although he talked about it some during the first weeks of school, it was not until his teacher's father died in October that he began to share his experiences openly with the group. It seemed to make him feel special that he and the teacher had this in common.

5. If children are old enough to behave appropriately at a funeral or memorial service, let them decide whether they want to attend. Children may feel left out and disconnected from the family if they are not allowed to attend. Explain in detail what will happen during the service. One of the books discussed in this section of the text might be used as a springboard for discussion.

6. Help children deal with death in concrete ways by drawing pictures, writing letters, or making a scrapbook about the person who has died. When a second-grade child was killed in an automobile accident, the kindergarten children in her school wrote letters and drew pictures for the family (the father had been a substitute teacher and school volunteer). They also made doughnuts for the second graders "to help them feel better."

7. Be sensitive to the ways different cultures face death. Rituals and responses to death vary among ethnic groups.

8. It takes a long time for children to come to terms with a death. At each stage of development, as they acquire new cognitive abilities, children may need to work through their understanding of death again. New questions will emerge and need to be answered by understanding adults. Joshua (see Item 4) pretended to "bury people" in sand. His teacher would sit near him on the edge of the sandbox, reflecting his feelings and listening if he began to talk about his mother.

FIGURE 6.7
Teacher to Teacher: Responding to Children's Feelings About Death

SUMMARY

All families undergo transitions and experience stressful times. The arrival of a new baby; a move to a new home; learning that a child has a disability; separation or divorce; or the death of a loved one are among the changes young children and families confront. We hope you will encourage families to relax together, taking time for simple activities they enjoy—watching the stars, picnics at the park, sledding, hiking, reading books, and talking together. The bonds that families build during ordinary times help them cope more effectively with change when it occurs. We also suggest that you build positive relationships with parents early in the year, so that if problems occur within families the adults and children will feel comfortable sharing them with you. The books recommended in this chapter can be used for informal bibliotherapy, helping children and families learn about issues and find ways to cope with the transitions in their own lives.

FOR PROFESSIONAL DEVELOPMENT

1. Develop a home living center that incorporates the theme "new baby." What types of physical and literacy props could be included? List some experiences in which you might expect children to engage. How could you facilitate the play, social interactions, and language development in this center?
2. Interview an adoptive family and ask them to share their experiences with you. Invite them to tell their adoption story with the children in your center, if they are comfortable doing so. Replace the usual "Family Tree" type of activities with ones that are inclusive of adopted children.
3. Develop a handout on divorce to share with families. Suggest simple strategies to help children at different ages adjust to divorce. Include a bibliography of books for parents to read (see Lansky, 2000), and list agencies in your community that support families of divorce.

INTERNET RESOURCES

http://www.pactadopt.org

A Web site about adoption, particularly aimed at biracial adoption. It also includes a section on gay/lesbian adoption. A magazine sponsored by the Web site is published quarterly.

http://www.childrenwithdisabilities.ncjrs.org/

The Children with Disabilities Web site offers information about advocacy, education, recreation, and national and local resources for families and teachers.

http://www.umbc.edu/education/programs/earlychildhood/childlit.html

Students in children's literature classes at the University of Maryland, Baltimore County, have compiled a comprehensive list of children's books containing many of the topics discussed in this chapter. Entries are updated as new books become available. A great resource list.

7

DAILY LIVES IN FAMILIES

Tommy, a 3-year-old, lives with his mom, Sandy, in a rented mobile home. Every morning they wake up at 5:30, dress, and prepare for the day ahead. By 6:15 A.M., Sandy leaves Tommy at a family daycare home, where he will eat breakfast and lunch. At 4 P.M. Sandy picks him up and together they often run errands. Their route includes weekly trips to the grocery store, Laundromat, or health department. Sometimes they shop at thrift stores for bargains on clothes, toys, and kitchen items. On warm days they stop occasionally at a park to play, but usually there are more pressing tasks to complete.

At home Tommy watches television while his mother prepares a quick supper. After eating he plays with his toy trucks while Mom cleans the kitchen. Following Tommy's bath, he may watch a little television with his mom. Often he falls asleep within a few minutes.

Tommy's child-care provider has sent home notes informing parents of the importance of reading to their children, and Sandy keeps telling herself she should start reading to her son. They have a few children's books they have picked up at yard sales and thrift stores, but they have rarely looked at them together. Their days seem so hectic that Sandy cannot imagine adding one more responsibility to her routine.

A family's everyday routines, customs, and events depend a great deal on the presence or absence of adults in the home, how well primary needs are being met, and what extended family and community support systems are in place. The daily lives of families are sometimes unpredictable or stressful and never the same from one family to the next; however, most families can enjoy the pleasure that reading aloud brings to their lives.

The daily rituals and routines of family life are often reflected in books for young children. Seeing familiar objects and reading about daily activities brings children comfort and allows them to identify with their own everyday experiences. Frequent readings and re-readings of favorite books about families give children a sense of stability and predictability, help illuminate the daily happenings in their lives, and forge connections between their own experiences and those outside the realm of their own families.

The social nature of sharing books significantly influences emergent literacy development as adults scaffold children's language and conceptual thinking during read-aloud sessions (Heath, 1982; Vygotsky, 1978). During story reading, adults often naturally supply information that extends children's understanding of language or concepts. They may also ask children to point to or name objects, ask questions about illustrations or story lines, make sounds to accompany text, or read with expression (Taylor & Strickland, 1986). Further, the language used in books frequently becomes incorporated into conversations between caregivers and children (Green & Halsall, 1991; Green, Lilly, & Barrett, 2002). Nate's mother reports that after reading Sendak's **In the Night**

Kitchen (1970) one day, she and 2-year-old Nate decided to make dumplings for supper. Seeing that they were out of milk—just like the bakers in the story—Dad was sent to the store to fetch it. As they stirred the batter for the dumplings, Nate began to chant, "Stir it! Stir it! Make it! Bake it!" adapting quotes from the story.

The lives of children younger than 6 generally focus on the home, neighborhood, and child care or preschool. Literature that describes families in these various contexts helps children make sense of their world while introducing new words, new concepts, and new connections. Everyday routines such as playing with friends at preschool, going shopping for groceries, enjoying the outdoors, or preparing dinner take on new meaning when viewed through the eyes and adventures of characters in a favorite book. Allison's mom has noticed that her 3-year-old daughter likes book situations that mirror her life. The topic of the book has to be relevant to Allison. For example, after having her teeth cleaned, Allison selected a library book about dentists. Nineteen-month-old Shay's mom agrees about the appeal of realistic books and states, "Once he has a life experience, he gravitates" to books about similar topics and events.

Sometimes an unpleasant or unexpected event can become less traumatic as children read related books. At age 3, Ary was fascinated with blocks, construction, and building. One evening as he and his family drove through the local university campus, they observed flames and smoke coming from the cafeteria. The experience made a big impression on Ary, and he talked about it for several weeks. At home, he connected the fire to familiar books, incorporating them into his play. He made a fire engine out of blocks and squirted other blocks, a take-off on *Changes, Changes* (Hutchins, 1971). Frequently, he built the cafeteria out of cardboard brick blocks, then made it collapse. Ary often looked at his books while making his block structures, especially *Building a House* (Barton, 1981). His teacher reported that he played in similar ways at preschool with the bristle blocks (Green & Halsall, 1991).

Although seeing oneself and one's family in literature is important for young readers, of equal significance is reading about others whose lives are different. Daily routines and events that are not part of a child's world, but are depicted in books, help young children understand others and glimpse life beyond their own experiences. Empathy and understanding, a broader perspective on life and the world, and appreciation for differences can be fostered as young children enjoy stories that provide windows into the larger community of families.

In the sections that follow, we will discuss the daily lives of families with young children and books that might relate to their experiences. Young children are in the process of "working out what their world means to them" (Pahl, 1999, p. 9). As they observe their communities and interact with the people around them, reading about ordinary families and everyday happenings can provide pleasure, entertainment, and information. Teachers and caregivers can use the recommended books to ease transitions among home, school, and community contexts, and engage children in experiences and activities that support emergent literacy development.

DAILY ROUTINES

The lives of children are centered in the home and family. In a study on routines in families with infants (Jensen, James, Boyce, & Hartnett, 1983), researchers found that the more families engage in predictable routines, the higher the overall adjustment to the expanded family unit. Additionally, the mother's sense of parenting competency increased as families settled into familiar patterns and routines.

The predictability of day-to-day events is usually the first concept about time that young children learn. Children feel safe and confident when they know what will happen at certain times during the day. Toddlers and preschoolers find stability and comfort in the repetition of daily events. In fact, many toddlers become so ritualistic that they "fall apart" when routines change. They may want only a certain color of towel to be used after bathing or insist that blankets and toys be arranged in a particular order before sleep. Books that portray familiar routines will appeal to the young child's need for order and may help families understand the importance routines play in child development.

Children first learn about time sequence as they observe the cycles of day and evening and the repeated activities of daily life. By experiencing these patterns, children gradually internalize a sense of continuance and a concrete understanding of past, present, and future. *Like Butter on Pancakes* (London, 1995) is an imaginative interpretation of a little boy's day on a farm. The poetic form will introduce young children to simile and metaphor, while the illustrations by Brian Karas sustain the mood from early morning until all is quiet at night.

Stunning nature paintings portray the activities of animals from dawn to dusk in Jean Craighead George's *Morning, Noon, and Night* (1999). Through short, soothing narration and large detailed pictures, children will come to know the continuity of life. George begins with illustrations of animals from the eastern United States, gradually depicting fauna from farther and farther west. Teachers and families can help children understand about time sequence through their own daily experiences.

Reciting poetry is a delightful way to include literature throughout the day with a newborn. Even the youngest babies respond well to the rhythm and cadence of simple rhymes. Many poems include simple movements, such as touching toes or gently tickling the tummy, that connect tactile stimulation to appealing language. A charming collection of rhymes for children age birth to 3 can be found in *Hippety-Hop, Hippety-Hay* (Dunn, 1999). The book, which includes poems about familiar activities like dressing and washing, is divided into three sections for each of the first three years. Parent notes at the beginning of each section describe language milestones for the year as well as suggestions for supporting language development and ways to use the rhymes.

MORE FAVORITES

Morning Time

The Baby's Good Morning Book (Chorao, 1986)

Buzz (Wong, 2000)

First Pink Light (Greenfield, 1991)

Flannel Kisses (Crotta, 1997)

When the Sun Rose (Berger, 1986)

Morning Time

For many families, with adults rushing to work and preparing children for school, mornings are stressful times. It may be difficult to convey to a preschooler the need for rising, dressing, and eating breakfast in what grown-ups consider a timely manner. And of course, we all have days when we would simply rather stay in bed than face the world.

Adults and children alike have mornings when they are grumpy or awaken "on the wrong side of the bed." In *Clara Ann Cookie* (Ziefert, 1999), when Clara Ann wakes up grouchy, her clever mother invents a face-making game in which Clara makes scary, ugly, sick, and snooty faces in the mirror. Distracted by the game, Clara does not notice that she has dressed herself (with Mother's help) by the end of the story. When her grandmother read this story, 2-year-old Amy imitated Clara's face game. Older children might act out the sequence of events, including both faces and dressing.

Sunshine (Omerod, 1981) is about a preschooler rising in the morning, waking her parents, watching Daddy shave, and helping to prepare breakfast. This wordless picture book entices children to tell their own stories to accompany the pictures. Looking at sequential pictures in storybooks also introduces story sequence, an important reading concept.

Evening Time

Most caregivers have struggled with putting reluctant toddlers or preschoolers to sleep at night. The predictability of a nighttime routine can help calm a restless youngster after an active day of play. Reading quiet stories or singing with children before they sleep have become cherished rituals in many families. Books that depict evening time for baby animals or children may support the goal of a tranquil bedtime.

Reading quiet stories or singing with children before they go to bed has become a cherished ritual in many families. One young mother calls this special routine "cuddle time."

The succession of activities children go through as they prepare for bed is depicted in ***A-Hunting We Will Go*** (Kellogg, 1998). Preschool and kindergarten children will surely love Kellogg's energetic and detailed animal pictures that illuminate the new verses for an old folksong. Some children who may need a bit more peaceful text at bedtime will be lulled to sleep by the tranquil illustrations and soothing verses in ***Little Donkey Close Your Eyes*** (Brown, 1995) or ***Time for Bed*** (Fox, 1993), which depict animal and human mothers putting their babies to bed.

Many young children have special toys that help them make the transition from active days to restful sleep. ***Where's Chimpy?*** (Rabe, 1988) is the story of Misty and her father hunting for a stuffed chimpanzee at bedtime. Photographs are interspersed to represent Misty's recollections of the day as she searches the house, yard, and car for her missing toy.

Hush! (Ho, 1996), a Thai lullaby, portrays a mother searching for and quieting the nearby animals who might disturb her baby's sleep. The cadence, repetition of phrases, and unusual animal sounds appeal to toddlers who are rapidly acquiring language. From the age of 1 Grace asked for the book by

MORE FAVORITES

Evening Time

And If the Moon Could Talk (Banks, 1998)

Asleep, Asleep (Ginsburg, 1992)

Bayou Lullaby (Applet, 1995)

Bearsie Bear and the Surprise Sleep-over Party (Waber, 1997)

Bedtime! (Swain, 1999)

Bedtime (Warnick, 1998)

Bernard's Nap (Goodman, 1999)

The Boy Who Wouldn't Go to Bed (Cooper, 1997)

Cowboy Baby (Heap, 1998)

Cowboy Dreams (Applet, 1999)

Golden Bear (Young, 1992)

Good Night, Gorilla (Rathman, 1995)

Goodnight Moon (Brown, 1947)

Grandfather Twilight (Burger, 1984)

I See the Moon and the Moon Sees Me (London, 1996)

Laura Charlotte (Galbraith, 1990)

Mad Summer Night's Dream (Brown, 1998)

Moonlight (Ormerod, 1982)

The Night the Moon Blew Kisses (Manual, 1996)

Sleepy-O! (Ziefert, 1997)

Some Babies (Schwartz, 2000)

Tell Me Something Happy Before I Go to Sleep (Dunbar, 1998)

10 Minutes till Bedtime (Rathman, 2000)

Time for Bed (Fox, 1993)

Treasure Nap (Havill, 1992)

Tucking Mommy In (Loh, 1987)

Tuck-Me-In Tales: Bedtime Stories from Around the World (MacDonald, 1996)

When I'm Sleepy (Howard, 1985)

---

name, seeming to enjoy the way her grandmother pronounced, "hush" with quiet emphasis throughout the story. At 20 months, as Grace listened to the story, she picked up a doll and said, "Baby's sleeping."

Parents who remember being rocked to sleep with lullabies but can't seem to remember the words to the tunes will enjoy **The Baby's Bedtime Book** by Kay Chorao (1984). More energetic rhymes can be found at the beginning of the book followed by several about reluctance to sleep, and finally some that depict little children and animals drifting off into slumber. The soft blues, greens, and lavenders of the illustrations are soothing and restful. After hearing the poems for several months, Emily began to adapt them. She rocked gently in her little rocker and sang, "Sleep my mommy and peace attend thee, all through the night."

Teachers are often asked for advice about children's developmental issues, such as fear of the dark or monsters. There are classic as well as contemporary books for young children in which a child overcomes fears. *Can't You Sleep, Little Bear?* (Waddell, 1988) presents the age-old issue of a child who has trouble going to sleep because of fear of the dark. When Big Bear lights three lanterns and Little Bear is still afraid of the dark outside, they go together into the night and see the bright, full moon and twinkling stars.

Developmental Milestones and Challenges

Children are continually growing and developing, as each new stage brings changes in the way they move, think, socialize, and behave. Each period in the child's life cycle can put new stresses and strains on relationships with siblings and caregivers. Children come to understand themselves in new ways as they grow and develop.

Sometimes it seems that each day with a young child brings developmental changes. In reality this is probably true, although the changes may not always be apparent on a daily basis. Babies lift their heads, respond to familiar faces, begin to roll over, start cooing and babbling, sit, pull up on furniture, follow simple directions, and finally walk and talk. In between these more notable milestones there are myriad other achievements that cause parents and grandparents to believe their baby is the most clever child ever.

Oh, Baby (Stein, 1993) shows the sequence of infant development, including initial reflexes. Charming photographs by Holly Anne Shelowitz capture the facial expressions, palmar reflex, walking reflex, nursing, and bathing of newborns. Older babies are pictured exploring Mother's pocketbook, crawling, and playing with pots and pans. The informative text and delightful photos make it appropriate for new siblings, toddlers, and even first-time parents. Crayon outlines around the photos and borders on each page add to the appeal of the book.

In *Step by Step,* Bruce McMillan (1987) chronicles the physical development of a baby from 4 months to 14 months. Major motor achievements, such as rolling over, sitting, standing, climbing, walking, and running are labeled with one or two words and depicted by large colored photographs. Young children who are in the process of accomplishing some of these developmental milestones themselves will enjoy seeing what the baby in the pictures can do and practicing the actions they observe.

A lively look at growing up—from the worldly viewpoint of a 4-year-old—is given in *When I Was Little: A Four-Year-Old's Memoir of Her Youth* (Curtis, 1993). The young narrator compares with obvious delight her numerous accomplishments as a 4-year-old, versus her inability to do much of anything when she was a baby. The text is wonderful and convincingly childlike, but it is the illustrations that make the book irresistible. Laura Cornell's expressionistic pictures almost dance off the page with the full range of emotions experienced by an active 4-year-old who considers herself to be very grown up. She goes to nursery school; eats pizza, noodles, fruit, and Cheetos; is helpful to her mom; and can paint her toenails pink. Preschool teachers and parents could use this book in many ways to encourage self-esteem and pride in oneself.

For many families, potty learning (or training) can be one of the most challenging developmental issues in the preschool years. Information abounds in books, on the Internet, and from well-meaning relatives and friends. Sometimes it is hard for new parents to sort through all the different advice they may receive. A few facts can guide new parents as they help their children with this process. Basically, children are not physiologically ready for voluntary elimination until at least age 18 months, with most children learning to use the toilet sometime between their second and third birthdays. The best way for parents to tell if their son or daughter is ready is by looking for clues from the child: understanding the meaning of the family's words for elimination, interest in the potty chair, and controlling the time of urination or bowel movements.

Reading books about potty learning will introduce language and concepts related to this new skill. When Lila was learning to use the potty, her mother and older sisters read ***Once Upon a Potty: Girl*** (Frankel, 1999) to her "several hundred times." Lila delighted in being smarter than Prudence, the book character, who thought her new potty might be a flower pot, a hat, or a

MORE FAVORITES

Potty Learning

Max's Potty (Ziefert, 1999)

My Big Boy Potty (Cole, 2000)

My Big Girl Potty (Cole, 2000)

Once Upon a Potty: Boy (Frankel, 1999)

Once Upon a Potty: Girl (Frankel, 1999)

The Potty Book—For Boys (Capucilli, 2000)

The Potty Book—For Girls (Capucilli, 2000)

Potty Time (Van Genechten, 2001)

The Princess and the Potty (Lewison, 1998)

Sara's Potty (Ziefert, 1999)

birdbath. The colorful, cartoonlike illustrations show that children do not learn to control elimination all at once. Success is gradual, but eventually, with patience and loving persistence, boys and girls do master this step toward independence. (**Once Upon a Potty: Boy**, Frankel, 1999, tells the identical story with a character named Joshua.)

Jason's favorite book about potty training happened to be **The Princess and the Potty** (Levison, 1998). Children of both sexes will delight in this humorous tale of a little princess who cannot be persuaded to renounce her diapers. While the king, queen, and court bring forth musical, polka dot, and glow-in-the-dark potties, the little princess resists. Even a royal demonstration by the king and queen cannot convince her of the benefits. Finally, in her own good time, the little princess decides that she would prefer fancy, lace pantalettes to diapers; and using the potty begins to please her. Told with light-hearted frivolity, this book conveys to parents that, in the end, it is the children who will decide when they are ready to use the potty.

In **Potty Time** (Van Genechten, 2000), a menagerie of animals all seem pleased to be sitting on potties just the right size for their bottoms. On the next to the last page a grinning toddler named Joe sits on his own orange potty, toilet paper and big boy pants nearby. On the final spread we witness little Joe congratulating himself on his new accomplishment. Boldly colored illustrations of Joe and the animals are innovatively painted with acrylics on newspaper.

Young children who have not yet learned to control their anger are sometimes frightened by their own uncontrollable feelings. **When Sophie Gets Angry—Really, Really, Angry . . .** (Bang, 1999) accurately depicts the strong emotions preschoolers sometimes experience, but may not be able to understand or handle. When Sophie's sister grabs her toy gorilla, her mother confirms that it is sister's turn. Sophie's explosion of anger is illustrated with pulsating red, orange, yellow, and purple acrylic paintings that quiver with rage. Sophie runs into her yard then walks and cries until she finally calms herself. Nestled in the arms of a tree overlooking a quiet blue lake, Sophie relaxes. On the last pages, she returns home to the welcoming arms of her family, and all is back to normal. Bang's portrayal of Sophie's experience may help children consider their own feelings and develop ways to cope with and express them appropriately.

The mother and daughter in **Harriet, You'll Drive Me Wild** (Fox, 2000) have a tender and tumultuous relationship, typical to families with toddlers. Energetic little Harriet's only flaw seems to be that she acts her age, again and again, throughout the day at home with her mother. When 3-year-old Grace Marie hears the story, she insists that her mother insert her name instead of Harriet's throughout the text, making it, "Grace Marie my *darling* child. Grace Marie you'll drive me wild." Obviously this is a book to which toddlers, preschoolers, and parents can relate. During the preschool years most children acquire minor illnesses about a half-dozen times a year. Children are more prone to illnesses than adults because they have been exposed to fewer viruses and bac-

The Sick Day (MacLachlan, 2001) begins with Emily complaining of a stomachache in her head and a headache in her throat. Her loving and patient father, who stays home to care for her, spends most of the morning hunting vainly for the lost thermometer and bringing the toys his young daughter demands. After a bout with an upset stomach, father brings clear soup, which Emily rejects because there is nothing floating in it. To appease her, father plops in a plastic giraffe! The next morning Emily is feeling better, but father is pictured next to her in bed with the found thermometer in his mouth, surrounded by Emily's toys and books.

Vera Rosenberry recalls a childhood stint with chicken pox in *When Vera Gets Sick* (1998). The frightening parts of illness (such as seeing scary monsters when she had a fever) as well as the warm memories of her father bringing flowers and playing Chinese checkers with her sister, are portrayed with charming ink and gouache illustrations. After several days in the sick room (reminiscent of the 1950s), Vera finally feels better and is pictured on the last page turning somersaults outside.

Families might find the following books of interest when their children are feeling "under the weather."

Germs Make Me Sick (Berger, 1985) New York: HarperCollins. (Ill. M. Hafner) (K)

Doctor Maisy (Cousins, 2001) Cambridge, MA: Candlewick Press. (I, T, pre-K)

The Sick Day (MacLachlan, 2001) New York: Random House. (Ill. J. Dyer) (pre-K, K)

When Vera Was Sick (Rosenberry, 1998) New York: Henry Holt. (pre-K, K)

Felix Feels Better (Wells, 2001) Cambridge, MA: Candlewick Press. (T, pre-K)

FIGURE 7.1
When Children Get Sick

teria, and have not yet built up resistance to them. We have suggested some books about childhood illnesses in Figure 7.1.

FOOD AND COOKING

Young children find such joy in eating! As you watch an infant nursing, a toddler savoring finger foods, or an older preschooler relishing dinner after a day at play, their pleasure and interest in food is obvious. Involving children in food preparation can have far-reaching values for many areas of development and learning. Through cooking children can acquire good nutritional habits, learn math skills such as measurement and numeration, expand their vocabularies, and develop emergent literacy by beginning to recognize print on labels and in recipes. Fine motor coordination is improved as children stir, pour, blend, and mix ingredients. Cooking also provides a sense of accomplishment in completing a task from beginning to end and enjoying the results.

Even very young children can help prepare food. Cooking provides a sense of accomplishment in completing a task and heightens enjoyment of the results.

Scientific knowledge can be gained by observing the effects of heating and cooling on substances and transformations from one state to another. Children can see how foods change when they are mixed together, separated (e.g., eggs), whipped (e.g., cream or meringue) or dried (e.g., fruit). They learn about cause and effect when they note how their actions change ingredients in a recipe, and they learn about prediction when they are asked to guess what they think will happen during a cooking experience.

The foods children eat reflect cultural and family conventions, as well as individual preferences. ***Yoko,*** by Rosemary Wells (1998), portrays the variety of foods eaten by children in our multicultural society. Yoko's school lunch consists of traditional Japanese fare—steamed rice in a bamboo mat, sushi, shrimp, and seaweed. When classmates tease Yoko because of her lunch, the teacher decides to host an international food day. Families could use this story as a springboard for trying new foods, as well as talking about their own cultural diet.

As children, many of us heard stories about food in traditional tales such as "The Little Red Hen." Did you ever wonder what became of the Little Red Hen's baby chicks? We have it on the best of authority that they grew up and had children of their own. One of the grandchildren of Little Red Hen is Rooster, the star of ***Cook-a-Doodle-Doo!*** by Jan Stevens and Susan Stevens

Crummel (1999). After many comical mishaps caused by homophones ("flower" or "flour") and malapropisms (beating an egg with a baseball bat), the cake is baked and eaten. Sidebars provide interesting information for older readers and clarify some of the cooking phrases such as "cut in" the butter.

While reading *Cook-a-Doodle-Doo!* to 2½-year-old Maggie, her mom asked if the red flower Turtle held in his hand was the right kind of "flour" for the cake. Having baked with Mom before, Maggie knew it was not. She felt clever about finding other mistakes the animal helpers in the story almost made. When Maggie and Mom decided to make strawberry shortcake using the recipe at the back of the book, Maggie brought her Sesame Street toys Big Bird, Zoe, and Elmo to the kitchen to help cook.

Children want to do grown-up things and enjoy activities that they can do *with* their parents or caregivers. If adults have been working all day and children have been in child care, preparing a meal together can be one way to reconnect. Figure 7.2 describes how an Even Start teacher and her preschoolers published their own cookbook. Two of their recipes are illustrated on pages 200 and 221. There are a number of noteworthy cookbooks for children, as well as many books that mention food or cooking within a

---

Elizabeth Childers, a teacher in an Even Start classroom, describes how her preschoolers became interested in recipes and decided to publish a cookbook:

We were talking about ordering (first, second, third, etc.) and we read *How to Make a Mudpie* (Williams, 1995). The adult classes were talking about recipes and cooking, so my paraprofessional and I had brought cookbooks for them to use. The children became very interested in the cookbooks, too, and started "reading" them together. We then began talking about the order of cooking, looking at the recipes. We made fruit smoothies together and afterwards, we wrote down what we had done. We also made and tasted banana bread, then wrote the recipe. At this point, the children were getting much better about sequencing and adding details.

We were emphasizing the fact that we can write down the recipes so that if we want to make the food later we could read the recipes. Isai, one of our Hispanic preschoolers, suggested that we write down all the recipes in a "book with the recipe papers for to cook!" Each child chose a food, drew pictures, and talked about it. We found that not all the children could express themselves verbally about the foods, so we did some recipes as a group.

We sent home a letter (in both English and Spanish) asking for recipes to be added to the cookbook. One of the parents translated Spanish to English and English to Spanish, so we would have the recipes in both languages. Each child wrapped their cookbook and addressed it to their family. I added their self-portraits and their names. The whole process, from reading *How to Make a Mudpie* to the completed cookbook, took three or four weeks.

FIGURE 7.2
Teacher to Teacher: A Cookbook Emerges

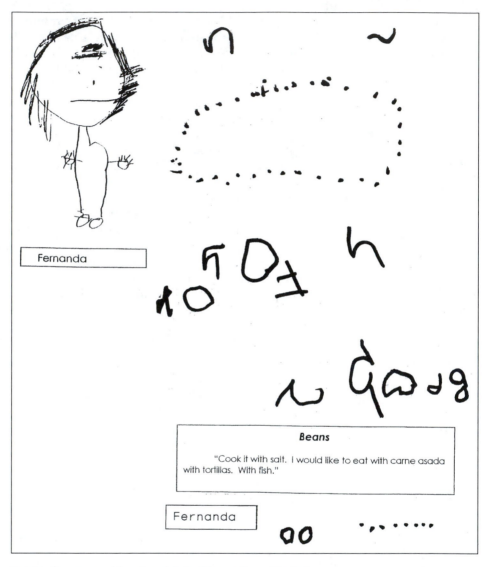

Fernanda

Beans

"Cook it with salt. I would like to eat with carne asada with tortillas. With fish."

Fernanda

Entries from a cookbook published by an Even Start class.

story and have recipes at the end. ***Pretend Soup and Other Real Recipes*** (1994) was written by Mollie Katzen and Ann Henderson, both of whom are experienced at cooking with children. Their combined talents have resulted in a delightful compilation of recipes kids will love to make and eat. Each section includes notes to the grown-up, hints, safety tips, a printed recipe, a pictorial recipe in a sequence, and praise or comments for young cooks. Some sure successes from *Pretend Soup* include noodle pudding, bagel faces, number salad, and hide-and-seek muffins. Foreword material for caregivers includes

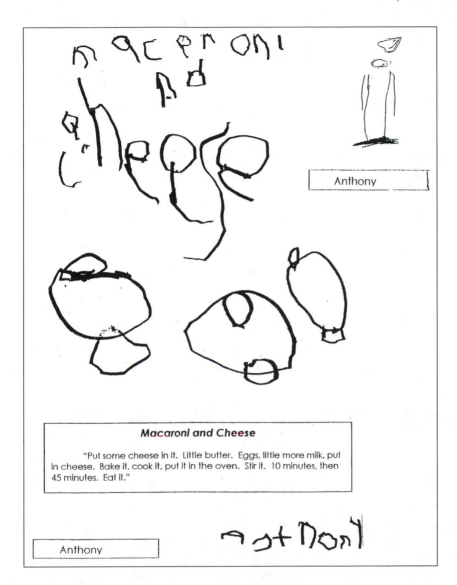

Macaroni and Cheese

"Put some cheese in it. Little butter. Eggs, little more milk, put in cheese. Bake it, cook it, put it in the oven. Stir it. 10 minutes, then 45 minutes. Eat it."

Anthony

information on the benefits of cooking with children and hints for managing cooking experiences.

The photo illustrations in ***Eating Fractions*** (McMillan, 1991) are absolutely dazzling. Child and adult readers will want to try all the mouth-watering delicacies pictured in the book. Complete recipes are provided at the end. While the book is designed to illustrate simple fractions (whole, halves, thirds, fourths), it also shows children helping to prepare and enjoy healthful foods such as bananas, corn, muffins, strawberry pie, and pizza.

MORE FAVORITES

Food and Cooking

Book Cooks: Literature-Based Classroom Cooking (Bruno, 1991)

Bread and Jam for Frances (Hoban, 1964)

A Cow, a Bee, a Cookie, and Me (Hooper, 1997)

Dumpling Soup (Rattigan, 1993)

Food and Recipes of Native Americans (Erdosh, 1997)

How to Make a Mudpie (Williams, 1995)

In the Night Kitchen (Sendak, 1970)

Kinder Krunchies (Jenkins, 1997)

Let's Eat (Zamorano, 1996)

Love as Strong as Ginger (Look, 1999)

The Mash and Smash Cookbook (Buck-Murray, 1998)

AT PLAY

As modern families rush from work and school to lessons, shopping, meetings, and other obligations, caregivers may lose sight of the importance of imaginative play in the lives of young children (Fortson & Reiff, 1995). The various forms of play are important for all areas of development—social, emotional, cognitive, and physical. As they play, children learn to negotiate and cooperate with others; work through frustrations; acquire concepts significant for later school achievement; and develop coordination, strength, and dexterity.

Through play, children develop a concept of "who they are, and who they are not" (Hendrick, 1998, p. 39). By taking on roles such as firefighter, mother, baby, or doctor, they are defining their own identity, as well as learning to take the perspective of someone else. Children also come to differentiate between reality and fantasy as they enter the world of "let's pretend." Imaginative thought will help children visualize material they will later read in literature and history, and will serve as a basis for original storytelling and writing.

Many books show children's creativity as they play alone or with others. Using a photo-collage technique, Nina Crews has created two fascinating books based on childhood adventures. In **One Hot Summer Day** (1995), a little girl dressed in lavender and pink chases her shadow, draws sidewalk pictures in the shade, and eats purple popsicles before fat drops of rain cool her. The two girls in **You Are Here** (1998) devise a magic game to keep themselves from boredom on a rainy day. The collage design of the book effectively illustrates the girls, the size of a teaspoon, taking a ride in a toy airplane. When the cat becomes a monster the girls invent magic chants to keep him at bay. On Mom's return, the spell is broken, the sun is out, and they all go to the park.

Even children as young as 2 can gain ideas for imitation and play from the books they hear. Nate's mother reported that **Pretend You're a Cat** (Pinkney, 1996) was just the right book to encourage Nate's pleasure in pretending to be animals. During a bath, Nate sometimes makes fish faces and every now and then he tries to balance a ball on his nose like the seal in the story!

Recent research on brain development emphasizes the importance of touch and massage for optimal mental development (Shore, 1997). A hilarious story that encourages adult–child play and positive touching is William Steig's **Pete's a Pizza** (1998). One rainy, boring day Father thinks he might cheer Pete up by making him into a pizza. He places Pete on the table, rolls him, twirls him, stretches him like dough, and adds checkers for pepperoni and paper scraps for cheese. Then Father pops Pete into the oven (sofa). After 2-year-old Grace's grandma read her *Pete's a Pizza*, her mom "made" her into a pizza by stretching, twisting, and gently patting her as she retold the story. Grace loved the book and enactment so much that she begged, "More, more!" until Mom repeated the play.

One goal of children's play is learning to enter an existing play scenario and imagine a role for oneself within that situation. Children who are identified as play leaders (Trawick-Smith, 1994) are very skilled at observing play situations and negotiating and creating roles for themselves that enhance other children's characters. In **Sand Castle,** a cumulative story by Brenda Shannon Yee (1999), one child starts building a sand castle at the lake and is soon joined by other children, each bringing a toy (e.g., bucket, spoon, rake) and an

MORE FAVORITES

At Play

It's Just Me, Emily (Grossnickle, 1987)

Madlenka's Dog (Sis, 2002)

The Magic Moonberry Jump Ropes (Hru, 1996)

Mud Is Cake (Ryan, 2002)

My Steps (Derby, 1996)

Play (Morris, 1998)

Stella & Roy (Wolff, 1993)

Tom and Pippo Go for a Walk (Oxenbury, 1998)

What Shall We Play? (Heap, 2002)

idea for elaborating on the castle (e.g., moat, road, wall). The children work cooperatively on their separate parts of the joint project until called away by their families. Their last shared activity is to jump into the sandcastle together and knock it down.

OUTDOORS

Watch a child in the yard—she stoops down close to the ground, digs around a minute with her fingers, and triumphantly holds up a tiny beetle in her grubby hand. Think about how children creatively incorporate mud, pine cones, bark, acorns, leaves, grass clippings, and other natural objects into their outdoor play. Take a walk with children and they will usually run ahead, exploring every nook and cranny along the pathway, smelling flowers, and urging you to hurry and come see what they have found.

Wilson (1995) believes that outdoor experiences are prime opportunities for nurturing developmental growth. As a child meets challenges in outdoor play—climbing a tree, learning to stay afloat in the water, or recognizing the dangers of certain plants or animals—adaptive behaviors are encouraged and mastered. Paying attention to light as it streams through the forest, observing the paint-box colors of autumn trees, or listening the symphony of early-morning birds enhances a child's aesthetic awareness and helps him become a more astute observer of the natural rhythms of nature. Close examination of the physical characteristics of the world, coupled with conversation, questions, and observations from an adult allows a child to develop communication and cognitive skills as concepts about nature become clearer. Taking care of a pet rabbit, being careful not to disturb a bird's nest, or learning ways to keep our streams and rivers from becoming polluted allow children to grow socioemotionally as they become other-centered and aware of larger environmental and social issues. Squishing mud through small fingers, savoring wild blackberries, smelling the pungent earth after a hard rain, digging in the vegetable garden—the outdoors are alive with sensory experiences that engage young children.

Children who collect every creepy crawly in the immediate environment or have to be called inside repeatedly after spending hours outdoors have highly developed "naturalist intelligences," according to Howard Gardner's theory of multiple intelligences (Gardner, 2000). He uses the term to describe the ability to recognize plants, animals, and other natural elements; clearly see and identify patterns in nature; and classify objects. Books that are packed with information about the natural world will be appealing to young naturalists. In our computer-saturated world it is important for children who spend large amounts of time indoors to read and listen to books that promote appreciation, understanding, and enjoyment of nature. Raising awareness and educating children about the outdoors is interesting and stimulating with the wide variety of books about the natural world available to families today.

Through playful explorations of the outdoors and reading books about nature, children learn about the environment and appreciate the natural world.

Learning About Nature and Animals

Books about nature and animals encourage budding naturalists and stimulate questions and conversations within families. In **Tadpoles** (James, 1999), the familiar story of adjusting to a new sibling is coupled with a story about how tadpoles become frogs. The nurturing relationship between Molly and her brother as she helps Davey learn to walk is combined with close-up insets in the illustrations that chronicle the growth of the tadpoles Molly is raising at home. At the end of the book, accurate information and drawings detail the life cycle of frogs.

At an early age, children become familiar with backyard inhabitants, usually encountering them during outdoor play or watching them through a window. One afternoon, 3-year-old Andrew ran into the kitchen to report an *inside* encounter shouting, "Mommy, Mommy, there's a 'squirdel' in the den!" There was, indeed, a squirrel in the den! He had come up through the heating ducts and was wreaking havoc as he scampered about on the furniture. A wonderful book about squirrels is **Nuts to You!** by Lois Ehlert (1993). Set in the city in summertime, Ehlert's clever story and mixed-media collage illustrations provide a closer look at a squirrel's habits. "Squirrel Talk" concludes the story, and

MORE FAVORITES

Nature and Animals

Baby Animals (Royston, 1992)

Barnyard Banter (Fleming, 1994)

Blueberries for Sal (McCloskey, 1948)

Counting on the Woods (Lyon, 1998)

Early Morning in the Barn (Tafuri, 1983)

The Earth Is Painted Green (Brenner, 1994)

Elephants Swim (Riley, 1995)

Feathers for Lunch (Ehlert, 1990)

Good Night, Gorilla (Rathmann, 1995)

I Took a Walk (Cole, 1998)

I Went Walking (Williams, 1990)

In the Tall, Tall Grass (Fleming, 1991)

Peck, Slither, and Slide (MacDonald, 1997)

Touch and Feel: Wild Animals (Brown, 1998)

gives the reader information about squirrels such as identification, teeth, feet, and food.

Very young children will enjoy the daily routines of Mama Cat and her kittens, Fluffy, Skinny, and Boris in **Mama Cat Has Three Kittens** (Fleming, 1998). Boris naps while Mama, Fluffy, and Skinny are shown in various cat activities such as washing and sharpening claws, chasing leaves, and digging in the sand. The repetitive phrase "Boris naps," the echoing text of the kittens' activities as they mimic Mama Cat, and the familiar ways the animals behave encourage participation and make this a great read-aloud for families with toddlers.

Nancy Tafuri's (1988) **Spots, Feathers, and Curly Tails** is a great read-aloud about animals that invites participation from infants and toddlers. A repetitive refrain, "Who has...?" gives clues and asks for the name of animals. The simple illustrations and predictable nature of the text make the book ideal for sharing with young children.

Daily walks are routine in some families and provide opportunities for young children to appreciate nature. **Stella Luna** (Cannon, 1993), a story about a baby bat who falls into a bird's nest and is raised as a bird, became a favorite of 4-year-old Moksha. Her mom, Katie, says that since reading the book, Moksha has been especially interested in bird eggs and nests, trying to spot nests as they go on their walks around the apartment complex. One day, after the yard service mowed the lawn, Moksha gathered bits of grass clippings, string, and twigs and made a nest that she put in her bedroom bookcase. A few days later, she and her mom found two robin eggs under the trees on the sidewalk and one rolling around in the parking lot, and Moksha put them in the little nest she had made. Mom thinks that *Stella Luna* appeals to Moksha's naturalist instincts and comforts her, since the baby bat eventually finds his real mother again.

Close observation of the natural world often promotes a sense of responsibility for maintaining it. Raising children's awareness about the environment will encourage them to become sensitive caretakers of our natural resources. Spending time as a family outdoors and extending conversations about nature during storybook reading will give children opportunities and information to become young conservationists. The rhythmic text of Denise Fleming's **Where Once There Was a Wood** (1996) beautifully describes the loss of wildlife habitats to urban development. Even very young children will identify with the animals' plight as their homes are taken over by subdivisions. As children explore environmental issues involved in maintaining natural areas, Fleming's book provides a wealth of information about wildlife issues and habitats.

Observing the Seasons and Weather

Books that capitalize on children's curiosity about the natural world connect and extend the everyday pleasures they encounter outdoors. **Out and About** (Hughes, 1988), a collection of poetry that affirms family life and nature, is sure to be a favorite with preschoolers. Beginning with spring, daily experiences in each season are presented through a child's eye, evoking the smells, sights, sounds, and feelings of the natural elements. The lilting rhythm, concise imagery, and descriptive language of Hughes's poems capture the essence of nature in all its glory.

Three-year-old Mei Ling and her mom, Karen, enjoy winter days even more when they read **In the Snow** (Lee, 1995). Karen, a single mom who adopted Mei Ling as an infant in China, often reads books that depict Mei Ling's Chinese heritage and is teaching her to write Chinese characters. In the story, a young boy's mother uses the snow as a canvas to write Chinese characters with a stick. The boy learns 10 Chinese characters while his mother compares them to objects in nature, such as a tree, rain, and the moon. When Mei Ling and Karen read *In the Snow*, their outside play is often followed by an inside treat, snow cream, which they make together with fresh snow.

With simple images, spare language, and bold colors, Taro Gomi depicts a baby calf growing through the seasons in **Spring Is Here** (1989). Gomi's book for infants and toddlers is a seasonal story illustrated with an interesting perspective as the calf's back becomes the stage for transforming the seasons. Children and families cavort through the seasons as the story takes us back to the baby calf, now a year older. Adult readers could help young ones role-play the seasonal changes described, such as storms raging, wind blowing, or flowers blooming.

MORE FAVORITES

Seasons and Weather

Bear Snores On (Wilson, 2001)

A Busy Year (Lionni, 1992)

Chicken Soup with Rice (Sendak, 1962)

Circle of Seasons (Muller, 1995)

Frozen Noses (Carr, 1999)

A Hat for Minerva Louise (Stoeke, 1994)

Is That You, Winter? (Gammell, 1997)

Kipper's Book of Weather (Inkpen, 1999)

Mud (Ray, 1996)

Red Leaf, Yellow Leaf (Ehlert, 1991)

Snow (Shulevitz, 1998)

Snowballs (Ehlert, 1995)

The Snowy Day (Keats, 1962)

Stories for All Seasons (Carle, 1998)

Gardening

Gardening is often a family affair. Eliza's mom remembers that as a toddler, Eliza's sandbox was placed next to the garden where she spent hours watching Mom and Dad plant, weed, hoe, and harvest vegetables for the family. Now at age 4, one of Eliza's favorite books is Janet Stevens' trickster tale ***Tops and Bottoms*** (1995), which appeals to her sense of humor as well as her knowledge about gardening. Mom says that while planting their spring garden she and Eliza have talked about the book, leading to extended conversations about spring rains, protection of the vegetables, and other related gardening topics.

A regional tale set in the American Southwest, ***Carlos and the Squash Plant*** (1993) by Jan Romero Stevens, is a humorous story about a young boy's resistance to taking a bath after gardening. His reluctance to bathe leads his mother to proclaim that a squash plant will grow out of his dirty ears. Glimpses of everyday life in this Hispanic household affirm the culture at the same time giving a sense of familiarity in the routines of mealtimes, bath time struggles, and tending to everyday chores. The Spanish translation follows the English version of the story on each page. A recipe for "Calabacitas" (a squash dish) is included at the end of the book.

"Eat your vegetables!" is a familiar phrase heard at dinnertime in many families. In ***Oliver's Vegetables*** (French, 1995), a young city boy visits his grandparents and promptly tells them he does not eat vegetables, only french fries—even

Gardening with young children is made more enjoyable by reading books such as Planting a Rainbow *or* Glenna's Seeds.

> be polite.
> Do not pike
> For food
> totet is no
> Ripe.

"Be polite. Do not pick food that is not ripe." Experiences in family gardening lead to respect for nature's bounty.

MORE FAVORITES

Gardening

Allison's Zinnia (Lobel, 1990)

Bumblebee, Bumblebee, Do You Know Me?: A Garden Guessing Game (Rockwell, 1999)

Butterfly House (Bunting, 1999)

The Carrot Seed (Krauss, 1993)

The Gardener (Stewart, 2000)

Glenna's Seeds (Edwards, 2001)

Grandma's Garden (Moore, 1994)

In Wibbly's Garden (Inkpen, 2000)

Jasper's Beanstalk (Inkpen, 1997)

Maisy's Garden (Cousins, 2001)

Moose in the Garden (Carlstrom, 1990)

Pickin' Peas (MacDonald, 1998)

Planting a Rainbow (Ehlert, 1988)

The Victory Garden Vegetable Alphabet Book (Pallotta & Thomson, 1992)

though Grandpa grows all his own vegetables. A bargain is struck that Oliver will try to find the potatoes in the garden to make french fries, but until he does he must eat any other vegetables he discovers. *Oliver's Vegetables* is sure to spark family conversations about growing vegetables, as well as eating them.

Katie and Moksha have no access to land for gardening but are planning their window garden to include flowering plants along with rosemary, tomatoes, and jade. Families like theirs may enjoy reading books such as Eve Bunting's (1994) **Flower Garden,** which describes a young girl's birthday surprise for her mother—a window flower box.

AT PRESCHOOL OR DAY CARE

"The first day of school." For adults, this phrase may elicit memories of new clothes, freshly sharpened pencils, and notebooks filled with clean, blue-lined paper. Children starting preschool or child care today may have very different experiences from those of their parents or grandparents, yet the transition from home to a group situation is still a milestone in their lives. Many factors influence a child's initial response to school: personality, preparation by parents and caregivers for the new experience, size and atmosphere of the classroom, and teacher attitudes and dispositions. Teachers can foster a smooth transition through frequent communication and by maintaining a strong sense of connection with families. Hearing stories about preschool may help children see that they are not alone in their feelings.

The little mouse in **School** (McCully, 1987) is so anxious to go to class with her brothers and sisters that she runs off to the nearby school. Told with pictures only, young children can relate to the mouse's feelings and make up a story to accompany the detailed illustrations. Wordless picture books provide an excellent avenue for language development, while providing practice with many reading skills, such as sequencing, comprehension, and vocabulary development.

Like the character in *School*, Lilly in **Lilly's Purple Plastic Purse** (Henkes, 1996), has been waiting with apprehension for her first day of school to arrive. Everything seems perfect until she and her teacher have a disagreement over Lilly's purple purse. Lilly writes a note to her teacher that she later regrets. Thanks to understanding parents and a remarkable teacher, all ends happily. This book could help children understand that it is okay to make mistakes and ask for forgiveness. It provides wonderful lessons in interpersonal communication.

In today's inclusive classrooms most children will attend school with children who have special abilities and challenges. How can teachers and parents help young children learn about individuals with special abilities and disabilities? Children will not learn to accept others simply by being in the same setting with them. Adults must model warm, enthusiastic attitudes toward all children and take a proactive role in teaching them to be informed and caring. When Martha, a 3-year-old without disabilities attended a program primarily aimed at children with disabilities, she was very shy at first. Soon her teachers encouraged her to push Liam's "stroller" (wheelchair) to the playground and help him with other physical tasks. Taking on a helping role smoothed Martha's transition to her new environment and let her feel needed at school. The following suggestions may assist teachers who wish to be proactive about including children with special needs in their classrooms:

1. Talk with children about ways we are all alike and different, what we have an easy time doing and what is hard for us. (See *Starting Small*, 1997.)

2. Become familiar with the characteristics of various disabilities and find ways to share basic information about disabilities with your students.

3. Borrow special equipment, such as child-size wheelchairs and walkers, for the children to play with and explore. Locate dolls with special equipment, such as braces, canes, and hearing aides. Play experiences will help demystify the equipment and the disabilities.

4. Encourage questions; let children know you are comfortable talking about disabilities.

5. Help children with and without disabilities develop the social skills they need for all to be included in play.

6. Invite guests with disabilities to share their experiences with the children.

7. Use literature about people with disabilities as a springboard for discussion.

In recent years, a number of books have been published that show children with disabilities in their regular classroom activities. Laura Dwight's books show children at home and school engaging in ordinary activities, as well as times with the speech therapist or physical therapist. These books are great for helping children learn how those with special challenges are more like other children than different. **We Can Do It!** (Dwight, 1997) and **Friends at School** (Bunnett, 1996) show school and child care including young children with challenges, while focusing on the children's capabilities. Both books depict children with disabilities enjoying books, blocks, and running through sprinklers as much as other youngsters do. Children with special challenges may identify with some of the photographs in these two books, while those who do not have special needs will come to understand that all children enjoy many of the same activities and games.

Moses Goes to a Concert (Millman, 1998) is the delightful story of a little boy and his classmates of hearing-impaired children who attend a children's concert. The hearing-impaired children hold balloons while the music is playing, to help them feel the vibrations. After the concert they meet with the percussionist, a woman who is deaf. She tells them about her career ambitions and how she worked hard to fulfill her dream. Each page shows Moses saying something in sign language with arrows to help the reader learn sign language.

MORE FAVORITES

At Preschool or Day Care

Chrysanthemum (Henkes, 1991)

Day Care Days (Barrett, 1999)

First Day Hooray! (Poydar, 1999)

I Need a Lunchbox (Caines, 1988)

The Kissing Hand (Penn, 1993)

Minerva Louise at School (Stoeke, 1996)

Off to School, Baby Duck! (Hest, 1999)

Rotten Teeth (Simms, 1998)

School (Arnold, 1997)

The Teeny Tiny Teacher (Calmenson, 1998)

When Will Sarah Come? (Howard, 1999)

When You Go to Kindergarten (Howe, 1991)

Will I Have a Friend? (Cohen, 1967)

ADULTS AT WORK

With more than half of mothers of young children in the workforce, evenings have become the focus for family interactions. The bond between a working mother and her child is beautifully portrayed in **When Mama Comes Home Tonight** (Spinelli, 1998). While preschool children and younger will be attracted by the familiar activities and soft illustrations, working parents will see the value of spending time with their young ones during these precious hours together.

Lizzie accompanies her mother to work as a children's librarian in **Red Light, Green Light, Mama and Me** (Best, 1995). The warm and loving relationship between Mama and Lizzie, the realistic ways Lizzie keeps herself busy while Mama works, and the kindness of the library workers who include Lizzie in "jobs" throughout the day combine to make this a special book for working moms to share with their children.

Two books about families working together are **Farmers' Market** (Johnson, 1997) and **We Keep a Store** (Shelby, 1990). Laura, the young girl in *Farmers' Market*, joins her family on a routine Saturday journey to sell their freshly picked produce at the busy open-air market. After working hard for a while, Laura joins her friend Betsy in exploring the market. The center double-page spread opens up to four panels and is visually inviting in its depiction of the stalls, people, and products for sale at the farmers' market. Families who frequent farmers' markets, either to sell or to buy, will be drawn in to the familiarity of the story and will enjoy the realistic representation of the daylong event.

We Keep a Store (Shelby, 1990) describes the daily events of an African American family who own a country store. The illustrations convey a sense of close family ties and respect from community members as seen through the eyes of the young daughter of the family. Pride in their business, the range of neighborhood personalities who are store patrons, and the realistic routines and responsibilities of a country store combine to make this story high quality.

MORE FAVORITES

Adults at Work

A Chair for My Mother (Williams, 1982)

Grandpa's Corner Store (DiSalvo-Ryan, 2000)

Just One More Story (Brutschy, 2002)

Night Shift Daddy (Spinelli, 2000)

Story Hour—Starring Megan! (Brillhart, 1992)

IN THE COMMUNITY

Children are naturally interested in the neighborhoods and communities where they live, beginning at very early ages. The mail carrier, the plumber, and the telephone repair person come to their homes and enter the immediate worlds of infants, toddlers, and preschoolers. Visits to the post office, doctor's office, health department, or social services agency give children opportunities to see people and places beyond their home environment and help them connect the roles and purposes of workers and jobs in the neighborhood and community. Multiple contexts exist in communities for supporting emergent literacy development. Many times museums, historical landmarks, parks, libraries, art galleries, and other community resources offer developmentally appropriate programs for children as young as 6 months and their families. Combined with literature, daily community life and special events can become prime occasions for learning about people and places in settings outside the family.

Neighborhood Workers

Neighborhood workers often fascinate young children. Two-year-old Christy stood by the window of her grandparents' porch on trash day, waiting for her friend the garbage collector to wave as he made his pick up and drove off. *Trashy Town* by Andrea Zimmerman and David Clemensha (1999) is a short, repetitive book with bold, paper-cut illustrations by Dan Yaccarino. The language and refrains, opportunities for response, and familiar topic would appeal to 2- and 3-year-olds. Caregivers could extend the book by helping children learn about recycling or pointing out trash receptacles as they drive through town.

When Curtis the mail carrier retires, the whole neighborhood throws a party in his honor. *Good-Bye Curtis* (Henkes, 1995) provides information on the work of mail carriers and tells how we show our appreciation to workers at their retirement as well as other times. The book shows a positive reciprocal relationship that developed between Curtis and the people on his mail route.

On a lighter note, another enjoyable book about the world of mail is *The Jolly Postman and Other People's Letters* (Ahlberg & Ahlberg, 1986). Filled with "real" envelopes and letters, the postman delivers mail to storybook characters. Children who already know traditional tales will enjoy reading the letters to Cinderella, the Three Bears, the Big Bad Wolf, and others. Families who have relatives in distant places could use these two books to engage preschoolers and kindergarten children in writing letters—a meaningful and functional use of literacy. Figure 7.3 suggests other books about letters and a related home-learning activity. See Figure 7.4 for ideas on involving the community in your reading program.

A clever way to learn about the jobs of neighborhood workers and community collaboration is presented in *Cat up a Tree* (1998) by John and Ann Has-

Dear Families,

Writing letters with children provides wonderful opportunities for learning about reading, writing, and communication. Included in the book bag are a book and materials to help you create letters with your child. Read *Mailbox Magic* together and use the note paper, crayons, envelopes, and stamps to write a letter to each other, friends, or family members. Help your child mail the letter, either at your home mailbox or at a nearby post office. Please return the book bag, book, and materials after one week. Other books about letters you may wish check out from our Family Lending Library are *Dear Juno, A Letter to Amy, Dear Annie,* and *The Jolly Postman.*

Sincerely,
[Teacher's Name]

FIGURE 7.3

Teacher to Teacher: "Magic Mailbox" Home Learning Activity

sett. Nana Quimby notices a cat stuck in a tree outside her window and calls the firehouse to come rescue it. Telling her to call back if the cat starts playing with matches, they refuse her request. Each time Nana looks outside more cats are up in the tree. She calls the police, the zoo, the library, the pet shop, and city hall to come help, but at each place someone says to call back. An unpredictable ending turns the tables and city hall asks for Nana's help—but now it is her turn to say, "Call back . . ." Young children will readily identify the community places and job descriptions, enjoy counting the cats as they multiply in the tree, and learn the importance of helping each other.

When recalling people who influenced their reading as young children, adults do not usually cite neighborhood or community workers. One of the reasons may be that they seldom had an opportunity to see them reading. At a family literacy program in one community, business people and community workers were invited to read aloud a favorite book to families and children. The mayor brought his grandson and read a Dr. Seuss book to the crowd, while the adult literacy coordinator at a local textile mill brought her granddaughter to help share her favorite book. In addition to reading aloud, each community reader posed for a local version of the celebrity "READ" posters, similar to those provided by the American Library Association. The posters were printed and distributed to schools and library branches in the area (Strickland, Dodd, & Newsom, 1999).

FIGURE 7.4

Teacher to Teacher: Community Readers

MORE FAVORITES

Neighborhood Workers

The Adventures of Taxi Dog
(Barracca & Barracca, 1990)

Fire Engines (Rockwell, 1986)

Make Way for Ducklings
(McCloskey, 1941)

Officer Buckle and Gloria
(Rathmann, 1995)

Daily Outings

Communities offer varying resources and services, and the degree to which children and families profit from the available organizations, services, businesses, and agencies depends on the financial, social, and emotional capital present in the family (Barbour & Barbour, 1997). Transportation, work and school schedules, child care, safety, and other family and social issues support or hinder the daily comings and goings of families within their communities; however, most families will make a trip to the grocery store at least once a week.

Where Are You? (Simon, 1998) provides a glimpse into a perennial childhood predicament associated with shopping: getting lost in the store. Harry, a young pup, takes his first trip to the grocery store with his grandpa and is immediately sidetracked by the smell of cupcakes. He hops off the cart to investigate and gets lost among the aisles and food displays. Harry's problem will be familiar to youngsters and the loving resolution of the story will provide comfort. Parents and caregivers could use the book as a starting point for discussing the importance of staying close by in an unfamiliar place, learning the functions of writing such as making out a grocery list, or recognizing environmental print on grocery items.

Urban environments offer worlds of print that children see every day as they walk to school, go to the park, or visit a playmate. Shop signs, traffic signs, billboards, and advertising circulars are ubiquitous and provide information as well as environmental print to support early literacy development. Parents and caregivers who point out environmental print daily are using a natural context to help their children "read the world." *Alphabet City* (1995) a Caldecott Honor book by Stephen T. Johnson, takes a unique look at daily scenes and "print" in the city. The author located and illustrated capital alphabet letters found in natural positions throughout the city; for example, the "A" on the side of a sawhorse or the "E" made by the side view of a traffic light. Some of the letters will be hard to recognize unless an adult is helping out, but the book is an interesting celebration of ordinary city scenes viewed through the eyes of a painter. Use of these struc-

Survey the community for places, special events, and other opportunities for family involvement in the business or arts community. Take photos of the sites and select appropriate children's literature to help prepare or extend opportunities for family participation in the places and activities you have located. Using the photographs, make a bulletin board for the classroom or a photo essay book to copy and give to families. Make a list of people associated with the community who could come into your center or classroom to share information, experiences, or favorite books with the children and families.

FIGURE 7.5

Teacher to Teacher: "Where Is It?"

tures and objects as a form of environmental print could lead to family "literacy walks" around the neighborhood or city (Orellana & Hernandez, 1999). See Figure 7.5 for ideas about featuring places and people in your community.

Taking a trip to the dentist will seem less painful after reading ***Dr. DeSoto*** (Steig, 1982). This classic tale about a clever dentist and his wife—who happen to be mice—offers lots of opportunities to talk about dentists, their tasks, and their equipment in a light-hearted way. The witty story line, comical illustrations, and interesting vocabulary (e.g., "morsel," "woozy," "shabby") will entertain young readers and perhaps demystify the first visit to the dentist.

Families who frequent the neighborhood or city library will enjoy ***Stella Louella's Runaway Book*** (Ernst, 1998). Locating the book she needs to return to the library puts Stella Louella in a jam because it has disappeared. Turning the house upside down, she is still unable to find it. Her brother says he read the book, loved it, and left it by the mailbox. Each person Stella Louella encounters on her search for the lost book has read it and sends her to another place to find it, taking the reader on a tour of the town. Any family who has experienced the library "due date" dilemma will relate to this story.

Figure 7.6 shows how parents can help children learn from their daily activities at home and in the community by taking photographs that can be used to create personal books.

Special Events

Art galleries, hands-on science museums, zoos, national parks, and theaters often present programs that engage children in learning. Families who have the financial means to take advantage of these opportunities profit more substantially from them. However, child-care centers, preschool and kindergarten programs, or after-school programs could be the avenue through which other children benefit. As parents and caregivers become more skilled at locating and using community services, their knowledge of the available cultural and natural resources will increase and they may more frequently use the programs and events connected with these resources. Barbour and Barbour (1997)

Emily's going sliding.

Plan a family night at school for book-making. Prior to the meeting, make home visits with the families. Take five to seven digital photographs of the child engaged in activities at home or in the neighborhood. Print out the photos and have them ready for family night.

During the meeting, provide the photos, book-making materials and directions to help families make a book. As the child dictates a sentence for each photo, have an adult transcribe. (You may need to furnish volunteers to help low-literate adults do the transcribing.) For children whose home language is not English, put the home language description first, then transcribe the sentence in English below.

Bind the books, have a sharing session, and let each family take their book home to read with their child and share with friends and relatives.

That's the dog that I love. I'm not afraid of that dog.

FIGURE 7.6
Teacher to Teacher: Making a Book About Daily Activities

MORE FAVORITES

Daily Outings

Around Town (Soentpiet, 1994)

The Bookshop Dog (Rylant, 1996)

Car Wash (Steen & Steen, 2001)

The Car-Washing Street (Patrick, 1993)

Cathedral Mouse (Chorao, 1988)

Check It Out! The Book About Libraries (Gibbons, 1985)

The Cookie-Store Cat (Rylant, 1999)

Don't Forget the Bacon! (Hutchins, 1989)

An Everyday Book (Rylant, 1997)

In the Park (Lee, 1998)

A Letter to Amy (Keats, 1968)

The Library Dragon (Deedy, 2001)

Library Lil (Williams, 2001)

This Little Baby Goes Out (Breeze, 1990)

Mailbox Magic (Poydar, 2000)

Sheep in a Shop (Shaw, 1991)

The Shopping Basket (Burningham, 1980)

Sunday Week (Johnson, 1999)

The Supermarket Mice (Gordon, 1984)

To Market, to Market (Miranda, 1997)

refer to "the curriculum of the community" and stress the vital role that communities play in a child's development and education. Figure 7.7 provides ideas for setting up literacy-based community centers in your classroom.

Dylan's mom reports that the 18-month-old became very excited when they went to the zoo, because he recognized familiar animals from reading ***1, 2, 3 to the Zoo*** (Carle, 1968) and talking about the animals. A counting book about animals on their way to the zoo, *1, 2, 3 to the Zoo* has double-page spreads that show the animals in boxcars and the correct numeral on the upper left corner. The last page folds out so children can see all the animals in their new home. ***Dear Zoo*** (Campbell, 1982), a participation book, is another zoo book to read to toddlers. Lift-the-flap crates and boxes partially hide the animals, and allow the child to predict and identify them. A familiar zoo song in storybook form, ***Going to the Zoo*** (Paxton, 1996) or Gail Gibbons' informational book ***Zoo*** (1987) are other books that provide pleasure and information about the zoo.

Fine art is the focus of a wonderful book for preschool and kindergarten children, ***I Spy a Lion: Animals in Art*** (Micklethwait, 1994). Large print, a simple repetitive phrase, and familiar animals are combined with art by Picasso, Chagall, Rousseau, and other masters to make this a visual treat for young children.

Set up "community centers" in your room and furnish children's books and literacy props in each. The books and materials will facilitate engagement in emergent language and literacy, social interaction, and expand children's knowledge about community places and workers. Partner with places in your community that may be willing to sponsor each center and donate materials. Ask family members who work in related jobs to help provide materials and come share their jobs with the children. The ideas below will help you begin to gather children's books and literacy materials for your community centers. Supplement with real items (e.g., clerk coats, postal worker outfits, instruments, plants, art easel/paints) and your children will be ready to work in their "community!"

Center	Children's Books	Literacy Materials
Library	• *Stella Louella's Runaway Book* • *Story Hour—Starring Megan!* • *Library Lil* • *The Library Dragon* • *Check It Out: The Book About Libraries*	• Pencils, crayons, markers, pens, paper • Books • Book stamp • Check-out cards and book pockets • Library membership cards • Book bags with library logo • "Quiet" sign • "Check-out" sign • Posters of children's books • Drawings of favorite books by children, labeled with the book titles
Post Office	• *Good-Bye Curtis* • *The Jolly Postman* • *Dear Juno* • *A Letter to Amy* • *Dear Mr. Blueberry*	• Pencils, crayons, markers, pens, paper • Stationary • Stamps • Envelopes • Manila envelopes • Stamp posters • Cancel stamp • Mailbag with logo • Mailing labels
Grocery Store	• *Where Are You?* • *To Market, to Market* • *The Shopping Basket* • *Don't Forget the Bacon!* • *Grandpa's Corner Store* • *We Keep a Store*	• Pencils, crayons, markers, pens, paper • Cash register and tape • Play money • Grocery bags with logos • Newspaper ads • Food containers • Signs for areas (e.g., "vegetables" "meats" "bread")

FIGURE 7.7

Teacher to Teacher: Using Literacy Props and Children's Books in "Community Centers"

Nursery/
Landscaping
Business
 	
	• *Glenna's Seeds*
	• *The Gardner*
	• *Flower Garden*
	• *Planting a Rainbow*
	• *Allison's Zinnia*
	• *Red Leaf, Yellow Leaf*
		• Pencils, crayons, markers,
		  pens, paper
		• Order forms
		• Labels for flowers
		• Garden catalogs and
		  advertisements
		• Seed packets
		• Tree and plant tags
		• Play money

Art Museum	• *I Spy a Lion* • *A Child's Book of Art* • *Visiting the Art Museum* • *Emma's Rug*	• Pencils, crayons, markers, pens • Admission tickets • Brochure of art displayed • Museum guide • Art prints with captions • Children's prints with dictation • Play money

FIGURE 7.7

Continued

At the end of the book there is a list of the animals and paintings, with additional information about each painting. Preparing for a trip to the art museum is a real pleasure when families read this book together. Once at the museum, extending the game of "I spy" to the paintings there or trying to locate some of the paintings in the book will promote visual literacy and discrimination skills as well as provide interest.

The lights, sights, and excitement of the fair are portrayed in Donald Crew's book, ***Night at the Fair*** (1998). The inky night is a perfect backdrop for highlighting the rides and treats offered. Crew's effective use of light in the many double-page illustrations adds warmth and throws shadows to make the reader feel uniquely a part of the crowd and nighttime activities. His wife, Ann Jonas, photographed him at the county fair, and Crews puts himself in the illustrations as well as on the jacket flap. A trip to the fair, even in daylight, will be more fun after reading this story.

Performances for children by musicians are becoming more frequent. A 1996 Caldecott Honor book about the orchestra that will quickly become a favorite is ***Zin! Zin! A Violin*** (Moss, 1995). The illustrations, by Marjorie Priceman are full of movement and seem to flow right along with the music. The text is rhyming and placed in various ways on the page to accent the content as the story takes us through a performance. As the instruments are introduced, the reader counts and learns to name combinations such as "quartet" and "sextet"

MORE FAVORITES

Special Events

Bantam of the Opera (Auch, 1997)

Charlie Parker Played Be Bop (Raschka, 1992)

A Child's Book of Art (Micklethwait, 1993)

Emma's Rug (Say, 1996)

Hip Cat (London, 1993)

Lili at Ballet (Isadora, 1993)

Lili Backstage (Isadora, 1997)

Meet the Orchestra (Hayes, 1991)

Olivia Saves the Circus (Falconer, 2000)

The Philharmonic Gets Dressed (Kuskin, 1982)

Visiting the Art Museum (Brown & Brown, 1986)

until the whole orchestra fills the stage. The range of musical vocabulary and instruments, as well as the lively illustrations, will give families interesting information about the orchestra. **The Philharmonic Gets Dressed** (Kuskin, 1982) is a book that takes a behind-the-scenes look at the orchestra members as they prepare for a performance. The illustrations by Marc Simont comically capture performers in their homes dressing in formal attire and take readers right to the stage with them for a night at the symphony.

SUMMARY

During the first five years of life, children are developing concepts about their homes, families, neighborhoods, and communities. Picture books help children come to understand their own family routines and neighborhood milieu and offer glimpses of other lifestyles and communities. Parents and caregivers can build on literature experiences by cooking with their children, enjoying the outdoors, or introducing them to community places and people. Home, school, and community literacy partnerships are strengthened as teachers guide families in the selection and use of quality books about everyday in families.

FOR PROFESSIONAL DEVELOPMENT

1. Read several books about young children at play, then observe children in a park or other outdoor setting. Do you think the books accurately depict children's play? Why or why not? How could you integrate the books on play into your curriculum?

2. How can books help young children as they develop an understanding of temporal sequencing? Locate books that show daily, weekly, or seasonal sequences. Share the books with young children and note their conceptual understanding as you read.

3. Interview a parent or caregiver about their child's daily routines and favorite books. Based on the information, recommend to the family a list of books to share together.

4. Plan a trip to one or more places in the community. Take photographs or digital pictures during the trip. After returning, have the children dictate captions for each photograph and make a book to be shared in the classroom and checked out by families.

INTERNET RESOURCES

www.zerotothree.org

> Sponsored by the National Center for Infants, Toddlers, and Families. This organization provides information on child development, tips for parents and professionals, and the latest research on early childhood topics.

www.parentsplace.com

> The site provides information and resources on a wide variety of parenting topics.

www.naeyc.org

> Sponsored by the National Association for the Education of Young Children. Primarily designed for early childhood teachers, there are many resources on family involvement and early literacy development.

www.edpsych.com

> Sponsored by Paideia Press, the site provides information to parents and early chidhood teachers and directors. Many links to useful Web sites.

PROFESSIONAL REFERENCES

Adams, M. (1990). *Beginning to read: Thinking and learning about print.* Cambridge, MA: MIT Press.

Adoptive Families. (1999). International adoption statistics released. *Adoptive Families, 32*(1), 6.

Allen, M. L., Brown, P., & Finlay, B. (1995). *Helping children by strengthening families.* Washington, DC: Children's Defense Fund.

Anderson, E. A., & Koblinsky, S. A. (1995). Homeless policy: The need to speak to families. *Family Relations, 44*(1), 13–18.

Aoki, E. M. (1981). "Are you Chinese? Are you Japanese? Or are you just a mixed-up kid?" Using Asian American children's literature. *The Reading Teacher, 34,* 382–385.

Ashabranner, B. (1991). *An ancient heritage: The Arab-American Minority.* New York: HarperCollins.

Banks, J. A., & Banks, C. A. (1997). *Multicultural education: Issues and perspectives.* Boston: Allyn & Bacon.

Barbara Bush Foundation. (2001). Lessons learned. Retrieved March 22, 2002, from http://www.barbarabushfoundation.org

Barbour, C., & Barbour, N. H. (1997). *Families, schools, and communities: Building partnerships for educating children.* Upper Saddle River, NJ: Merrill/Prentice Hall.

Barbour, C., & Barbour, N. H. (2001). *Families, schools, and communities: Building partnerships for educating children* (2nd ed.). Upper Saddle River, NJ: Merrill/Prentice Hall.

Barclay, K. D., & Walwer, L. (1992). Linking lyrics and literacy through song picture books. *Young Children, 47*(4), 76–85.

Barton, B. (1986). *Tell me another.* Portsmouth, NH: Heinemann.

Beaty, J. (1997). *Building bridges with multicultural picture books for children 3–5.* Upper Saddle River, NJ: Merrill/Prentice Hall.

Belton-Owens, J. (1999). Multicultural issues confronted by parents and families. In G. Boutte (Ed.), *Multicultural education: Raising consciousness* (pp. 232–260). Belmont, CA: Wadsworth.

Bennett, C. (1999). *Comprehensive multicultural education.* Needham Heights, MA: Allyn & Bacon.

Berger, E. H. (2000). *Parents as partners in education: Families and schools working together* (5th ed.). Upper Saddle River, NJ: Merrill/Prentice Hall.

Berk, L. E., & Windsler, A. (1995). *Scaffolding children's learning: Vygotsky and early childhood education.* Washington, DC: National Association for the Education of Young Children.

Bettleheim, B. (1976). *The uses of enchantment.* New York: Knopf.

Between the Lines. (2002). *The Motheread Newsletter, 7*(1). Retrieved April 8, 2002, from http://www.motheread.org.

Blaska, J. K., & Lynch, E. C. (1998). Is everyone included? Using children's literature to facilitate the understanding of disabilities. *Young Children, 53,* 36–38.

Bodrova, E., & Leong, D. (1996). *Tools of the mind: A Vygotskian approach to early childhood education.* Upper Saddle River, NJ: Merrill/Prentice Hall.

Boudouris, J. (1996). *Parents in prison: Addressing the needs of families.* Lanham, MD: American Correctional Association.

Boutte, G. (Ed.). (1999). *Multicultural education: Raising consciousness.* Belmont, CA: Wadsworth.

Boutte, G. S., & McCormick, C. B. (1992). Authentic multicultural activities: Avoiding pseudomulticulturalism. *Childhood Education, 68*(3), 140–144.

Brock, D. R., & Dodd, E. L. (1994). A family lending library: Promoting early literacy development. *Young Children, 49*(3), 16–21.

Brodkin, A. M. (1998). Why is Joey so sad? *Scholastic Early Childhood Today, 7*(10), 15–16.

Bronfenbrenner, U. (1979). *The ecology of human development: Experiments by nature and design.* Cambridge, MA: Harvard University Press.

Bubolz, M. M., & Sontag, M. S. (1993). *Human ecology theory.* In P. G. Boss, W. J. Doherty, R. LaRossa, W. R. Schumm, & S. K. Steinmetz (Eds.), *Sourcebook of family theories and methods: A contextual approach* (pp. 419–448). New York: Plenum Press.

Buchoff, R. (1995). Family stories. *The Reading Teacher, 49,* 230–233.

Buirski, N. (1994). *Earth angels: Migrant children in America.* San Francisco: Pomegranate Artbooks.

Burke, R. W. (1999). Diverse family structures: Implications for P–3 teachers. *Journal of Early Childhood Teacher Education, 20*(3), 245–251.

Burns, M. S., Griffin, P., & Snow, C. E. (Eds.). (1999). *Starting out right: A guide to promoting children's reading success.* Washington, DC: National Academy Press.

Butler, D. (1998). *Babies need books.* Portsmouth, NH: Heinemann.

Butler, J., Liss, C., & Sterner, P. (1999). Starting on the right foot: Helping parents understand how children learn to read and write. *Texas Child Care,* 2–9.

Butterfield, F. (1999, April 11). Prison parents critical factor in creating new criminals. *The Miami Herald.* Retrieved January 16, 2001, from www.herald.com/content/archive/specialreport/docs/067028.htm

Cahill, B. J., & Theillheimer, R. (1999). Can Tommy and Sam get married? Questions about gender, sexuality, and young children. *Young Children, 54*(1), 27–31.

Calkins, L. (1997). *Raising lifelong learners.* Reading, MA: Perseus.

Cambourne, B. (1988). *The whole story: Natural learning and the acquisition of literacy in the classroom.* Auckland, NZ: Ashton Scholastic.

Campbell, R. (1999). *Reading with Alice.* Wiltshire, UK: Trentham Press.

Charkow, W. B. (1998). Inviting children to grieve. *Professional School Counseling, 2*(2), 117–122.

Cheng, L. L. (1998). *Enhancing the communication skills of newly arrived Asian American students.* New York: ERIC Clearinghouse on Urban Education. (ERIC/CUE Digest No. ED420726)

Child Welfare League of America. (n.d.). *What happens to children?* Retrieved January 1, 2001, from http://www.cwla.org/programs/incarcerated/whathappens.htm

Children's Defense Fund. (2000). *The state of America's children.* Boston: Beacon Press.

Christian, L. G. (1997). Children and death. *Young Children, 54*(4), 76–80.

Clay, J. W. (1990). Working with lesbian and gay parents and their children. *Young Children, 45*(3), 31–35.

Clay, M. M. (1975). *What did I write?* Portsmouth, NH: Heinemann.

Clay, M. M. (1991). *Becoming literate.* Portsmouth, NH: Heinemann.

Cochran-Smith, M. (1984). *The making of a reader.* Norwood, NJ: Ablex.

Cohen, O., & Ronen, T. (1999). Young children's adjustment to their parents' divorce as reflected in their drawings. *Journal of Divorce and Remarriage, 30* (1/2), 47–70.

Coleman, J. S. (1991). *Policy perspectives: Parental involvement in education.*

Washington, DC: U.S. Department of Education, Office of Educational Research and Improvement.

Cullinan, B. E., & Galda, L. (1998). *Literature and the child* (4th ed.). Fort Worth, TX: Harcourt Brace.

Darigan, D. L., Tunnell, M. O., & Jacobs, J. S. (2002). *Children's literature: Engaging teachers and children in good books.* Upper Saddle River, NJ: Merrill/Prentice Hall.

De Gaetano, Y., Williams, L. R., & Volk, D. (1998). *Kaleidoscope.* Upper Saddle River, NJ: Merrill/Prentice Hall.

DeFlorimonte, D., Boutte, G., & LaPoint, S. (1999). The elementary years. In G. Boutte (Ed.), *Multicultural education: Raising consciousness.* Belmont, CA: Wadsworth.

Dejong, L., & Cottrell, B. H. (1999). Designing infant child care programs to meet the needs of children born to teenage parents. *Young Children, 54*(1), 37–45.

Derman-Sparks and the ABC Task Force. (1989). *Anti-Bias curriculum: Tools for empowering young children.* Washington, DC: National Association for the Education of Young Children.

Dodd, E. L. (1990). From bedtime stories to the shared book experience: Supporting emergent literacy with big books. *Georgia Journal of Reading, 16*(1), 27–32.

Dodd, E. L. (1999). Echoes of the past: Jackdaws and historical fiction bring history to life. *Childhood Education, 75*(3), 136–141.

Dodd, E. L., & Brock, D. R. (1994). Building partnerships with families through home learning activities. *Dimensions of Early Childhood Education, 22*(2), 37–38, 46.

Dodd, E. L., & Lilly, D. H. (1997). Family portfolios: Portraits of children and families. *Preventing School Failure, 41*(2), 57–62.

Dodd, E. L., & Lilly, D. H. (2000). Learning within communities: An investigation of community service-learning in teacher education. *Action in Teacher Education, 23*(3), 77–85.

Dombro, A. L., Colker, L. J., & Dodge, D. T. (1997). *The creative curriculum for infants and toddlers.* Washington, DC: Teaching Strategies.

Duarte, G., & Rafanello, D. (2001). The migrant child: A special place in the field. *Young Children, 56*(2), 26–34.

Durkin, D. (1966). *Children who read early.* New York: Teachers College Press.

Eastern Stream Center on Resources and Training. (1998). *Help! They don't speak English starter kit.* Oneonta, NY: Author.

Eddowes, E. A., & Hranitz, J. R. (1989). Educating children of the homeless. *Childhood Education, 65*(4), 197–200.

Edwards, P. A., Pleasants, H. M., & Franklin, S. H. (1999). *A path to follow: Learning to listen to parents.* Portsmouth, NH: Heinemann.

Elkind, D. (1994). *Ties that stress: The new family imbalance.* Cambridge, MA: Harvard University Press.

Epstein, J. (1995). School/family/community partnerships: Caring for the children we serve. *Phi Delta Kappan, 76*, 701–712.

Feng, J. (1994). *Asian-American children: What teachers should know.* Urbana, IL: ERIC Clearinghouse on Elementary and Early Childhood Education. (ERIC Document Reproduction Service No. ED369577)

Fisher, B. (1991). *Joyful learning: A whole language kindergarten.* Portsmouth, NH: Heinemann.

Fitzgerald, J. (1999). What is this thing called "balance?" *The Reading Teacher, 53*, 100–107.

Fortson, L. R., & Reiff, J. C. (1995). *Early childhood curriculum: Open structures for integrative learning.* Boston: Allyn and Bacon.

Fox, M. (2001). *Reading magic.* San Diego: Harcourt.

Fox, M. (1993). *Dear Mem Fox, I have read all your books, even the pathetic ones.* San Diego: Harcourt, Brace, Jovanovich.

Franklin, C. (1999). Grandparents as parents. *Social Work in Education, 21*(3), 131–135.

Freire, P. (1985). Reading the world and reading the word: An interview with Paulo Freire. *Language Arts, 62*(1), 15–21.

Friedlander, M. L., Larney, L. C., Skau, M., Hotaling, M., Cutting, M. L., & Schwam, M. (2000). Bicultural identification: Experiences of internationally adopted children and their parents. *Journal of Counseling Psychology, 47,* 187–198.

Garcia, E. (1997). The education of Hispanics in early childhood: Of roots and wings, *Young Children, 52*(3), 5–14.

Gardner, H. (2000). *Intelligence reframed: Multiple intelligences for the 21st century.* New York: Basic Books.

Gee, J. P. (1990). *Social linguistics and literacies: Ideology in discourses.* Philadelphia: Falmer Press.

Gee, J. P. (1996). *Social linguistics and literacies: Ideology in discourse* (2nd ed.). Bristol, PA: Taylor & Francis.

Genisio, M. H. (1996). Breaking barriers with books: A fathers' book-sharing program from prison. *Journal of Adolescent & Adult Literacy, 40*(2), 92–100.

Geraci, P. M. (2000). Reaching out the right way. *Journal of Adolescent and Adult Literacy, 43,* 632–634.

Gesell, A. (1925). *The mental growth of the preschool child.* New York: Macmillan.

Gestwicki, C. (1987). *Home, school, and community relations: A guide to working with parents.* Albany, NY: Delmar.

Giardini, L. (1990). I carried you in my heart. *Children Today, 19,* 6–7.

Gilligan, C. (1982). *In a different voice: Psychological theory and women's development.* Cambridge, MA: Harvard University Press.

Glazer, S. M. (1989). Oral language and literacy development. In D. S. Strickland, & L. M. Morrow, *Emerging literacy: Young children learn to read and write* (pp. 16–34). Newark, DE: International Reading Association.

Goldman, L. E. (1996). We can help children grieve: A child-oriented model for memorializing. *Young Children, 51*(6), 69–73.

Goodman, K. S. (1967). Reading: A psycholinguistic guessing game. *Journal of the Reading Specialist, 4,* 126–135.

Goodman, Y. (1997). Multiple roads to literacy. In D. Taylor (Ed.), *Many families, many literacies* (p. 56). Portsmouth, NH: Heinemann.

Green, C. (1998). This is my name. *Childhood Education, 78,* 226–231.

Green, C. (2002). Moving to literature. *Texas Child Care Quarterly, 26*(1), 12–21.

Green, C., & Halsall, S. (1991). Literature's role in the language and cognition of the young child. *Early Child Development and Care, 67,* 39–52.

Green, C., Lilly, E., & Barrett, T. (2002). Families reading together: Connecting literature and life. *Journal of Research in Childhood Education, 16,* 248–262.

Greenbaum, J., Varas, M., & Markel, G. (1980). Using books about handicapped children. *The Reading Teacher, 33,* 16–19.

Grimes, B. F. (Ed.). (2002). Ethnologue: Languages of the world (14th ed.). SIL International. [On-line]. Available: http://www.ethnologue.com/show_country.asp?name=Mexico

Hale, J. (1991). The transmission of cultural values to young African American children. *Young Children, 46*(6), 7–15.

Hannigan, I. (1998). *Off to school.* Washington, DC: National Association for the Education of Young Children.

Hansen, D., & Bernstorf, E. (2002). Linking music learning to reading instruction. *Music Educators Journal, 88*(5), 17–21, 52.

Harding, N. (1996). Family journals: The bridge from home to school and back again. *Young Children, 51*(2), 27–30.

Harste, J., Woodward, V., & Burke, C. (1984). *Language stories and literacy lessons.* Portsmouth, NH: Heinemann.

Heath, S. B. (1982). What no bedtime story means: Narrative skills at home and at school. *Language in Society, 11,* 49–76.

Heath, S. B. (1983). *Ways with words: Language, life, and work in communities and classrooms.* Cambridge, UK: Cambridge University Press.

Helm, J. (1994). Family theme bags: An innovative approach to family involvement in the school. *Young Children, 49* (4), 48–52.

Hendrick, J. (1998). *Total learning* (5th ed.). Upper Saddle River, NJ: Merrill/Prentice-Hall.

Hiebert, E. H., & Coffey, M. (1983, November). *Parents involving their children with environmental print.* Paper presented at the annual meeting of the National Reading Conference, Dallas, TX.

Hiebert, E. H., & Raphael, T. E. (1998). *Early literacy instruction.* Fort Worth, TX: Harcourt Brace.

Hildebrand, V., Phenice, L. A., Gray, M. M., & Hines, R. P. (1996). *Knowing and serving diverse families.* Upper Saddle River, NJ: Merrill/Prentice Hall.

Hodgkinson, H. (1992). *The current condition of Native Americans.* Charleston, WV: ERIC Clearinghouse on Rural Education and Small Schools. (ERIC Document Reproduction Service No. ED348202)

Hoffbauer, D., & Prenn, M. (1996). A place to call one's own: Choosing books about homelessness. *Social Education, 60*(3), 167–169.

Holdaway, D. (1979). *The foundations of literacy.* Sydney: Ashton Scholastic.

Hones, D. F., & Cha, C. S. (1999). *Educating Americans.* Mahwah, NJ: Erlbaum.

Huang, G. (1993). *Beyond culture: Communicating with Asian American children and families.* New York: ERIC Clearinghouse on Urban Education. (ERIC/CUE Digest No. ED366673)

Huck, C. S., Hepler, S., Hickman, J., & Kiefer, B. Z. (2001). *Children's literature in the elementary school.* (7th ed.). Boston: McGraw-Hill.

Humphryes, J. (1998). The developmental appropriateness of high-quality Montessori programs. *Young Children, 54*(4), 4–16.

Hunsaker, R. A. (1990). *Understanding and developing the skills of oral communication: Speaking and listening.* (2nd ed.). Englewood, CO: Morton.

Isom, B. A., & Casteel, C. P. (1997/1998). Hispanic literature: A fiesta for literacy instruction. *Childhood Education, 74*(2), 83–89.

Jackson, M. (1997). Counseling youth of Arab ancestry. In C. C. Lee (Ed.), *Counseling for diversity.* (pp. 41–60). Needham Heights, MA: Allyn & Bacon.

Jaffe, M. L. (1997). *Understanding families.* Boston: Allyn & Bacon.

Jalongo, M. R. (1985). When young children move. *Young Children, 40*(6), 51–57.

Jalongo, M. (1988) *Young children and picture books.* Washington, DC: National Association for the Education of Young Children.

Jalongo, M. R. (1994/1995). Helping children cope with relocation. *Childhood Education, 71*(2), 80–85.

Jalongo, M. (2000). *Early childhood language arts* (2nd ed.). Boston: Allyn & Bacon.

Jalongo, M. R., & Ribblett, D. (1997). Using song picture books to support emergent literacy. *Childhood Education, 74*(1), 15–22.

Jendrek, M. P. (1994). Grandparents who parent their grandchildren. *Gerontologist, 34,* 206–216.

Jensen, E. (1998). *Teaching with the brain in mind.* Alexandria, VA: Association for Supervision and Curriculum Development.

Jensen, E. W., James, S. A., Boyce, W. T., & Hartnett, S. A. (1983). The family routines inventory: Developmental and validation. *Social Science Medicine, 14,* 201–211.

Joe, J. R., & Malach, R. S. (1998). Families with Native American roots. In E. W. Lynch & M. J. Hanson (Eds.), *Developing cross-cultural competence* (pp. 127–164). Baltimore, MD: Brookes.

Johnson, J., Christie, J., & Yawkey, T. (1999). *Play and early childhood development.* New York: Addison-Wesley Longman.

Keeler-Wolf, V. (1998). Why children don't talk (much) about adoption. [on-line]. Available: http://www.pactadopt.org/press/articles/talk-much.html

Kieff, J., & Wellhousen, K. (2000). Planning family involvement in early childhood programs. *Young Children, 55*(3), 18–25.

Kieff, J., & Wellhousen, K. (2000). Using "tool kits" to develop anti-bias teaching strategies among preservice early childhood educators. *Journal of Early Childhood Teacher Education, 21,* 227–233.

Klein, T., Bittel, C., & Molnar, J. (1993). No place to call home: Supporting the needs of homeless children in the early childhood classroom. *Young Children, 48*(6), 22–31.

Kleist, D. M. (1999). Single-parent families: A difference that makes a difference? *Family Journal, 7,* 373–379.

Koblinsky, S. A., & Anderson, E. A. (1993). Serving homeless children and families in Head Start. *Children Today, 22*(3), 19–23, 36.

Kramer, P. A., & Smith, G. G. (1998). Easing the pain of divorce through children's literature. *Early Childhood Education Journal, 26*(2), 89–94.

Lamme, L. L., & McKinley, L. (1992). Creating a caring classroom with children's literature. *Young Children, 48*(1), 65–71.

Lansky, V. (2000). *Vicki Lansky's divorce book for parents.* Minnetonka, MN: Book Peddlers.

Lass, B., & Bromfield, M. (1981). Books about children with special needs: An annotated bibliography. *The Reading Teacher, 34,* 30–38.

Lee, F. Y. (1995). Asian parents as partners. *Young Children, 50*(3), 4–8.

Lutton, A. (1998). "Well, what are you?" Naming and belonging in early childhood. *Child Care Information Exchange* (122), 48–50.

Lynch, E. W., & Hanson, M. J. (1998). *Developing cross-cultural competence.* Baltimore, MD: Brookes.

Lyons, J. (2000, July 26–August 2). Faith of their fathers. *Metro Santa Cruz.* Retrieved January 16, 2001, from http://www.metroactive.com/papers/cruz/07.26.00/migrantworkers-0030.html

Marshall, C. S. (1998). Using children's storybooks to encourage discussions among diverse populations. *Childhood Education, 74*(4), 194–199.

Martin, P. (1994). *Migrant farmworkers and their children.* Charleston, WV: ERIC Clearinghouse on Rural Education and Small Schools. (ERIC Document Reproduction Service No. ED376997)

McBride, J. (1996). *The color of water.* New York: Riverhead Books.

McCormick, L., & Holden, R. (1992). Homeless children: A special challenge. *Young Children, 47*(6), 61–67.

McDonnell, L. M., & Hill, P. T. (1993). Immigrant education: The incredible shrinking priority. *The Education Digest, 59,* 35–39.

McGee, L., & Richgels, D. (2000). *Literacy's beginnings.* Needham Heights, MA: Allyn & Bacon.

McLane, J., & McNamee, A. (1991). Parent information the beginnings of literacy. *Zero to Three, 12*(1), 1–8.

Meacham, J. (2000, September 18). The new face of race. *Newsweek,* pp. 38–41.

Menchana, V., Ruiz-Escalante, J. (n.d.). Instructional strategies for migrant students. Charleston, WV: ERIC Clearinghouse on Rural Education and Small Schools. (ERIC Document Reproduction Service No. ED388491)

Minkler, M., & Roe, K. (1993). *Grandparents as caregivers: Raising children of the crack cocaine epidemic.* Newbury Park, CA: Sage.

Moll, L. C., & Greenberg, J. (1990). Creating zones of possibilities: Combining social contexts for instruction. In L. C. Moll (Ed.), *Vygotsky and education* (pp. 319–348). Cambridge, UK: Cambridge University Press.

Moll, L. C., Amanti, C., Neff, D., & Gonzalez, N. (1992). Funds of knowledge for teaching: Using a qualitative approach to connect homes and classrooms. *Theory into Practice, 21*(2), 132–141.

Moosa, S., & Adams, L. (2001). Teacher perception of Arab parent involvement in elementary schools. *The School-Community Journal, 11*(2), 7–26.

Morningstar, J. W. (1999). Home response journals: Parents as informed contributors in the understanding of their child's literacy development. *The Reading Teacher, 52,* 690–697.

Morris, D. (1999). *The Howard Street tutoring manual.* New York: Guilford.

Morrison, J. W., & Borders, T. (2001). Supporting biracial children's identity development. *Childhood Education, 77*(3), 134–138.

Morrow, L. M. (1997). *Literacy development in the early years* (3rd ed.). Boston: Allyn & Bacon.

Munger, R., & Morse, W. C. (1992). When divorce rocks a child's world. *The Educational Forum, 43*(4), 100–103.

Nabhan, G. P., & Trimble, S. (1994). *The geography of childhood.* Boston: Beacon Press.

National Association for the Education of Young Children. (1996). NAEYC position statement: Responding to linguistic and cultural diversity—recommendations for effective early childhood education. *Young Children, 51*(2), 4–12.

National Coalition for the Homeless. (1999). Education of homeless children and youth. NCH Fact Sheet #10. [On-line]. Available: http://nch.ari.net/edchild.html

Neuman, S. B., & Celano, D. C. (2001). Access to print in middle- and low-income communities: An ecological study of four neighborhoods. *Reading Research Quarterly, 36,* 8–26.

Neuman, S., Copple, C., & Bredekamp, S. (2000). *Learning to read and write.* Washington, DC: National Association for the Education of Young Children.

Neuman, S. B., Celano, D. C., Greco, A. N., & Shue, P. (2001). *Access for all: Closing the book gap in early childhood education.* Newark, DE: International Reading Association.

Nieto, S. (1992). We have stories to tell: A case study of Puerto Ricans in children's books. In V. J. Harris (Ed.), *Teaching multicultural literature in grades K–8* (pp. 171–201). Norwood, MA: Christopher Gordon.

Norton, D. E. (1999). *Through the eyes of a child* (5th ed.). Upper Saddle River, NJ: Merrill/Prentice Hall.

Nunez, R., & Collignon, K. (1997). Creating a community of learning for homeless children. *Educational Leadership, 55,* 56–60.

Okagaki, L., & Diamond, K. E. (2000). Responding to cultural and linguistic differences in the beliefs and practices of families with young children. *Young Children, 55*(3), 74–80.

Olkowski, T. T., & Parker, L. (1992). *Helping children cope with moving.* York, PA: William Gladden Foundation.

Orellana, M. F., & Hernandez, A. (1999). Talking the walk: Children reading urban environmental print. *The Reading Teacher, 52,* 612–619.

Packer, A., Hoffman, S., Bozler, B., & Bear, N. (1976). Home learning activities for children. In I. J. Gordon & W. F. Breivogel (Eds.), *Building effective home–school relationships* (pp. 130–147). Boston: Allyn & Bacon.

Pahl, K. (1999). *Transformations: Meaning making in nursery education.* Staffordshire, UK: Trentham Books.

Paley, V. (1997). *The girl with the brown crayon.* Cambridge, MA: Harvard University Press.

Pang, V. O., Colvin, C., Tran, M., & Barba, R. H. (1992). Beyond chopsticks and dragons: Selecting Asian-American literature for children. *The Reading Teacher, 46,* 216–224.

Pappas, C. C. (1993). Is narrative "primary"? Some insights from kindergartners' pretend reading of stories and information books. *Journal of Reading Behavior, 25,* 97–129.

Paratore, J. R. (2001). *Opening doors, opening opportunities: Family literacy in an urban community.* Boston: Allyn & Bacon.

Pardeck, J. T. (1996). Recommended books for helping children deal with separation and divorce. *Adolescence, 31*(121), 233–237.

Pedro-Carroll, J. L., Sutton, S. E., & Wyman, P. A. (1999). A two-year follow-up evaluation of a preventive intervention for young children of divorce. *School Psychology Review, 28,* 467–477.

Piaget, J. (1926). *The language and thought of the child.* London: Routledge & Kegan Paul.

Pipher, M. B. (1996). *The shelter of each other: Rebuilding our families.* New York: Putnam.

Prewitt-Diaz, J. O., Trotter, R. T., & Rivera, V. A. (1990). Effects of migration on children. *The Educational Digest, 55,* 26–29.

Ramsey, P. (1998). *Teaching and learning in a diverse world* (2nd ed.). New York: Teachers College Press.

Richgels, D. J. (2001). Phonemic awareness. *The Reading Teacher, 55,* 274–278.

Richgels, D. J. (2002). Informational texts in kindergarten. *The Reading Teacher, 55,* 586–595.

Rockwell, R. E., Andre, L. C., & Hawley, M. K. (1996). *Parents and teachers as partners: Issues and challenges.* Fort Worth, TX: Harcourt Brace.

Rong, X. L., & Preissle, J. (1998). *Educating immigrant students.* Thousand Oaks, CA: Corwin.

Rosenblatt, L. (1976). *Literature as exploration.* New York: Noble & Noble.

Rosenblatt, L. M. (1978). *The reader, the text, and the poem.* Carbondale: Southern Illinois University Press.

Rothenberg, D. (1996). *Grandparents as parents: A primer for schools.* Urbana, IL: ERIC Clearinghouse on Elementary and Early Childhood Education. (ERIC Document Reproduction Service No. ED401044)

Rothenburg, D. (1998). *With these hands: The hidden world of migrant farmworkers today.* Berkeley: University of California Press.

Rowe, D. W. (1998). The literate potentials of book-related dramatic play. *Reading Research Quarterly, 33,* 10–35.

Sammons, W. A. H., & Lewis, J. M. (2000). What schools are doing to help the children of divorce. *Young Children, 55*(5), 64–65.

Schickendanz, J. (1999). *Much more than the ABCs.* Washington, DC: National Association for the Education of Young Children.

Schwartz, W. (1999). Arab American students in public schools. (ERIC Digest No. 142, ED429144).

Seymour, C. (1998). Children with parents in prison: Child welfare policy, program, and practice issues. *Child Welfare, 77,* 469–493.

Shannon, P. (1998). *Reading poverty.* Portsmouth, NH: Heinemann.

Sharkey, P. B. (1998). Being adopted: Books to help children understand. *Emergency Librarian, 25*(4), 8–10.

Shen, W., & Mo, W. (1990). *Reaching out to their cultures—Building communication with Asian-American families.* Urbana, IL: Educational Resources Information Center. (ERIC Document Reproduction Service No. ED351435)

Shockley, B., Michalove, B., & Allen, J. (1995). *Engaging families: Connecting home and school literacy communities.* Portsmouth, NH: Heinemann.

Shore, R. (1997). *Rethinking the brain: New insights into early development.* Washington, DC: Families and Work Institute.

Simmons, M. P. (1996). Bibliotherapy with children's books. *The Delta Kappa Gamma Bulletin, 62,* 53–55.

Sims Bishop, R. (1992). Multicultural literature for children: Making informed choices. In V. Harris (Ed.), *Teaching multicultural literature in grades K–8* (pp. 37–54). Norwood, MA: Christopher-Gordon.

Smith, A. B., Dannison, L. L., & Vach-Hasse, T. (1998). When "Grandma" is "Mom": What today's teachers need to know. *Childhood Education, 75*(1), 12–16.

Smolen, L. A., & Ortiz-Castro, V. (2000). Dissolving borders and broadening perspectives through Latino traditional literature. *The Reading Teacher, 53,* 566–578.

Snell, T. (1994). *Women in Prison.* (Special report). Washington, DC: U.S. Department of Justice, Bureau of Justice Statistics.

Snow, C. E., Burns, M. S., & Griffin, P. (1998). *Preventing reading difficulties in young children.* Washington, DC: National Academy Press.

Somerindyke, J. (2000). Homeless, not hopeless: Understanding children who live in poverty. *Dimensions of Early Childhood, 28*(1), 11–15.

Spiegel, D. L. (1998). Silver bullets, babies, and bath water: Literature response groups in a balanced literacy program. *The Reading Teacher, 52,* 114–124.

Spitz, E. (1999). *Inside picture books.* New Haven, CT: Yale University Press.

Springate, K. W., & Stegelin, D. A. (1999). *Building school and community partnerships through parent involvement.* Upper Saddle River, NJ: Merrill/Prentice Hall.

Stacey, J. (1998). Gay and lesbian families: Queer like us. In M. A. Mason, A. Skolnick, & S. D. Sugarman (Eds.), *All our families: New policies for a new century.* New York: Oxford University Press.

Staley, L. (2000). Time to say good-bye. *Childhood Education, 76*(3), 170–171.

Stanovich, K. (2000). *Progress in understanding reading.* New York: Guilford.

Stern, D. (1977). *The first relationship: Infant and mother.* Cambridge, MA: Harvard University Press.

Strickland, R., Dodd, E. L., & Newsom, L. (1999). Recipe for love: A family literacy program. *Georgia Journal of Reading, 23*(2), 14–22.

Sulzby, E. (1985). Children's emergent reading of favorite storybooks: A developmental study. *Reading Research Quarterly, 20,* 458–481.

Swick, K. (1991). *Teacher–parent partnerships to enhance school success in early childhood education.* Washington, DC: National Education Association.

Tabors, P. O. (1997). *One child, two languages.* Baltimore, MD: Brookes.

Tatum, B. D. (2000). Examining racial and cultural thinking. *Educational Leadership, 57*(8), 54–57.

Taylor, D. (1983). *Family literacy.* Exeter, NH: Heinemann.

Taylor, D. (Ed.) (1997). *Many families, many literacies.* Portsmouth, NH: Heinemann.

Taylor, D., & Strickland, D. (1986). *Family storybook reading.* Portsmouth, NH: Heinemann.

Teale, W. H., & Sulzby, E. (Eds.). (1986). *Emergent literacy: Writing and reading.* Norwood, NJ: Ablex.

Temple, C., Martinez, M., Yokota, J., & Naylor, A. (1998). *Children's books in children's hands: An introduction to their literature.* Boston: Allyn & Bacon.

The new face of race. (2000, September 18). *Newsweek,* pp. 38–46.

The Teaching Tolerance Project. (1997). *Starting small: Teaching tolerance in preschool and the early grades.* Montgomery, AL: Southern Poverty Law Center.

Thompkins, G. E. (2003). *Literacy for the 21st century* (3rd ed.). Upper Saddle River, NJ: Merrill/Prentice Hall.

Tomlinson, C. M., & Lynch-Brown, C. (1996). *Essentials of children's literature* (2nd ed.). Boston: Allyn & Bacon.

Trawick-Smith, J. (1994). *Interactions in the classroom: Facilitating play in the early years.* New York: Macmillan.

U.S. Census Bureau. (2000). *USA statistics in brief.* Retrieved January 16, 2001, from http://www.census.gov

Van Kleek, A., Alexander, E., Vigil, A., & Templeton, K. (1996). Verbally modeling thinking for infants: Middle-class mothers' presentation of information structures during book sharing. *Journal of Research in Childhood Education, 10*(2), 101–113.

Vandergrift, K. (1980). *Child and story: The literacy connection.* New York: Neal-Schuman Publishers.

Velasquez, L. C. (1994). Migrant and seasonal farmworkers: An invisible population. Charleston, WV: ERIC Clearinghouse on Rural Education and Small Schools. (ERIC Document Reproduction Service No. ED386355)

Vopat, J. (1994). *The parent project: A workshop approach to parent involvement.* York, ME: Stenhouse.

Voss, M. (1996). *Hidden literacies: Children learning at home and at school.* Portsmouth, NH: Heinemann.

Vygotsky, L. S. (1978). *Mind and society: The development of higher mental processes.* Cambridge, MA: Harvard University Press.

Waggoner, D. (1994). Language minority school age population now totals 9.9 million. *National Association for Bilingual Education News, 18*(1), 1, 24–26.

Wardle, F. (1992). Supporting biracial children in the school setting. *Education and Treatment of Children, 15*(2), 163–172.

Wardle, F. (1998) Belonging. *Child Care Information Exchange* (122), 57.

Washington, V., & Andrews, J. D. (1998). *Children of 2010.* Washington, DC: National Association for the Education of Young Children.

West, R., & Stanovich, K. (1991). The incidental acquisition of information from reading. *Psychological Science, 2,* 325–330.

Whitehurst, G., Arnold., D., Epstein, J., Angell, A., Smith, M., & Fischel, J. (1994). A picture book reading intervention in day care and home for children from low-income families. *Developmental Psychology, 30,* 679–689.

Wickens, E. (1993). Penny's question: "I will have a child in my class with two moms–What do you know about this?" *Young Children, 48*(3), 25–28.

Wilson, M. (1996). Arab speaker: Language and culture, here and abroad. *Topics in Language Disorders, 16,* 65–80.

Wilson, R. A. (1995). Nature and young children: A natural connection. *Young Children, 50*(6), 4–11.

Wingfield, M., & Karaman, B. (1995). Arab stereotypes and American educators. *Social Studies and the Young Learner, 7*(4), 7–10.

Winston, L. (1997). *Keepsakes: Using family stories in elementary classrooms.* Portsmouth, NH: Heinemann.

Wolf, S., & Heath, S. B. (1992). *The braid of literature.* Cambridge, MA: Harvard University Press.

Yoest, C. C. (1990) The lucky ones. *Children Today, 19,* 12–13.

York, S. (1991). *Roots and wings.* Mt. Rainier, MD: Gryphon House.

York, S. (1992). *Developing roots and wings.* Mt. Rainier, MD: Gryphon House.

CHILDREN'S REFERENCES

I = Infant

T = Toddler

P = Preschool

K = Kindergarten

Aardema, V. (1998). *Borrequita and the coyote: A tale from Ayutla, Mexico.* New York: Dragonfly. (P, K)

Ada, A. F. (1995). *Mediopollito/Half-chicken* (K. Howard, Ill.). New York: Doubleday. (P, K)

Ada, A. F. (1997). *Gathering the sun: An alphabet in Spanish and English* (S. Silva, Ill.; R. Zubizarreta, Trans.). New York: Lothrop, Lee, & Shepard. (P, K)

Adoff, A. (1973). *Black is brown is tan.* (E. A. McCulley, Ill.). New York: Harper-Collins. (P, K)

Adoff, A. (1988). *Whiskers and rhymes.* New York: Morrow. (K)

Ahlberg, J., & Ahlberg, A. (1978). *Each peach pear plum.* New York: Viking.

Ahlberg, J., & Ahlberg, A. (1986). *The jolly postman or other people's letters.* Boston: Little, Brown. (P, K)

Ahlberg, J., & Ahlberg, A. (1988). *Starting school.* London: Puffin. (P, K)

Aliki. (1979). *The two of them.* New York: Greenwillow. (K)

Aliki. (1986). *Go tell Aunt Rhody.* New York: Simon & Schuster. (T, P, K)

Aliki. (1998). *Painted memories, painted words.* New York: Greenwillow. (K)

Aliki. (2000). *All by myself!* New York: HarperCollins. (T, P)

Allen, C. (1988). *My first dentist visit.* New York: Children's Press. (P)

Ancona, G. (1998). *Let's dance.* New York: Morrow Junior Books. (P, K)

Anderson, L. (1988). *Stina.* New York: Greenwillow. (P, K)

Andrews, J. (2002). *Very last first time* (I. Wallace, Ill.). Vancouver, BC: Douglas & McIntyre. (K)

Applet, K. (1995). *Bayou lullaby* (N. Waldman, Ill.) New York: Morrow. (P, K)

Applet, K. (1999). *Cowboy dreams.* (B. Boot, Ill.) New York: HarperCollins. (P, K)

Arnold, E. A. (1997). *School.* New York: HarperCollins. (T, P, K)

Ashbe, J. (2000). *What's inside?* Brooklyn, NY: Kane/Miller.

Ashbe, J. (2002). *And after that. . . .* La Jolla, CA: Kane/Miller. (P, K)

Ashley, B. (1991). *Cleversticks.* New York: Crown. (P, K)

Ata, T. (1996). *Baby rattlesnake/Viborita de Cascabel* (M. Reisberg, Ill.). Emeryville, CA: Children's Book Press. (P, K)

Auch, M. J. (1997). *Bantam of the opera.* New York: Holiday House. (K)

Aylesworth, J. (1992). *Old black fly* (S. Gammell, Ill.). New York: Henry Holt.

Aylesworth, J. (1998). *The gingerbread man* (B. McClintock, Ill.). New York: Scholastic Trade.

Azarian, M. (1981). *A farmer's alphabet.* New York: Godine. (K)

Bailey, L. (1999). *When Addie was scared.* Toronto: Kids Can Press. (K)

Baker, J. (1991). *Window.* New York: Penguin. (K)

Baker, K. (1994). *Big fat hen.* San Diego: Harcourt Brace. (P, K)

Ballard, R. (1993). *Gracie.* New York: Greenwillow. (P, K)

Ballard, R. (1998). *When I am a sister.* New York: Greenwillow. (P)

Bang, M. (1983). *Ten, nine, eight*. New York: Greenwillow. (T, P)

Bang, M. (1999). *When Sophie gets angry—Really, really, angry. . . .* New York: Blue Sky Press. (P)

Banks, K. (1998). *And if the moon could talk* (G. Hallensleben, Ill.). New York: Farrar, Straus & Giroux. (P, K)

Barber, B. (1994). *Saturday at the new you* (A. Rich, Ill.). New York: Lee & Low. (K)

Barbour, K. (1991). *Mr. Bow Tie*. San Diego: Harcourt Brace Jovanovich. (P, K)

Barracca, D., & Barracca, S. (1990). *The adventures of taxi dog* (M. Buehner, Ill.). New York: Dial. (P, K)

Barrett, J. (1978). *Cloudy with a chance of meatballs* (R. Barrett, Ill.). New York: Aladdin. (P, K)

Barrett, M. B. (1999). *Day care days* (P. Murphy, Ill.). Boston: Little, Brown. (P)

Barron, T. (2000). *Where is Grandpa?* (C. Soentpiet, Ill.). New York: Philomel. (P)

Barton, B. (1992). *Building a house*. Carmel, CA: Hampton-Brown.

Barton, B. (1995). *Buzz, buzz, buzz*. New York: Simon & Schuster Children's Books. (I, T)

Barton, B. (1997). *Machines at work*. New York: HarperCollins.

Barton, B. (1998). *Planes*. New York: HarperCollins. (T, P)

Barton, B. (1998). *Trucks*. New York: HarperCollins. (T, P)

Barton, B. (2001). *My car*. New York: Greenwillow.

Bateson-Hill, M. (1996). *Lao-Lao of Dragon Mountain* (F. Pelizzoli, Ill.). New York: Stewart, Tabori, & Chang. (K)

Bayer, J., & Kellogg, S. (1992). *A my name is Alice*. New York: Dutton.

Beaton, C. (1999). *Zoe and her zebra*. New York: Scholastic. (P, K)

Belton, S. (1994). *May'naise sandwiches and sunshine tea* (G. Carter, Ill.). New York: Four Winds. (K)

Bemelmans, L. (1976). *Madeline*. New York: Viking Penguin. (P, K)

Berger, B. (1984). *Grandfather Twilight*. New York: Philomel. (P, K)

Berger, B. (1986). *When the sun rose*. New York: Philomel. (P, K)

Best, C. (1996). *Getting used to Harry* (D. Palmisciano, Ill.). New York: Orchard. (P, K)

Best, L. (1995). *Red light, green light, Mama and me*. (N. Daly, Ill.). New York: Orchard. (P, K)

Bider, D. (1989). *A drop of honey* (A. Kojoyian, Ill.) New York: Simon & Schuster. (P, K)

Bierman, C., & Hehmer, B. (1998). *Journey to Ellis Island: How my father came to America* (L. McGaw, Ill.). New York: Hyperion. (K)

Blanc, F. (1997). *I am Vietnamese American*. New York: PowerKids. (P, K)

Bond, R. (1999). *Just like a baby*. Boston: Little, Brown. (P, K)

Bousman, C. (2000). *Pete and P. J.: Sing, dance, and read with me*. Kindermusic International. (T, P)

Boynton, S. (2000). *Pajama time!* New York: Workman. (I, T)

Breckler, R. K. (1992). *Hoang breaks the lucky teapot*. Boston: Houghton Mifflin. (K)

Brodinsky, A. (1996). *The mulberry bird* (D. Stanley, Ill.). Indianapolis: Perspectives. (K)

Breeze, L. (1990). *This little baby goes out*. London: Orchard. (I, T)

Brenner, B. (Ed.). (1994). *The earth is painted green* (S. D. Schindler, Ill.). New York: Scholastic. (K)

Brett, J. (1990). *The mitten: A Ukranian folktale*. New York: Putnam. (P, K)

Brett, J. (1994). *Town mouse, country mouse*. New York: Scholastic. (P, K)

Brett, J. (1999). *The gingerbread baby*. New York: Putnam. (P, K)

Briggs, R. (1973). *Father Christmas*. New York: Coward, McCann, & Geoghegan. (P, K)

Briggs, R. (1978). *The snowman*. New York: Random House. (P, K)

Brillhart, J. (1992). *Story hour—Starring Megan!* Morton Grove, IL: Whitman. (P, K)

Brooks, D. (Ed.). (2000). *The wheels on the bus* (P. Zelinsky, Ill.). New York: Dutton.

Brothers Grimm. (1987). *Little Red Riding Hood* (T. S. Hyman, Ill.). New York: Holiday House. (P, K)

Brothers Grimm. (1993). *Red Riding Hood* (J. Marshall, Ill.). New York: Puffin. (P, K)

Brown, D. (1998). *Touch and feel: Wild animals.* New York: DK Publishing. (I, T)

Brown, L., & Brown, M. (1986). *Visiting the art museum.* New York: Dutton. (P, K)

Brown, M. W. (1947). *Goodnight moon* (C. Hurd, Ill.). New York: Harper & Row. (I, T, P)

Brown, M. W. (1959). *Little donkey close your eyes* (A. Wolff, Ill.). New York: HarperCollins. (P, K)

Brown, M. W. (1972). *The runaway bunny* (C. Hurd, Ill.). New York: Harper & Row. (I, P)

Brown, R. (1998). *Mad summer night's dream.* New York: Penguin Putnam. (P, K)

Brown, T. (1995). *Konnichiwa! I am a Japanese-American girl.* New York: Henry Holt. (K)

Bruchac, J. (1997). *Many nations: An alphabet of Native America* (R. Goetzl, Ill.). Bridgewater, NJ: Bridgewater Paperbacks.

Bruno, J. (1991). *Book cooks: Literature-based classroom cooking* (R. E. Herrera, Ill.). Cypress, CA: Creative Teaching. (P, K)

Brutschy, J. (2002). *Just one more story* (C. B. Smith, Ill.). New York: Orchard. (P, K)

Bryant-Mole, K. (1999). *Talking about death.* New York: Raintree/Steck Vaughn. (P, K)

Buckley, H. (1994). *Grandfather and I* (J. Omerod, Ill.). New York: HarperCollins. (P)

Buck-Murray, M. (1998). *The mash and smash cookbook* (R. Butler, Ill.). New York: Wiley. (K)

Buffett, J., & Buffett, S. J. (1988). *The jolly mon.* Fort Worth, TX: Harcourt Brace. (P, K)

Bunnett, R. (1996). *Friends at school.* (M. Brown, Photo.). New York: Star Bright. (P, K)

Bunting, E. (1991). *Fly away home* (R. Himler, Ill.). New York: Clarion. (K)

Bunting, E. (1993). *Someday a tree* (R. Himler, Ill.). Boston: Houghton Mifflin. (K)

Bunting, E. (1994). *Flower garden.* (K. Hewitt, Ill.). Orlando, FL: Harcourt Brace. (P, K)

Bunting, E. (1994). *Sunshine home* (D. DeGroat, Ill.). New York: Clarion. (P, K)

Bunting, E. (1996). *Going home* (D. Diaz, Ill.). New York: HarperCollins. (K)

Bunting, E. (1996). *No nap* (S. Meddaugh, Ill.). Boston: Houghton Mifflin. (K)

Bunting, E. (1997). *December* (D. Diaz, Ill.). San Diego: Harcourt Brace Jovanovich. (K)

Bunting, E. (1999). *Butterfly house* (G. Shed, Ill.). New York: Scholastic. (K)

Bunting, E. (1999). *A picnic in October* (N. Carpenter, Ill.). San Diego: Harcourt Brace. (K)

Burningham, J. (1980). *The shopping basket.* New York: Crowell. (P, K)

Butterworth, O. (1993). *A visit to the big house* (S. Avishai, Ill.). Boston: Houghton Mifflin. (K)

Cain, S., & Speed, M. (1999). *Dad's in prison* (C. Heronneau, Ill.; Z. Mukhida, Photo.). London: U A & C. Black. (P, K)

Caines, J. (1988). *I need a lunchbox* (P. Cummings, Ill.). New York: HarperCollins. (P, K)

Cairo, S. (1997). *Our brother has Down syndrome: An introduction for children.* Willowdale, ON: Annick Press. (P, K)

Caldecott, R. (1978). *The diverting history of John Gilpin.* New York: Warne. (Originally published 1878)

Calmenson, S. (2002). *The teeny tiny teacher* (D. Roche, Ill.) New York: Scholastic. (P, K)

Calmenson, S. (2000). *Welcome baby: Baby rhymes for baby times* (M. Sweet, Ill.). New York: HarperCollins Juvenile books.

Campbell, R. (1982). *Dear zoo.* New York: Puffin. (T, P)

Cannon, J. (1993). *Stella Luna*. New York: Harcourt Brace. (P, K)

Capucilli, A. S. (2000). *The potty book—for boys*. (D. Stot, Ill.). Hauppauge, NY: Barron's Juveniles.

Capucilli, A. S. (2000). *The potty book—for girls*. (D. Stott, Ill.). Hauppauge, NY: Barron's Juveniles.

Carle, E. (1968). *1, 2, 3 to the zoo*. New York: Philomel. (T, P)

Carle, E. (1969). *The very hungry caterpillar*. New York: Philomel. (T, P, K)

Carle, E. (1985). *My very first book of colors*. New York: HarperCollins. (I, T)

Carle, E. (1995). *The very lonely firefly*. New York: Philomel. (P, K)

Carle, E. (1998a). *Stories for all seasons*. New York: Simon & Schuster. (P, K)

Carle, E. (1998b). *Catch the ball!* New York: Scholastic. (I, T)

Carle, E. (1999). *From head to toe*. New York: HarperCollins. (T, P, K)

Carlson, L. (1998). *Sol a sol* (E. Lisker, Ill.). New York: Henry Holt. (P, K)

Carlson, N. L. (2001). *My best friend moved away*. New York: Penguin Putnam Books for Young Readers. (K)

Carlstrom, N. (1990). *Moose in the garden* (L. Desimini, Ill.). New York: Harper & Row. (P, K)

Carlstrom, N. (1992a). *Northern lullaby* (L. & D. Dillon, Ill.). New York: Philomel. (P, K)

Carlstrom, N. (1992b). *Baby-O* (S. Stevenson, Ill.). Boston: Little, Brown. (T, P)

Carlstrom, N. (1996). *Let's count it out, Jesse Bear* (B. Degen, Ill.). New York: Simon & Schuster.

Carr, J. (1999). *Frozen noses* (D. Donohue, Ill.). New York: Holiday House. (P, K)

Carrick, C. (1976). *Accident*. New York: Seabury. (P, K)

Carroll, L. (1989). *Alice's adventures in wonderland* (John Tenniel, Ill.). New York: St. Martin's. (K) (Originally published 1865)

Carson, J. (1992). *You hold me and I'll hold you* (A. Carson, Ill.). New York: Orchard. (T, P)

Caseley, J. (1986). *When Grandpa came to stay*. New York: Morrow. (P, K)

Caseley, J. (1991). *Dear Annie*. New York: Greenwillow. (K)

Cauley, L. B. (1992). *Clap your hands*. New York: Putnam. (T, P)

Cha, D. (1996). *Dia's story cloth* (C. & N. Thao Cha, Ills.). New York: Lee & Low. (K)

Charlip, R., Beth, M., & Acona, G. (1987). *Handtalk birthday: A number and story book in Sign Language*. New York: Four Winds. (K)

Charlip, R. (2000). *Sleepytime rhyme*. New York: Scholastic.

Cheng, A. (2000). *Grandfather counts* (A. Zhang, Ill.). New York: Lee & Low. (K)

Chinn, K. (1995). *Sam and the lucky money* (C. Wright & Y. Hu, Ills.). New York: Lee & Low. (K)

Chocolate, D. (1995). *On the day I was born* (M. Rosales, Ill.). New York: Scholastic. (P, K)

Chocolate, D. (1996). *Kente colors* (J. Ward, Ill.). New York: Walker. (P, K)

Choi, S. N. (1993). *Halmoni and the picnic*. Boston: Houghton Mifflin. (K)

Choi, Y. (2001). *The name jar*. New York: Knopf. (P, K)

Chorao, K. (1984). *The baby's bedtime book*. New York: Dutton. (I, T)

Chorao, K. (1986). *The baby's good morning book*. New York: Dutton. (I, T)

Chorao, K. (1988). *Cathedral mouse*. New York: Dutton. (P, K)

Christiansen, C. (1989). *My mother's house, my father's house* (I. Trivas, Ill.). New York: Atheneum. (P, K)

Church, C. (2002). *Do your ears hang low? A love story*. New York: Scholastic. (I, T, P)

Cimarusti, M. (1998). *Peek-a-moo!* (S. Peterson, Ill.). New York: Dutton. (I, T)

Clifton, L. (1991). *Everett Anderson's Christmas coming* (J. Gilchrist, Ill.). New York: Henry Holt. (P, K)

Climo, S. (1989). *The Egyptian Cinderella* (R. Heller, Ill.). New York: HarperCollins. (P, K)

Climo, S. (1993). *Korean Cinderella* (R. Heller, Ill.). New York: HarperCollins. (P, K)

Cohen, M. (1967). *Will I have a friend?* New York: Macmillan/McGraw-Hill. (P, K)

Cohen, M, & Yohen, M. (1984). *Jim's dog muffins* (L. Hoban, Ill.). New York: Greenwillow. (K)

Cole, H. (1998). *I took a walk.* New York: Greenwillow. (P, K)

Cole, J. (1995). *My new kitten* (Margaret Miller, Ill.). New York: Morrow. (T, P)

Cole, J. (1997). *I'm a big brother.* (M. Chambliss, Ill.). Out of print.

Cole, J. (1997). *I'm a big sister.* (M. Chambliss, Ill.). Out of print.

Cole, J. (1998). *The new baby at your house* (M. Miller, Ill.). New York: Morrow. (T, P)

Cole, J. (2000). *My big boy potty* (M. Chambliss, Ill.). New York: HarperCollins Juvenile Books.

Cole, J. (2000). *My big girl potty* (M. Chambliss, Ill.). New York: Morrow.

Collins, S. H. (1995). *Songs in sign.* Eugene, OR: Garlic Press. (P, K)

Combs, B. (2001). *ABC: A family alphabet book* (D. Keane, Ill.). Ridley Park, PA: Two Lives. (P, K)

Combs, B. (2001). *1,2,3: A family counting book* (D. Keane, Ill.). Ridley Park, PA: Two Lives. (P, K)

Cooke, T. (1994). *So much* (H. Oxenbury, Ill.). Cambridge, MA: Candlewick. (T, P, K)

Cooney, B. (1991). *Island boy.* New York: Penguin Putnam Books for Young Readers. (P, K)

Cooney, B. (1982). *Miss Rumphius.* New York: Viking. (K)

Cooper, H. (1997). *The boy who wouldn't go to bed.* New York: Dial. (P, K)

Cousins, L. (1995). *Maisy's ABC.* Cambridge, MA: Candlewick. (P)

Cousins, L. (2001). *Maisy's garden.* Cambridge, MA: Candlewick. (T, P)

Cowan-Fletcher, J. (1993). *Mama zooms.* New York: Scholastic. (T, P)

Crews, D. (1978). *Freight train.* New York: Greenwillow. (T, P)

Crews, D. (1980). *Truck.* New York: Greenwillow. (T, P)

Crews, D. (1984). *School bus.* New York: Morrow. (T, P)

Crews, D. (1986). *Ten black dots.* New York: Morrow. (P, K)

Crews, D. (1991). *Bigmama's.* New York: Greenwillow. (P, K)

Crews, D. (1998). *Night at the fair.* New York: Greenwillow. (P, K)

Crews, N. (1995). *One hot summer day.* New York: Morrow. (P, K)

Crews, N. (1998). *You are here.* New York: Greenwillow. (P, K)

Crews, N. (1999). *A high, low, near, far, loud, quiet story.* New York: Greenwillow. (P, K)

Cristini, E., & Puricelli, L. (1984). *In the pond.* Natick, MA: Picture Book Studios. (P, K)

Crotta, L. (1997). *Flannel kisses.* Boston: Houghton Mifflin. (T, P, K)

Curtis, J. (1996). *Tell me again about the night I was born* (L. Cornell, Ill.). New York: HarperCollins. (P, K)

Cutler, J. (1993). *Darcy and Gran don't like babies* (S. Ryan, Ill.). New York: Scholastic. (P, K)

Czech, J. M. (2002). *The coffee can kid* (M. J. Manning, Ill.). Washington, DC: Child and Family Press. (P, K)

D'Antonio, N. (1997). *Our baby from China: An adoption story.* Morton Grove, IL: Whitman. (K)

Davol, M. (1993). *Black, white, just right* (I. Trivas, Ill.). Morton Grove, IL: Whitman. (P, K)

Day, A. (1985). *Good dog Carl.* New York: Green Tiger. (T, P)

Deedy, C. A. (2001). *The library dragon* (M. P. White, Ill.). Atlanta: Peachtree. (K)

Degan, B. (1983). *Jamberry.* New York: HarperTrophy. (T, P)

Delacre, L. (1989). *Arroz con leche: Popular songs and rhymes from Latin America.* New York: Scholastic. (P, K)

Delacre, L. (1993). *Vejigante/Masquerader.* New York: Scholastic. (K) dePaola, T. (1975). *Strega Nona*. New York: Scholastic. (P, K)

dePaola, T. (1981). *Now one foot, now the other*. New York: Putnam. (P, K)

dePaola, T. (1985). *Tomie dePaola's Mother Goose*. New York: Putnam.

dePaola, T. (1985). *Watch out for the chicken feet in your soup*. New York: Aladdin. (P, K)

dePaola, T. (1990). *Pancakes for breakfast*. San Diego: Harcourt Brace.

dePaola, T. (1997). *Mice squeak, we speak*. New York: Putnam. (T, P)

Derby, S. (1996). *My steps* (A. Burrowes, Ill.). New York: Lee & Low. (P, K)

DiSalvo-Ryan, D. (1991). *Uncle Willie and the soup kitchen*. New York: Morrow. (K)

DiSalvo-Ryan, D. (2000). *Grandpa's corner store*. New York: Morrow. (P, K).

Dooley, N. (1991). *Everybody cooks rice*. Minneapolis: Carolrhoda. (P, K)

Dooley, N. (1996). *Everybody bakes bread*. Minneapolis: Carolrhoda. (P, K)

Dorros, A. (1991). *Abuela* (E. Kleven, Ill.). New York: Penguin. (P, K)

Dorros, A. (1993). *Radio man* (S. Dorros, Trans.). New York: HarperCollins. (K)

Dotlich, R. K. (1999). *What is round?* (M. Ferrari, Photo.). New York: HarperCollins. (T, P)

Dotlich, R. K. (1999). *What is square?* (M. Ferrari, Photo.). New York: HarperCollins. (T, P)

Doyle, C. (1998). *You can't catch me*. New York: HarperFestival. (T, P)

Dunbar, J. (1998). *Tell me something happy before I go to sleep* (D. Gliori, Ill.). New York: Scholastic. (P, K)

Dunn, O. (1999). *Hippety-hop hippety-hay* (S. Lambert, Ill.). New York: Henry Holt. (I, T)

Dwight, L. (1997). *We can do it!* New York: Star Bright. (P, K)

Edens, C. (1998). *The glorious Mother Goose*. New York: Atheneum. (T, P, K)

Edwards, N. (2001). *Glenna's seeds*. Washington, DC: Child and Family Press. (P, K)

Egielski, R. (2000). *The gingerbread boy*. New York: HarperTrophy. (T, P, K)

Ehlert, L. (1987). *Growing vegetable soup*. Orlando, FL: Harcourt Brace. (T, P, K)

Ehlert, L. (1988). *Planting a rainbow*. Orlando, FL: Harcourt Brace. (T, P, K)

Ehlert, L. (1989). *Color zoo*. New York: HarperCollins. (P, K)

Ehlert, L. (1989). *Eating the alphabet*. San Diego: Harcourt Brace. (K)

Ehlert, L. (1990). *Color farm*. New York: HarperCollins. (P, K)

Ehlert, L. (1990). *Feathers for lunch*. San Diego: Harcourt Brace. (T, P)

Ehlert, L. (1991). *Red leaf, yellow leaf*. San Diego: Harcourt Brace. (P, K)

Ehlert, L. (1992). *Moon rope: A Peruvian folktale*. (A. Prince, Trans.). San Diego: Harcourt Brace. (P, K)

Ehlert, L. (1993). *Nuts to you!* Orlando, FL: Harcourt Brace. (T, P)

Ehlert, L. (1995). *Snowballs*. San Diego: Harcourt Brace. (P, K)

Ehlert, L. (1997). *Cuckoo/Cucu* (G. Andujar, Trans.). New York: Harcourt Brace. (T, P, K)

Ehlert, L. (2000). *Market day*. New York: Harcourt Brace. (T, P)

Elya, S. M. (2002). *Home at last* (F. Davalos, Ill.). New York: Lee & Low. (K)

Emberly, E. (1993). *Go away, big green monster!* New York: Little, Brown.

English, K. (1998). *Just right stew* (A. Rich, Ill.). Honesdale, PA: Boyds Mills Press. (K)

Erdosh, G. (1997). *Food and recipes of Native Americans*. New York: Rosen. (K)

Ernst, L. C. (1998). *Stella Louella's runaway book*. New York: Simon & Schuster. (P, K)

Fain, K. (1993). *Handsigns: A Sign Language alphabet*. San Francisco: Chronicle. (P, K)

Falconer, I. (2000). *Olivia*. New York: Atheneum. (P, K)

Falconer, I. (2001). *Olivia saves the circus*. New York: Atheneum. (P, K)

Falwell, C. (1993). *Feast for ten*. New York: Clarion. (P, K)

Feelings, M. (1974). *Jambo means hello* (T. Feelings, Ill.). New York: Dial. (K)

Figuerdo, D. (1999). *When this world was new* (E. Sanchez, Ill.). New York: Lee & Low. (K)

Fisher, V. (2002). *My big brother.* New York: Atheneum Books for Young Readers. (P, K)

Fleming, D. (1991). *In the tall, tall grass.* New York: Henry Holt. (T, P)

Fleming, D. (1992). *Count!* New York: Henry Holt. (P)

Fleming, D. (1993). *In the small, small pond.* New York: Henry Holt. (T, P)

Fleming, D. (1994). *Barnyard banter.* New York: Scholastic. (P, K)

Fleming, D. (1996). *Where once there was a wood.* New York: Henry Holt. (P, K)

Fleming, D. (1998). *Mama Cat has three kittens.* New York: Henry Holt. (T, P)

Fleming, V. (1993). *Be good to Eddie Lee* (F. Cooper, Ill.). New York: Philomel. (K)

Frankel, A. (Ill.). (1999). *Once upon a potty: Boy.* New York: Harper Festival.

Frankel, A. (Ill.). (1999). *Once upon a potty: Girl.* New York: Harper Festival.

Ford, J. G. (1997). *K is for Kwanzaa* (K. Wilson-Max, Ill.). New York: Scholastic.

Ford, M. (1999). *My day in the garden* (A. Lobel, Ill.). New York: Greenwillow. (T, P)

Fox, M. (1985). *Wilfrid Gordon McDonald Partridge* (J. Vivas, Ill.). New York: Kane/Miller. (P, K)

Fox, M. (1989). *Shoes from Grandpa* (P. Mullins, Ill.). New York: Orchard. (P, K)

Fox, M. (1993). *Time for bed* (J. Dyer, Ill.). San Diego: Gulliver Books. (T, P)

Fox, M. (1994). *Koala Lou* (P. Lotts, Ill.). New York: Harcourt Brace. (P, K)

Fox, M. (1997). *Whoever you are* (L. Staub, Ill.). San Diego: Harcourt Brace. (P, K)

French, V. (1995). *Oliver's vegetables.* New York: Orchard. (P, K)

Gag, W. (1928). *Millions of cats.* New York: Coward-McCann. (P, K)

Galbraith, K. (1990). *Laura Charlotte* (F. Cooper, Ill.). New York: Philomel. (P, K)

Gammell, S. (1997). *Is that you, Winter?* Orlando, FL: Harcourt Brace. (P, K)

Garland, S. (1992). *Billy and Belle.* New York: Viking. (P, K)

Garza, C. (1996). *In my family/En mi familia.* San Francisco: Children's Book Press. (K)

Gelsanliter, W., & Christian, F. (1998). *Dancin' in the kitchen.* New York: Putnam. (P, K)

George, L. B. (1995a). *In the snow: Who's been here?* New York: Scholastic. (P, K)

George, L. B. (1995b). *In the woods: Who's been here?* New York: Scholastic. (P, K)

George, J. C. (1999). *Morning, noon, and night* (W. Minor, Ill.). New York: HarperCollins. (P, K)

Gibbons, G. (1984). *Fire! Fire!* New York: HarperCollins. (P, K)

Gibbons, G. (1985). *Check it out! The book about libraries.* San Diego: Harcourt Brace. (P, K)

Gibbons, G. (1985). *The milk makers.* New York: Atheneum. (P, K)

Gibbons, G. (1987). *Zoo.* New York: HarperTrophy. (P)

Gibbons, G. (1993). *Spiders.* New York: Holiday House. (P, K)

Gibbons, G. (2000). *Apples.* New York: Scholastic. (K)

Gilmore, R. (1999). *A screaming kind of day* (G. Sauve, Ill.). Toronto: Fitzhenry & Whiteside.

Ginsburg, M. (1992). *Asleep, asleep* (N. Tafuri, Ill.). New York: Greenwillow. (I, T)

Girnis, M. (2000). *ABC for you and me* (S. Green, Photo.). Morton Grove, IL: Whitman. (P, K)

Godard, A. (1998). *Mama, across the sea* (adapted from French by G. Wen.). New York: Henry Holt. (K)

Goff, B. (1988). *Where's Daddy?* London: Olympic Marketing Corp. (T, P)

Gomi, T. (1989). *Spring is here.* San Francisco: Chronicle. (I, T)

Gonzalez, L. (1994). *The bossy Gallito* (L. Delacre, Ill.). New York: Scholastic. (P, K)

Goodman, J. (1999). *Bernard's nap* (D. Catalano, Ill.). Honesdale, PA: Boyds Mill Press. (T)

Gordon, M. (1984). *The supermarket mice.* New York: Dutton. (P, K)

Gould, D. (1987). *Grandpa's slide show* (C. Harness, Photo.). New York: Lothrop, Lee, & Shepard. (K)

Greenaway, K. (1993). *A apple pie.* New York: Derrydale books. (P, K)

Greenfield, E. (1978). *Honey, I love and other love poems* (L. & D. Dillon, Ill.). New York: HarperCollins. (P, K)

Greenfield, E. (1991). *First pink light* (J. S. Gilchrist, Ill.). New York: Harper & Row. (P, K)

Grindley, S. (2002). *A new room for William* (C. Thompson, Ill.). Cambridge, MA: Candlewick. (P, K)

Grossnickle, A. (1987). *It's just me, Emily.* New York: Clarion. (T)

Groth, B. L. (1995). *Home is where we live.* Chicago: Cornerstone. (K)

Grover, E. (Ed.). (1984). *The original Volland edition Mother Goose* (F. Richardson, Ill.). New York: Derrydale.

Guarino, D. (1989). *Is your mama a llama?* (S. Kellogg, Ill.). New York: Scholastic.

Guback, G. (1994). *Luka's quilt.* New York: Greenwillow. (K)

Hague, K. (1999). *Ten little bears: A counting rhyme* (M. Hague, Ill.). New York: Morrow. (P, K)

Hale, S. J. (1990). *Mary had a little lamb* (B. McMillan, Photo.). New York: Scholastic. (T, P, K)

Haley, G. (1970). *A story, a story.* New York: Atheneum. (P, K)

Haley, G. (1996). *Two bad boys.* New York: Dutton. (K)

Hall, D. (1979). *The ox-cart man* (B. Cooney, Ill.). New York: Viking.

Hall, F. (1998). *Appalachian ABC's* (K. Oehm, Ill.). Johnson City, TN: Overmountain. (P, K)

Hallworth, G. (Ed.) (1996). *Down by the river: Afro-Caribbean rhymes, games, and songs for children.* New York: Scholastic. (P, K)

Harris, R. (2000). *Hi, new baby.* Cambridge, MA: Candlewick. (T, P)

Hassett, J., & Hassett, A. (1998). *Cat up a tree.* Boston: Houghton Mifflin & Walter Lorraine. (P, K)

Hausherr, R. (1997). *Celebrating families.* New York: Scholastic. (P, K)

Havill, J. (1989). *Jamaica tag-along* (A. S. O'Brien, Ill.). Boston: Houghton Mifflin. (P)

Havill, J. (1992). *Treasure nap* (E. Savadier, Ill.). Boston: Houghton Mifflin. (P, K)

Hayes, A. (1991). *Meet the orchestra* (K. Thompson, Ill.). San Diego: Harcourt Brace. (K)

Hayes, J. (1996). *A spoon for every bite* (R. Leer, Ill.). New York: Orchard. (P, K)

Heap, S. (1998). *Cowboy baby.* Cambridge, MA: Candlewick. (T, P)

Heap, S. (2002). *What shall we play?* Cambridge, MA: Candlewick. (P)

Helldorfer, M. C. (1999). *Silver Rain Brown* (T. Flavin, Ill.). Boston: Houghton Mifflin. (P, K)

Heller, R. (1999). *Chickens aren't the only ones.* New York: Penguin Putnam. (P, K)

Henkes, K. (1990). *Julius, the baby of the world.* New York: Greenwillow. (P, K)

Henkes, K. (1991). *Chrysanthemum* (W. Morrow, Ill.). New York: Greenwillow. (P, K)

Henkes, K. (1993). *Owen.* New York: Greenwillow. (P, K)

Henkes, K. (1995). *Goodbye Curtis* (M. Russo, Ill.). New York: Greenwillow. (P, K)

Henkes, K. (1996). *Lilly's purple plastic purse.* New York: Greenwillow. (P, K)

Hennessey, B. (1990). *Jake baked the cake.* (M. Morgan, Ill.). New York: Viking.

Heo, Y. (1995). *Father's rubber shoes.* New York: Orchard. (K)

Herron, C. (1997). *Nappy hair.* (J. Cepeda, Ill.). New York: Knopf. (P, K)

Hest, A. (1999). *Off to school, Baby Duck!* (J. Barton, Ill.). Cambridge, MA: Candlewick. (P, K)

Highwater, J. (1981). *Moonsong lullaby* (M. Keegan, Photo.). New York: Lothrop, Lee & Shepard. (P, K)

Hill, E. (1980). *Where's Spot?* New York: Putnam. (I, T)

Hill, E. (1985). *Spot goes to the beach.* New York: Putnam. (I, T)

Hill, E. (1986). *Spot's first words.* New York: Putnam. (I, T)

Hill, E. (1996). *Donde esta Spot?* New York: Putnam. (I, T, P)

Hill, E. (1999). *Goodnight Spot.* New York: Putnam. (I, T)

Hill, E. (2001a). *Spot goes to school.* New York: Putnam. (P, K)

Hill, E. (2001b). *Spot goes to the farm.* New York: Putnam. (T, P)

Hindley, J. (1999). *Eyes, nose, fingers, and toes.* (B. Granstrom, Ill.). Cambridge, MA: Candlewick.

Hines, A. (1996). *When we married Gary.* New York: Greenwillow. (P, K)

Hiser, B. T. (1986). *Charlie and his wheat straw hat.* (M. Szilagyi, Ill.). New York: Dodd, Mead. (K)

Ho, M. (1996). *Hush! A Thai lullaby.* New York: Orchard.

Hoban, R. (1964). *Bread and jam for Frances* (L. Hoban, Ill.). New York: Harper. (P, K)

Hoban, T. (1972). *Count and see.* New York: Simon & Schuster. (P)

Hoban, T. (1985). *1, 2, 3.* New York: Morrow. (T, P)

Hoban, T. (1986). *Red, blue, yellow shoe.* New York: Greenwillow. (I, T)

Hoban, T. (1987). *Over, under, and through: And other spatial concepts.* New York: Aladdin Paperbacks. (T, P)

Hoban, T. (1990). *Exactly the opposite.* New York: Greenwillow. (T, P)

Hoban, T. (1996). *Just look.* New York: Greenwillow. (P)

Hoban, T. (1997). *Look book.* New York: Greenwillow. (T, P)

Hoberman, M. (1991). *Fathers, mothers, sisters, brothers: A collection of family poems* (M. Hafner, Ill.). New York: Puffin. (P, K)

Hoberman, M. (1997). *One of each* (M. Priceman, Ill.). Boston: Little, Brown. (P, K)

Hoberman, M. (1998). *Miss Mary Mack* (N. Westcott, Ill.). Boston: Little, Brown.

Hobson, S. (2000). *Chicken Little.* New York: Aladdin Picture Books. (P, K)

Hoffman, E. (1999). *The best of colors/Los mejores colores* (C. Henriquez, Ill.). St. Paul, MN: Redleaf Press. (P)

Hoffman, M. (1991). *Amazing Grace* (C. Binch, Ill.). New York: Dial. (P, K)

Hoguet, S. R. (1986). *Solomon Grundy.* New York: Dutton. (K)

Hong, L. (1993). *Two of everything: A Chinese folktale.* Morton Grove, IL: Whitman. (P, K)

Hooper, M. (1997). *A cow, a bee, a cookie, and me* (A. Bartlett, Ill.). New York: Kingfisher. (P, K)

Hopkins, L. (Ed.) (1988). *Side by side* (H. Knight, Ill.). New York: Simon & Schuster. (P, K)

Houston, G. (1988). *The year of the perfect Christmas tree: An Appalachian story* (B. Cooney, Ill.). New York: Dial. (K)

Howard, E. F. (1999). *When will Sarah come?* (N. Crews, Ill.). New York: Greenwillow. (K)

Howard, J. (1985). *When I'm sleepy* (L. Cherry, Ill.). New York: Dutton. (P)

Howe, J. (1991). *When you go to kindergarten* (B. Imershein, Photo.). New York: Knopf. (P, K).

Hru, D. (1996). *The magic moonberry jump ropes* (E. Lewis, Ill.). New York: Dial. (K)

Hubbell, P. (1998a). *Pots and pans.* New York: HarperCollins. (I, T)

Hubbell, P. (1998b). *Wrapping paper romp.* New York: HarperCollins. (I, T)

Hubbell, P. (2000). *Bouncing time.* New York: HarperCollins. (I, T)

Hudson, C. W., & Ford, B. G. (1990). *Bright eyes, brown skin.* East Orange, NJ: Just Us. (P)

Hughes, S. (1985). *An evening at Alfie's.* New York: Lothrop, Lee, & Shepard. (P, K)

Hughes, S. (1988). *Moving Molly.* New York: Morrow. (P, K)

Hughes, S. (1988). *Out and about*. New York: Lothrop, Lee, & Shepard. (T, P)

Hughes, S. (1998). *Alfie's ABC*. New York: Lothrop, Lee, & Shepard. (P, K)

Hurd, T. (1984). *Mama don't allow*. New York: Harper & Row. (P, K)

Hurwitz, J. (1993). *New shoes for Silvia*. New York: Morrow. (P, K)

Hutchins, P. (1971). *Changes, changes*. New York: Scholastic.

Hutchins, P. (1989). *Don't forget the bacon!* New York: Mulberry. (P, K)

Hutchins, P. (1998). *Rosie's walk*. New York: Simon & Schuster Children's Books. (I, P, K)

Hyman, T. S. (1983). *Little Red Riding Hood*. New York: Holiday. (P, K)

Igus, T. (1996). *Two Mrs. Gibsons* (D. Wells, Ill.). San Francisco: Children's Book Press. (P, K)

Inkpen, M. (1994). *Where, oh where, is Kipper's bear?* New York: Harcourt Brace. (T, P)

Inkpen, M. *Jasper's beanstalk*. (N. Butterworth, Ill.). New York: Simon & Schuster Children's Books.

Inkpen, M. (1999). *Kipper's book of weather*. San Diego: Harcourt Brace. (I, T)

Inkpen, M. (2000). *In Wibbly's garden*. New York: Penguin Putnam. (I, T)

Intrater, R. (1995). *Two eyes, a nose, and a mouth*. New York: Cartwheel. (I, T)

Isadora, R. (1993). *Lili at ballet*. New York: Putnam. (K)

Isadora, R. (1997). *Lili backstage*. New York: Putnam. (K)

Jam, T. (1998). *This new baby* (K. Reczuch, Ill.). Toronto: Douglas & McIntyre. (T, P)

James, B. (1999). *Tadpoles*. New York: Dutton. (K)

James, S. (1991). *Dear Mr. Blueberry*. New York: Macmillan. (K)

Jenkins, K. S. (1997). *Kinder Krunchies* (D. Austin, Ill.). Livermore, CA: Discovery Toys. (P, K)

Jimenez, F. (2000). *La Mariposa* (S. Silva, Ill.). Boston: Houghton Mifflin. (K)

Johnson, A. (1989). *Tell me a story, mama* (D. Soman, Ill.). New York: Orchard. (P, K)

Johnson, A. (1991). *One of three* (D. Soman, Ill.). New York: Orchard. (K)

Johnson, A. (1992). *The leaving morning* (D. Soman, Ill.). New York: Orchard. (P, K)

Johnson, D. (1999). *Sunday week* (T. Geter, Ill.). New York: Henry Holt. (K)

Johnson, D. (2000). *Quinnie Blue* (J. Ransome, Ill.). New York: Henry Holt. (K)

Johnson, J. (1997). *My stepfamily*. Brookfield, CT: Copper Beach. (K)

Johnson, P. (1997). *Farmers' market*. New York: Orchard. (P, K)

Johnson, S. (1995). *Alphabet city*. New York: Viking. (K)

Johnson, T. (1994). *The tale of rabbit and coyote* (T. dePaola, Ill.). New York: Putnam. (K)

Jonas, A. (1989). *Color dance*. New York: Greenwillow. (T, P)

Jones, R. C. (1991). *Matthew and Tilly* (B. Peck, Ill.). New York: Dutton. (P, K)

Joosse, B. (1991). *Mama, do you love me?* (B. Lavallee, Ill.). San Francisco: Chronicle. (T, P)

Joyce, W. (1985). *George shrinks*. New York: HarperCollins. (P, K)

Kasza, K. (1996). *The wolf's chicken stew*. New York: Putnam. (P, K)

Katz, K. (1999). *The colors of us*. New York: Henry Holt. (P, K)

Katz, K. (2000). *Where is baby's belly button?* New York: Little Simon. (I, T)

Katz, K. (2001). *Over the moon: An adoption tale*. New York: Henry Holt. (K)

Katzen, M., & Henderson, A. (1994). *Pretend soup and other real recipes*. Berkeley, CA: Tricycle. (K)

Kaye, B., Wise, F., & Lippman, S. (1998). *"A" you're adorable* (M. Alexander, Ill.). Cambridge, MA: Candlewick.

Keats, E. (1962). *The snowy day*. New York: Viking. (P, K)

Keats, E. (1967). *Peter's chair*. New York: HarperCollins. (T, P, K)

Keats, E. (1968). *A letter to Amy*. New York: Harper & Row. (P, K)

Keats, E. (1969). *Goggles!* New York: Macmillan. (P, K)

Keats, E. (1971). *Over in the meadow*. New York: Four Winds. (P, K)

Keats, E. (1972). *Pet show*. New York: Macmillan. (P, K)

Keats, E. (1999). *One red sun*. New York: Viking. (P, K)

Keller, H. (1991). *Horace*. New York: HarperCollins. (P, K)

Kellogg, S. (1991). *Jack and the beanstalk*. New York: Morrow. (P, K)

Kellogg, S. (1998). *A hunting we will go*. New York: Morrow. (P, K)

Kennedy, J. (2002). *The teddy bears' picnic* (M. Hague, Ill.). New York: Henry Holt. (I, T, P)

Kennedy, J., & Canemaker, J. (1998). *Lucy goes to the country*. Los Angeles: Alyson Wonderland. (P)

Kennedy, X. J., & Kennedy, D. M. (1992). *Talking like the rain: A first book of poems* (J. Dyer, Ill.). Boston: Little, Brown. (P, K)

Kids Livin' Life. (1993). *The homeless hibernating bear*. Placerville, CA: Gold Leaf. (P, K)

Kimmel, E. (2000). *The runaway tortilla* (R. Cecil, Ill.). Delray Beach, FL: Winslow. (P, K)

King-Smith, D. (1997). *Puppy love* (A. Jeram, Ill.). Cambridge, MA: Candlewick. (P)

Komaiko, L. (1987). *Annie Bananie*. (L. Cornell, Ill.). New York: HarperTrophy. (P, K)

Krauss, R. (1993). *The carrot seed* (C. Johnson, Ill.). New York: HarperFestival.

Kroll, V. (1995). *Jaha and Jamil went down the hill: An African Mother Goose*. (K. Roundtree, Ill.). Watertown, MA: Charlesbridge. (P, K)

Kuklin, S. (1992). *How my family lives in America*. New York: Bradbury. (K)

Kunhardt, D. (1968). *Pat the bunny*. New York: Western. (I, T)

Kurtz, J. (2000). *Faraway home* (E. B. Lewis, Ill.). San Diego: Gulliver. (K)

Kuskin, K. (1982). *The Philharmonic gets dressed* (M. Simont, Ill.). New York: Harper & Row. (P, K)

Laminack, L. (1998). *The sunsets of Miss Olivia Wiggins* (C. Bergum, Ill.). Atlanta: Peachtree. (P, K)

Lansky, V. (1998). *It's not your fault, Koko Bear: A read-together book for parents and young children during divorce* (J. Prince, Ill.). Minnetonka, MN: Book Peddlers. (T, P, K)

Lee, H. (1995). *In the snow*. New York: Henry Holt. (P, K)

Lee, H. (1998). *In the park*. New York: Henry Holt. (P, K)

Lee, J. M. (1991). *Silent Lotus*. New York: Farrar, Straus & Giroux. (K)

Lerner, H., & Goldhor, S. (2001). *Frannie B. Kranny, there's a bird in your hair!* (H. Oxenbury, Ill.). New York: HarperCollins. (K)

Lesser, R. (1989). *Hansel and Gretel* (P. O. Zelinsky, Ill.). New York: Putnam. (P, K)

Levinson, R. (1990). *I go with my family to Grandma's*. (Diane Goode, Ill.). New York: Dutton. (P, K)

Levy, J. (1999). Totally uncool. (C. Monroe, Ill.). Minneapolis: Carolrhoda. (K)

Lewis, R. (2000). *I love you like crazy cakes*. (J. Dyer, Ill.). Boston: Little, Brown. (P, K)

Lewison, W. C. (1998). *The princess and the potty* (R. Brown, Ill.). New York: Alladin.

Lillie, P. (1993). *Everything has a place* (N. Tafuri, Ill.). New York: Greenwillow. (T, P)

Lillie, P. (1993). *When this box is full* (D. Crews, Ill.). New York: Greenwillow. (P, K)

Lindbergh, R. (1987). *The midnight farm* (S. Jeffers, Ill.). New York: Dutton. (T, P)

Lindgren, B. (1981). *The wild baby* (J. Prelutsky, Ill.). New York: HarperCollins. (T, P)

Lionni, L. (1973). *Frederick*. New York: Knopf. (P, K)

Lionni, L. (1992). *A busy year*. New York: Scholastic. (P, K)

Little, J. (2001). *Emma's yucky brother* (J. Plecas, Ill.). New York: HarperCollins. (P, K)

Lobel, A. (1981). *On market street*. (A. Lobel, Ill.). New York: Greenwillow.

Lobel, A. (1990). *Allison's zinnia*. New York: Greenwillow. (P, K)

Loh, M. (1987). *Tucking Mommy in* (D. Rawlins, Ill.). New York: Orchard. (P, K)

London, J. (1993). *Hip cat* (W. Hubbard, Ill.). San Francisco: Hubbard. (P, K)

London, J. (1993). *A koala for Katie* (C. Jabar, Ill.). Morton Grove, IL: Whitman. (pre–K, K)

London, J. (1995). *Like butter on pancakes*. (G. B. Karas, Ill.). New York: Viking. (P, K)

London, J. (1996). *I see the moon and the moon sees me* (P. Fiorre, Ill.). New York: Viking. (T)

Long, S. (1997). *Hush little baby*. New York: Trumpet.

Long, S. (1999). *Sylvia Long's Mother Goose*. San Francisco: Chronicle. (P, K)

Look, L. (1999). *Love as strong as ginger* (S. Johnson, Ill.). New York: Atheneum. (P, K)

Louie, A. (1990). *Yeh-Shen: A Cinderella story from China* (Ed Young, Ill.). New York: Philomel. (P, K)

Low, W. (1997). *Chinatown*. New York: Henry Holt. (P, K)

Lowery, L. (1995). *Twist with a burger, jitter with a bug*. New York: Houghton, Mifflin. (T, P, K)

Lyon, G. E. (1991). *Cecil's story*. (P. Catalanotto, Ill.). New York: Orchard. (K)

Lyon, G. E. (1998). *Counting on the woods* (A. Olson, Photo.). New York: DK Publishing. (P, K)

MacDonald, A. (1993). *Rachel Fister's blister* (M. Priceman, Ill.). Boston: Houghton Mifflin. (P, K)

MacDonald, M. (1996). *Tuck-me-in tales: Bedtime stories from around the world* (Y. Davis, Ill.). New York: August House for Littlefolk. (P, K)

MacDonald, M. (1998). *Pickin' peas* (P. Cummings, Ill.). New York: HarperCollins. (P, K)

MacDonald, S. (1986). *Alphabetics*. New York: Bradbury.

MacDonald, S. (1997). *Peck, slither, and slide*. San Diego: Gulliver. (T, P)

MacLachlan, P. (2001). *The sick day* (J. Dyer, Ill.). New York: Random House. (P, K)

Mandelbaum, P. (1990). *You be me, I'll be you*. Brooklyn, NY: Kane/Miller. (P, K)

Manning, J. (1997). *This little piggy*. New York: HarperFestival.

Manual, L. (1996). *The night the moon blew kisses* (R. Spowart, Ill.). Boston: Houghton Mifflin. (P, K)

Marshall, J. (1987). *Red riding hood*. New York: Dutton.

Marshall, J. (1988). *Goldilocks and the three bears*. New York: Dial. (P, K)

Martin, B. (1992). *Brown bear, brown bear, what do you see?* (E. Carle, Ill.). New York: Henry Holt. (T, P)

Martin, B., & Archambault, J. (1989). *Chicka chicka boom boom* (L. Ehlert, Ill.). New York: Simon & Schuster. (T, P)

Martin, J. (1991). *Carrot/parrot*. New York: Trumpet Club.

Martin, R. (1985). *Foolish rabbit's big mistake* (E. Young, Ill.). New York: Putnam. (P, K)

Martin, R. (1989). *Will's mammoth* (S. Gammell, Ill.). New York: Putnam. (P, K)

Martin, R. (1992). *The rough-face girl* (D. Shannon, Ill.). New York: Putnam. (K)

Marzollo, J. (1990). *Pretend you're a cat* (J. Pinkney, Ill.). New York: Dial Books for Young Readers. (T, P)

Marzollo, J. (1994). *Ten cats have ten hats: A counting book* (D. McPhail, Ill.). New York: Scholastic. (P, K)

Marzollo, J. (1998). *Close your eyes* (S. Jeffers, Ill.). New York: Penguin. (T, P)

Marzollo, J. (1999). *I love you: A rebus poem* (S. MacDonald, Ill.). New York: Scholastic. (P, K)

Matze, C. (1999). *The stars in my geddoh's sky* (B. Farnsworth, Ill.). Morton Grove, IL: Whitman. (P, K)

Mayer, M. (1974). *Frog goes to dinner.* New York: Dial. (P, K)

Mayer, M. (1977). *Oops!* New York: Dial. (P, K)

McCloskey, R. (1941). *Make way for ducklings.* New York: Viking. (P, K)

McCloskey, R. (1948). *Blueberries for Sal.* New York: Viking. (P, K)

McCully, E. (1985). *First snow.* New York: HarperCollins. (P, K)

McCully, E. (1987). *School.* New York: HarperCollins. (P, K)

McCully, E. (2001). *Four hungry kittens.* New York: Dial. (T, P)

McDermott, G. (1993). *Raven.* San Diego: Harcourt Brace. (K)

McGovern, A. (1997). *The lady in the box.* (M. Backer, Ill.). New York: Turtle. (P, K)

McMillan, B. (1987). *Step by step.* New York: Lothrop, Lee, & Shepard. (I, T, P)

McMillan, B. (1991). *Eating fractions.* New York: Scholastic. (P, K)

McMillan, B. (2001). *Puffins climb, penguins rhyme.* San Diego: Harcourt Brace (T, P)

Medearis, A. (1994). *Our people* (M. Bryant, Ill.). New York: Atheneum. (P, K)

Melmed, L. K. (1997). *Little Oh.* (J. LaMarche, Ill.). New York: Morrow. (K)

Merriam, E. (1990). *What in the world?* (B. Philips-Duke, Ill.). New York: Harper-Festival. (P, K)

Merriam, E. (1994). *Higgle wiggle happy rhymes* (H. Wilhelm, Ill.). New York: Mulberry. (T, P, K)

Merriam, E. (1999). *Ten rosy roses* (J. Gorton, Ill.). New York: HarperCollins. (K)

Micklethwait, L. (1993). *A child's book of art.* New York: DK Publishing. (P, K)

Micklethwait, L. (1994). *I spy a lion: Animals in art.* New York: Greenwillow. (P, K)

Miller, W. (1997). *A house by the river* (C. Van Wright & Y. Hu, Ill.). New York: Lee & Low. (K)

Miller, M. (1998). *What's on my head?* New York: Simon & Schuster. (I, T)

Miller, M. (1998). *My five senses.* New York: Simon & Schuster. (I, T)

Millman, I. (1998). *Moses goes to a concert.* New York: Farrar, Straus & Giroux. (K)

Millman, I. (2000). *Moses goes to school.* New York: Farrar, Straus & Giroux. (K)

Milne, A. (1926). *Winnie-the-pooh.* New York: Dutton.

Mitchell, B. (1996). *Red bird* (T. Doney, Ill.). New York: HarperCollins Children's Books. (K)

Miranda, A. (1997). *To market, to market* (J. Stevens, Ill.). New York: Harcourt Brace. (T, P)

Moon, N. (1997). *Lucy's picture.* New York: Puffin. (P, K)

Mora, P. (1992). *A birthday basket for Tia* (C. Lang, Ill.). New York: Macmillan. (P, K)

Mora, P. (1994). *Pablo's tree.* New York: Macmillan. (P, K)

Mora, P. (2001). *Bakery lady.* Houston, TX: Arte Publico. (P, K)

Moore, E. (1994). *Grandma's garden* (D. Andreasen, Ill.). New York: Lothrop, Lee & Shepard. (P, K)

Morris, A. (1992). *Tools* (K. Heyman, photo.). New York: Lothrop, Lee & Shepard. (P, K)

Morris, A. (1998). *Play.* New York: Lothrop, Lee & Shepard-Morrow. (P, K)

Mosel, A. (1987). *Tikki tikki tembo.* New York: Scholastic Trade. (P, K)

Moss, L. (1995). *Zin! Zin! Zin! a violin.* (M. Priceman, Ill.). New York: Scholastic. (P, K)

Moss, T. (1998). *I want to be* (J. Pinkney, Ill.). New York: Puffin. (P, K)

Muller, G. (1995). *Circle of seasons.* New York: Dutton. (T, P)

Munsch, R. (1994). *Where is Gah-Ning?* Buffalo, NY: Firefly. (P, K)

Murphy, S. (1996). *A pair of socks* (L. Ehlert, Ill.). New York: Scholastic. (T)

Myers, S. (2001). *Everywhere babies.* (M. Frazee, Ill.). San Diego: Harcourt Brace. (T, P)

Neitzel, S. (1989). *The jacket I wear in the snow.* (N. W. Parker, Ill.). New York: Greenwillow. (P, K)

Neitzel, S. (1995). *The bag I'm taking to Grandma's.* (N. W. Parker, Ill.). New York: Greenwillow. (P, K)

Newman, L. (2000). *Heather has two mommies.* (D. Souza, Ill.). Los Angeles: Alyson Wonderland. (T, P)

Numeroff, L. J. (1985). *If you give a mouse a cookie* (F. Bond, Ill.). New York: HarperCollins.

Nye, N. S. (1994). *Sitti's secret* (N. Carpenter, Ill.). New York: Four Winds. (P, K)

O'Donnell, E. (1987). *Maggie doesn't want to move* (A. Schwartz, Ill.). New York: Simon & Schuster. (P, K)

Okimoto, J. D. (1993). *A place for Grace* (D. Keith, Ill.). Seattle: Sasquatch. (P, K)

Osofsky, A. (1992). *Dreamcatcher* (E. Young, Ill.). New York: Orchard. (P, K)

Onyefulu, I. (1993). *A is for Africa.* New York: Cobblehill. (P, K)

Opie, I. (Ed.). (1999). *Here comes Mother Goose* (R. Wells, Ill.). Cambridge, MA: Candlewick.

Oppenheim, S. (1994). *Fireflies for Nathan* (J. Ward, Ill.). New York: Morrow. (P, K).

Ormerod, J. (1981). *Sunshine.* New York: Lothrop, Lee & Shepard. (T, P, K)

Ormerod, J. (1982). *Moonlight.* New York: Morrow. (T, P, K)

Orozco, J. L. (1999). *De colores and other Latin-American folk songs for children.* New York: Puffin.

Oxenbury, H. (1981a). *Dressing.* New York: Wanderer. (I, T)

Oxenbury, H. (1981b). *Family.* New York: Wanderer. (I, T)

Oxenbury, H. (1981c). *Friends.* New York: Little Simon.

Oxenbury, H. (1981d). *Playing.* New York: Little Simon. (I, T)

Oxenbury, H. (1981e). *Working.* New York: Little Simon. (I, T)

Oxenbury, H. (1983). *Helen Oxenbury's ABC of things.* New York: Delacorte. (T, P)

Oxenbury, H. (1984). *Grandma and Grandpa.* (P. Mullins, Ill.). New York: Orchard. (I, T)

Oxenbury, H. (1987). *Tickle, tickle.* New York: Simon & Schuster.

Oxenbury, H. (1994). *First nursery stories.* New York: Macmillan.

Oxenbury, H. (1995). *Helen Oxenbury's favorite nursery stories.* New York: Little Simon.

Oxenbury, H. (1998a). *Pippo gets lost.* New York: Little Simon. (T)

Oxenbury, H. (1998b). *Tom and Pippo go for a walk.* New York: Simon & Schuster. (T)

Pak, S. (1999). *Dear Juno* (S. K. Hartung, Ill.). New York: Viking. (P, K)

Pallotta, J., & Thomson, B. (1992). *The victory garden vegetable alphabet book* (E. Stewart, Ill.). Watertown, MA: Charlesbridge. (K)

Paschkis, J. (2001). *Happy adoption day!* (J. McCutcheon, Ill.). Boston: Little, Brown. (P, K)

Patrick, D. (1993). *The car-washing street.* (J. Ward, Ill.). New York: Scholastic. (P, K)

Paxton, T. (1996). *Going to the zoo.* (K. Schmidt, Ill.). New York: Morrow. (P, K)

Peek, M. (1998). *Mary wore her red dress and Henry wore his green sneakers.*

Peek, M. (1999). *Roll over: A counting song.* Boston: Houghton Mifflin.

Pellegrini, N. (1991). *Families are different.* New York: Holiday House. (P, K)

Penn, A. (1993). *The kissing hand* (R. Harper & N. Leak, Ills.). Washington, DC: Child Welfare League of America. (T, P, K)

Perez, A. I. (2000). *My very own room* (M. Gonzalez, Ill.). San Francisco: Children's Book Press. (K)

Pfister, M. (1991). *I see the moon: Goodnight poems and lullabies.* New York: North-South. (P, K)

Philip, N. (Ed.). (2002). *The fish is me: Bathtime rhymes* (C. Henley, Ill.). Boston: Houghton Mifflin. (P, K)

Pienkowski, J. (1986). *Little monsters.* Los Angeles: Price/Stern/Sloan.

Pinkney, A., & Pinkney, B. (1997). *I smell honey.* San Diego: Harcourt Brace. (T, P)

Pinkney, S. (2002). *A rainbow all around me* (M. Pinkney, photo.). New York: Cartwheel.

Plourde, L. (1997). *Pigs in the mud in the middle of the rud.* (J. Schoenherr, Ill.). New York: Blue Sky. (P, K)

Pogany, W. (2000). *Willy Pogany's Mother Goose.* New York: Seastar. (P, K)

Polacco, P. (1996). *I can hear the sun.* New York: Philomel. (K)

Pomerantz, C. (1989) *The piggy in the puddle.* New York: Simon & Schuster. (T, P)

Potter, B. (1974). *The tale of two bad mice.* New York: Penguin. (P, K)

Poydar, N. (1999). *First day hooray!* New York: Holiday House. (K)

Poydar, N. (2000). *Mailbox magic.* New York: Holiday House. (K)

Prelutsky, J. (1986). *Read-aloud rhymes for the very young* (M. Brown, Ill.). New York: Knopf. (T, P)

Price, H. L. (1999). *These hands* (B. Collier, Ill.). New York: Hyperion. (T, P)

Rabe, B. (1988). *Where's chimpy?* (K. Tucker, Ill.). Morton Grove, IL: Whitman. (P)

Raczek, L. T. (1998). *The night the grandfathers danced.* Flagstaff, AZ: Northland.

Raczek, L. T. (1999). *Rainy's powwow* (G. Bennett, Ill.). Flagstaff, AZ: Rising Moon.

Raffi. (1992). *Baby beluga* (A. Wolff, Ill.). New York: Crown. (T, P, K)

Raffi. (1998). *Five little ducks* (A. Dewey & J. Aruego, Ill.). New York: Random House. (I, T, P)

Rahaman, V. (1997). *Read for me, Mama* (L. McElrath-Eslick, Ill.). Honesdale, PA: Boyds Mills. (K)

Ransome, C. (1995). *The big green pocketbook.* New York: HarperTrophy. (P)

Raschka, C. (1992). *Charlie Parker played be bop.* New York: Orchard. (T, P, K)

Raschka, C. (1993). *Yo! Yes?* New York: Orchard. (T, P, K)

Rathmann, P. (1995). *Officer Buckle and Gloria.* New York: Putnam. (P, K)

Rathmann, P. (1995). *Good night, gorilla.* New York: Putnam. (I, T)

Rathmann, P. (2000). *10 minutes till bedtime.* New York: Scholastic. (T, P)

Rattigan, J. (1993). *Dumpling soup* (L. Hsu-Flanders, Ill.). Boston: Little, Brown. (P, K)

Ray, M. L. (1996). *Mud* (L. Stringer, Ill.). San Diego: Harcourt Brace. (P, K)

Reiser, L. (1993). *Margaret and Margarita/Margarita y Margaret.* New York: Greenwillow.

Reiser, L. (1998). *Tortillas and lullabies/Tortillas y cancioncitas* (C. Valientes, Ill.). New York: Greenwillow. (P, K)

Rey, H. A. (1973). *Curious George.* Boston: Houghton Mifflin. (P, K)

Ricker, J. (1999). *Russ and the apple tree surprise* (P. McGahan, Ill.). Bethesda, MD: Woodbine House. (P, K)

Ricker, J. E. (2000). *Russ and the almost perfect day* (P. McGahan, Photo.). Bethesda, MD: Woodbine House. (T, P, K)

Riecken, N. (1996). *Today is the day* (C. Stock, Ill.). Boston: Houghton Mifflin. (K)

Riley, L. C. (1995). *Elephants swim* (S. Jenkins, Ill.). Boston: Houghton Mifflin. (P, K)

Rockwell, A. (1986). *Fire engines.* New York: Dutton. (T, P)

Rockwell, A. (1999). *Bumblebee, bumblebee, do you know me?: A garden guessing game.* New York: HarperCollins. (T, P)

Rogers, F. (1996). *Let's talk about divorce.* New York: Putnam. (P, K)

Rogers, F. (1997). *Stepfamilies* (J. Judkis, Photo.). New York: Putnam. (P, K)

Rollings, S. (2000). *New shoes, red shoes.* New York: Orchard. (P, K)

Rosa-Casanova, S. (1997). *Mama Provi and the pot of rice.* (R. Roth, Ill.). New York: Simon & Schuster. (P, K)

Rosen, M. (1989). *We're going on a bear hunt.* New York: Macmillan, McElderry. (P, K)

Rosen, M. (1993). *Poems for the very young* (B. Graham, Ill.). New York: Kingfisher. (P, K)

Rosenberg, L. (1999). *The silence in the mountains.* New York: Orchard. (P, K)

Rosenberry, V. (1998). *When Vera was sick.* New York: Henry Holt. (P, K)

Ross, G. (1995). *How Turtle's back was cracked* (M. Jacob, Ill.). New York: Dial. (K)

Rotner, S. (1996). *Action alphabet.* New York: Atheneum Books for Young Readers. (K)

Round, G. (1991). *Cowboys.* New York: Holiday House. (P, K)

Royston, A. (1992). *Baby animals* (D. Brown, Ill.). New York: Simon & Schuster. (T, P)

Ryan, P. M. (2002). *Mud is cake.* (D. McPhail, Ill.). New York: Hyperion Books for Children. (P, K)

Rylant, C. (1982). *When I was young in the mountains* (D. Goode, Ill.). New York: Dutton. (P, K)

Rylant, C. (1996). *The bookshop dog.* New York: Blue Sky. (P, K)

Rylant, C. (1997). *An everyday book.* New York: Simon & Schuster. (P)

Rylant, C. (1999). *The cookie-store cat.* New York: Blue Sky. (P, K)

Rylant, C. (2001). *Good morning, sweetie pie: And other poems for little children.* New York: Simon & Schuster. (T, P)

Sabuda, R. (1999). *The movable Mother Goose.* New York: Simon & Schuster.

San Souci, R. (1994). *Sootface: An Ojibwa Cinderella Story* (D. San Souci, Ill.). New York: Bantam Doubleday Dell. (K)

Sandved, K. (1996). *The butterfly alphabet.* New York: Scholastic. (P, K)

Sardegna, J. (1994). *K is for kiss good night: A bedtime alphabet.* New York: Delacorte. (P, K)

Say, A. (1988). *A river dream.* Boston: Houghton Mifflin. (K)

Say, A. (1996). *Emma's rug.* Boston: Houghton Mifflin. (P, K)

Say, A. (1997). *Allison.* Boston: Houghton Mifflin. (P, K)

Schaefer, C. (1996). *The squiggle* (P. Morgan, Ill.). New York: Crown. (P)

Schick, E. (1996). *My Navajo sister.* New York: Simon & Schuster. (K)

Schindel, J. (1998). *Frog Face: My little sister and me* (J. Delaney, Ill.). New York: Henry Holt.

Schwartz, A. (2000). *Some babies.* New York: Scholastic. (I, T)

Scott, A. (1992). *On Mother's lap* (G. Coalson, Ill.). New York: Clarion. (T, P)

Seeger, P. (1994). *Abiyoyo* (M. Hays, Ill.). New York: Aladdin Books.

Sendak, M. (1962). *Chicken soup with rice.* New York: HarperCollins. (P, K)

Sendak, M. (1963). *Where the wild things are.* New York: HarperCollins. (T, P, K)

Sendak, M. (1970). *In the night kitchen.* New York: Harper & Row. (T, P, K)

Seuss, Dr. (1966). *Yertle the turtle and other stories.* New York: Random House. (P, K)

Shannon, D. (1999). *No, David!* New York: Scholastic. (T, P)

Shannon, G. (2000). *Frog legs: A picture book of action verse.* New York: HarperCollins. (T, P, K)

Shaw, N. (1986). *Sheep in a jeep* (M. Apple, Ill.). New York: Trumpet Club.

Shaw, N. (1991). *Sheep in a shop.* (M. Apple, Ill.). Boston: Houghton Mifflin. (T, P, K)

Shelby, A. (1990). *We keep a store.* New York: Orchard. (P, K)

Shulevitz, U. (1998). *Snow.* New York: Farrar, Straus & Giroux. (P, K)

Sierra, J. (1999). *Tasty baby belly buttons* (M. So, Ill.). New York: Bantam Doubleday. (P, K)

Simms, L. (1998). *Rotten teeth* (D. Catrow, Ill.). Boston: Houghton Mifflin. (K)

Simon, F. (1998). *Where are you?* (D. Melling, Ill.). Atlanta: Peachtree. (P, K)

Simont, M. (2001). *The stray dog.* New York: HarperCollins Children's Books. (P, K)

Sis, P. (2002). *Madlenka's dog.* New York: Farrar, Straus & Giroux. (K)

Sloat, T. (1998). *There was an old lady who swallowed a trout!* (R. Ruffins, Ill.). New York: Henry Holt. (P, K)

Slobodkina, E. (1947). *Caps for sale.* Glenview, IL: Scott Foresman. (T, P, K)

Small, D. (1986). *Imogene's antlers*. New York: Crown. (P,K)

Smalls, I. (1992). *Jonathan and his mommy*. New York: Little, Brown. (P)

Snyder, D. (1988). *The boy of the three-year nap* (A. Say, Ill.). Boston: Houghton Mifflin. (K)

Soentpiet, C. (1994). *Around town*. New York: Lothrop, Lee & Shepard. (P, K)

Soto, G. (1993). *Too many tamales*. (E. Martinez, Ill.). New York: Putnam. (P, K)

Soto, G. (1997). *Snapshots of a wedding* (S. Garcia, Ill.). New York: Putnam. (P, K)

Soto, G. (2000). *Chato and the party animals* (S. Guevara, Ill.). New York: Putnam.

Spier, P. (1982). *Peter Spier's rain*. New York: Doubleday. (P, K)

Spinelli, E. (1998). *When Mama comes home tonight* (J. Dyer, Ill.). New York: Simon & Schuster. (P, K)

Spinelli, E. (2000). *Night shift daddy* (M. Iwai, Ill.). New York: Hyperion. (P, K)

Steen, S., & Steen, S. (2001). *Car wash*. (B. Karas, Ill.). New York: Penguin. (P, K)

Steig, W. (1982). *Dr. DeSoto*. New York: Scholastic. (P, K)

Steig, W. (1998). *Pete's a pizza*. New York: HarperCollins. (T, P, K)

Stein, K. S. (1995). *Oh, baby!* (H. A. Shelowitz, Ill.). New York: Walker

Steptoe, J. (1987). *Mufaro's beautiful daughters: An African tale*. New York: Lothrop, Lee & Shepard. (K)

Steptoe, J. (1988). *Baby says*. New York: Mulberry Press. (T)

Stevens, J. (1993). *Carlos and the squash plant/Carlos y la planta de calabaza*. Flagstaff, AZ: Northland. (P, K)

Stevens, J. (1995). *Tops and bottoms*. San Diego: Harcourt Brace. (P, K)

Stevens, J., & Crummel, S. (1999). *Cook-a-doodle-doo* (J. Stevens, Ill.). San Diego: Harcourt Brace. (P, K)

Stewart, S. (2000). *The gardener* (Reprinted.) New York: Sunburst, imprint of Farrar, Straus & Giroux. (K)

Stinson, K. (1988). *Red is best* (R. Lewis, Ill.). Toronto: Firefly. (T, P)

Stoeke, M. (1996). *Minerva Louise at school*. New York: Dutton. (T, P, K).

Stoeke, J. (1994). *A hat for Minerva Louise*. New York: Dutton. (T)

Strom, M. (1999). *Rainbow Joe and me*. New York: Lee & Low.

Stutson, C., & Patent, D. H. (1999). *Prairie primer A to Z* (S. C. Lamb, Ill.). New York: Penguin Putnam Books for Young Readers. (P, K)

Stuve-Bodeen, S. (1998). *Elizabeti's doll* (C. Hale, Ill.). New York: Lee & Low. (P, K)

Stuve-Bodeen, S. (1998). *We'll paint the octopus red* (P. Devito, Ill.). Bethesda, MD: Woodbine House. (P, K)

Stuve-Bodeen, S. (2000). *Mama Elizabeti* (C. Hale, Ill.). New York: Lee & Low. (P, K)

Surat, M. (1983). *Angel child, dragon child* (V. Mai, Ill.). New York: Scholastic. (K)

Swain, R. (1999). *Bedtime!* (C. B. Smith, Ill.). New York: Holiday House. (K).

Sweet, M. (2002). *Fiddle-I-fee: A farmyard song for the very young*. Boston: Little, Brown. (I, T)

Taback, S. (1997). *There was an old lady who swallowed a fly*. New York: Viking. (P, K)

Taback, S. (1999). *Joseph had a little overcoat*. New York: Viking. (P, K)

Tafuri, N. (1983). *Early morning in the barn*. New York: Greenwillow. (I, T)

Tafuri, N. (1988). *Spots, feathers, and curly tails*. New York: Greenwillow. (I, T)

Tafuri, N. (1994). *This is the farmer*. New York: Greenwillow.

Tafuri, N. (1998). *Counting to Christmas*. New York: Scholastic.

Tafuri, N. (2000). *I love you little one*. New York: Scholastic. (I, T)

Tapahonso, L., & Schick, E. (1995). *Navajo ABC: A Dine alphabet book* (E. Schick, Ill.). New York: Simon & Schuster. (P, K)

Tarpley, N. A. (1997). *I love my hair!* Boston: Little, Brown. (P, K)

Testa, M. (1996). *Nine candles*. Minneapolis: Carolrhoda. (K)

Thiesing, L. (1998). *Me and you: A mother-daughter album*. New York: Hyperion.

Tompert, A. (1990). *Grandfather Tang's story* (R. Parker, Ill.). New York: Crown. (K)

Turkle, B. (1976). *Deep in the forest.* New York: Dutton. (P, K)

Udry, J. (1966) *What Mary Jo shared* (E. Mill, Ill.). Morton Grove, IL: Whitman. (P, K)

Updike, J. (1999). *A child's calendar* (T. S. Hyman, Ill.). New York: Holiday House. (P, K)

Van Fleet, M. (1995). *Fuzzy yellow ducklings.* New York: Dial. (I, T)

Van Genechten, G. (2001). *Potty time.* New York: Simon & Schuster.

Vigna, J. (1995). *My two uncles.* Morton Grove, IL: Whitman. (K)

Viorst, J. (1995). *Alexander, who's not (Do you hear me? I mean it!) going to move* (R. Glasser, Ill.). New York: Atheneum. (P, K)

Waber, B. (1972). *Ira sleeps over.* Boston: Houghton Mifflin. (P, K)

Waber, B. (1988). *Ira says good-bye.* Boston: Houghton Mifflin. (K)

Waber, B. (1997). *Bearsie Bear and the surprise sleepover party.* New York: Houghton Mifflin. (P, K)

Waddell, M. (1988). *Can't you sleep, Little Bear?* London: Walker. (T, P)

Waddell, M. (1990). *Rosie's babies* (P. Dale, Ill.). Cambridge, MA: Candlewick. (P)

Waddell, M. (1992). *Farmer duck* (H. Oxenbury, Ill.). Cambridge, MA: Candlewick. (P, K)

Walsh, E. (1989). *Mouse paint.* San Diego: Harcourt Brace. (T, P, K)

Walsh, E. (1995). *Mouse count.* New York: Voyager.

Warnick, E. (1998). *Bedtime.* Orlando, FL: Harcourt Brace. (I, T)

Watkins, S. (1995). *Green snake ceremony.* Tulsa, OK: Council Oak Books. (P, K)

Watson, W. (1989). *Wendy Watson's Mother Goose.* New York: Lothrop, Lee & Shepard. (I, T)

Weeks, S. (1998). *Mrs. McNosh hangs out her wash* (N. Westcott, Ill.). New York: Scholastic. (P, K)

Wells, R. (1977). *Don't spill it again, James.* New York: Dial. (P, K)

Wells, R. (1989). *Hazel's amazing mother.* New York: Viking Penguin. (P, K)

Wells, R. (1997a). *Bunny cakes.* New York: Scholastic. (P, K)

Wells, R. (1997b). *Bunny money.* New York: Dial. (P, K)

Wells, R. (1997c). *McDuff and the baby* (S. Jeffers, Ill.). New York: Hyperion Books for Children. (T, pre–K, K)

Wells, R. (1998). *The bear went over the mountain.* New York: Scholastic. (I, T, P)

Wells, R. (1998). *Yoko.* New York: Hyperion. (P, K)

Wells, R. (1999). *Bingo.* New York: Scholastic. (I, T)

Wells, R. (Ed.). (2000). *Goodnight Max.* New York: Viking. (T, P)

Wells, R. (2001). *Yoko's paper cranes.* New York: Hyperion. (P, K)

Weninger, B. (1995). *Good-bye, Daddy!* (A. Marks, Ill.). New York: North-South. (P, K)

Weninger, B. (2000). *Happy birthday, Davy* (E. Tharlet, Ill.; R. Lanning, Trans.). New York: North-South. (P)

Westcott, N. (1998). *The lady with the alligator purse.* Boston: Little, Brown. (P, K)

Wheeler, B. (1986). *Where did you get your moccasins?* (H. Bekkering, Ill.). Winnipeg, Canada: Peguis. (P, K)

White, E. (1952). *Charlotte's web* (Garth Williams, Ill.). New York: HarperCollins. (Elementary)

Wild, M. (1993). *Our granny* (J. Vivas, Ill.) Boston: Hougton Mifflin. (P, K)

Wilkin, E. (Ed.). (2001). *Poems to read to the very young.* New York: Random House. (I, T)

Willhoite, M. (1990). *Daddy's roommate.* Los Angeles: Alyson Wonderland. (P, K)

Willhoite, M. (1995). *Daddy's wedding.* Los Angeles: Alyson Wonderland. (P, K).

Williams, B. (1975). *Kevin's grandma* (K. Chorao, Ill.). New York: Dutton. (P, K)

Williams, R. L. (1995). *How to make a mudpie.* Cypress, CA: Creative Teaching. (P, K)

Williams, S. (1990). *I went walking* (J. Vivas, Ill.). San Diego: Harcourt Brace. (I, T)

Williams, S. A. (1992). *Working cotton* (C. Byard, Ill.). New York: Harcourt Brace. (K)

Williams, S. (1996). *Mommy doesn't know my name* (A. Sachat, Ill.). New York: Houghton Mifflin. (T, P)

Williams, S. (1998). *Let's go visiting* (J. Vivas, Ill.). San Diego: Harcourt Brace. (I, T)

Williams, S. (1999). *Girls together* (S. James, Ill.). Orlando, FL: Harcourt Brace. (K)

Williams, S. (2001). *Library Lil* (S. Kellogg, Ill.). New York: Penguin Putnam. (K)

Williams, V. B. (1982). *A chair for my mother*. New York: Greenwillow. (P, K)

Williams, V. B. (1986). *Cherries and cherry pits*. New York: Greenwillow. (P, K)

Williams, V. B. (1990). *"More, more, more" said the baby*. New York: Greenwillow. (I, T, P)

Wilmer, I. (2000). *The baby's game book*. New York: HarperCollins. (I, T)

Wilson, A. (1999). *April Wilson's magpie magic: A tale of colorful mischief*. New York: Dial. (P, K)

Wilson, K. (2001). *Bear snores on* (J. Chapman, Ill.). New York: McElderry Books. (P, K)

Wing, N. (1996). *Jalepeno bagels*. New York: Atheneum. (K)

Winter, J. (1999). *Hey diddle diddle*. Orlando, FL: Red Wagon. (I, T)

Winter, J. (1999). *Rock-a-bye baby*. Orlando, FL: Red Wagon. (I, T)

Wishinsky, F. (1998). *Oonga boonga* (C. Thompson, Ill.). New York: Dutton. (P, K)

Wojciechowski, S. (2000). *The best Halloween of all*. Cambridge, MA: Candlewick. (P, K)

Wolff, A. (1993). *Stella & Roy*. New York: Dutton. (T, P, K)

Wong, J. (2000). *The trip back home* (B. Jia, Ill.). San Diego: Harcourt Brace. (K)

Wong, J. S. (2000). *Buzz* (M. Chodos-Irvine, Ill.). San Diego: Harcourt Brace. (P, K)

Wood, A. (1984). *The napping house* (D. Wood, Ill.). San Diego: Harcourt Brace. (P, K)

Wood, A. (1985). *King Bidgood's in the bathtub* (D. Wood, Ill.). San Diego: Harcourt Brace. (P, K)

Wood, A., & Wood, D. (1991). *Piggies* (D. Wood, Ill.). San Diego: Harcourt Brace. (I, T, P)

Wood, A. (1992). *Silly Sally*. New York: Scholastic. (P, K)

Woodson, J. (2000). *Sweet, sweet memory* (F. Cooper, Ill.). New York: Hyperion. (K)

Woodson, J. (2002). *Visiting day* (J. Ransome , Ill.). New York: Scholastic.

Wright, B. (1981). *The real Mother Goose*. Chicago: Rand McNally. (T, P, K)

Wright, B. (1994). *The real Mother Goose*. New York: Scholastic.

Wyeth, S. (1995). *Always my dad* (R. Colon, Ill.). New York: Knopf. (K)

Xiong, B. (1989). *Nine-in-one Grr! Grr!* (adapted by C. Spagnoli; N. Hom, Ill.). San Francisco: Children's Book Press. (P, K)

Yarbrough, C. (1979). *Cornrows* (C. Byard, Ill.). New York: Howard-McCann. (P, K)

Yashima, T. (1958). *Umbrella*. New York: Viking. (P)

Yee, B. (1999). *Sand castle* (T. Kliros, Ill.). New York: Greenwillow. (P, K)

Yolen, J. (1987). *Owl moon* (J. Schoenherr, Ill.). New York: Philomel. (K)

Yolen, J. (1987). *The three bears rhyme book* (J. Dyer, Ill.). San Diego: Harcourt Brace. (P, K)

Yolen, J. (2000). *Off we go!* (L. Molk, Ill.). Boston: Little, Brown. (I, T)

Young, E. (1989). *Lon Po Po: A Red Riding Hood story from China*. New York: Philomel. (P, K)

Young, R. (1992). *Golden Bear* (R. Isadora, Ill.). New York: Viking. (T)

Zamorano, A. (1996). *Let's eat* (J. Viva, Ill.). New York: Scholastic. (P, K)

Zelinsky, P. (1986). *Rumplestiltskin*. New York: Dutton. (P, K)

Zelinsky, P. (1990). *The wheels on the bus: The traditional song*. New York: Dutton. (P, K)

Zelinsky, P. (1999). *Hansel and Gretel.* New York: Dutton. (K)

Zelinsky, P., & Grimm, J. (1997). *Rapunzel.* New York: Dutton. (P, K)

Ziefert, H. (1997). *Sleepy-O!* (L. Rader, Ill.). Boston: Houghton Mifflin. (T, P, K)

Ziefert, H. (1999). *Clara Ann Cookie* (E. Bolam, Ill.). New York: Houghton Mifflin. (T, P)

Ziefert, H. (1999). *Max's potty* (E. Bolan, Ill.). New York: DK publishing.

Ziefert, H. (1999). *Sarah's potty* (E. Bolan, Ill.). New York: DK publishing.

Ziefert, H., & Taback, S. (2002). *Where is my baby?* Brooklyn, NY: Handprint. (I, T)

Ziefert, H. (1998). *Waiting for baby.* (E. Bolam, Ill.). New York: Henry Holt. (T, pre–K)

Ziefert, H. (2000). *Pushkin minds the bundle* (D. Saaf, Ill.). New York: Atheneum. (T, pre–K, K)

Ziefert, H., & Taback, S. (2002). *Who said moo?* Brooklyn, NY: Handprint. (I, T)

Zimmerman, A., & Clemesha, D. (1999). *Trashy town* (D. Yaccarino, Ill.). New York: HarperCollins. (T, P)

Zolotow, C. (1972). *William's doll.* New York: Harper & Row. (P, K)

Zolotow, C. (1985). *My grandson Lew.* New York: HarperTrophy. (P, K)

Zolotow, C. (1992). *This quiet lady* (A. Lobel, Ill.). New York: Greenwillow. (P, K)

Name Index

NAME INDEX

Subject Index